Executive's Guide to Cloud Computing

Executive's Guide to Cloud Computing

Eric A. Marks
Bob Lozano

WILEY

John Wiley & Sons, Inc.

Library of Congress Cataloging-in-Publication Data:

Marks, Eric A.
   Executive's guide to cloud computing / Eric A. Marks, Bob Lozano.
       p. cm.
   Includes bibliographical references and index.
   ISBN 978-0-470-52172-4 (cloth)
   1. Business enterprises—Computer networks—Management. 2. Information technology—Management. 3. Cloud computing. I. Lozano, Bob, 1957- II. Title.
   HD30.37.M36427 2010
   004.3'6—dc22   2010002002

Printed in the United States of America

10 9 8 7 6 5 4 3 2 1

Eric Marks
For my wife, Diane, and my great children, Jonathan and Jessica. Thanks, as always, for enduring another business book project. Someday, I'll write one that you'll read and enjoy!

Bob Lozano
In deepest gratitude for my wife Carol and all who make up La Familia Lozano, including in a particular way Raul Jorge Lozano, mi padre who completed his journey more than 30 years ago, my nephew David and my father-in-law James Huckaba who both completed their journeys within the past year . . . words can never suffice.

Contents

Preface   **xi**

CHAPTER 1   THE SOUND OF INEVITABILITY   1

                  A Persistent Vision   5
                  A Little History   6
                  Three Ages of Computing   6
                  Broad Enablers   15
                  Big Contributions   20
                  Limitations   21
                  I Want One of Those   22
                  Back to the Future?   22
                  Notes   23

CHAPTER 2   CONCEPTS, TERMINOLOGY,
                  AND STANDARDS   25

                  Basic Concepts: The Big Stuff   27
                  Major Layers   34
                  Where They Live (Deployment Models)   36
                  Geographic Location   39
                  Datacenter Innovation   39
                  The Quest for Green   40
                  Standards   41
                  Much Sound and Fury . . .   42
                  Parting Thoughts   42
                  Notes   43

CHAPTER 3   CLOUD COMPUTING AND
EVERYTHING ELSE   45

The Neighborhood   45
Parting Thoughts   66
Notes   67

CHAPTER 4   STRATEGIC IMPLICATIONS OF CLOUD
COMPUTING   69

A Survey of Cloud Implications   70
Business Benefits of Cloud Computing   78
Cloud-Based Business Models   82
Cloud-Enabled Business Models   83
Strategic Implications of Cloud
Computing   86
Evolving from SOA into the Cloud   91
When to Do SOA versus Cloud?   98
Cloud Computing Adoption Obstacles   107
Parting Thoughts: Things to Do Tomorrow   109
Notes   110

CHAPTER 5   CLOUD ADOPTION
LIFECYCLE   111

Cloud Adoption Lifecycle and Cloud
Modeling Framework: Two Necessary
Tools for Cloud Success   112
Cloud Adoption Lifecycle   114
Cloud Adoption Lifecycle Summary   144
Parting Thoughts   145

CHAPTER 6   CLOUD ARCHITECTURE, MODELING,
AND DESIGN   147

Cloud Adoption Lifecycle Model:
Role of Cloud Modeling and Architecture   147
Cloud Industry Standards   149
Standards Monitoring Framework   154
A Cloud Computing Reference Model   155
Exploring the Cloud Computing Logical
Architecture   157

Developing a Holistic Cloud Computing
Reference Model 162
Cloud Deployment Model 170
Cloud Governance and
Operations Model 174
Cloud Ecosystem Model (Supporting
the Cloud Reference Model) 179
Consumption of Cloud-Enabled and
Cloud Enablement Resources 184
Cloud Computing Reference
Model Summary 187
Cloud Computing Technical
Reference Architecture 188
Parting Thoughts 192
Notes 193

CHAPTER 7 WHERE TO BEGIN WITH
CLOUD COMPUTING 195

Cloud Adoption Lifecycle 195
Where to Begin with Cloud: Using the
Cloud Adoption Lifecycle 199
Where to Begin with Cloud: Deployment
Model Scenarios 200
Cloud Business Adoption Patterns 204
Where to Begin with Cloud: Consumers
and Internal Cloud Providers 209
Cloud Patterns Mapped to Common
Cloud Use Cases 213
Parting Thoughts 224

CHAPTER 8 ALL THINGS DATA 227

The Status Quo 228
Cracks in the Monolith 230
Cloud Scale 232
The Core Issues 234
Lessons Learned 237
Solutions and Technologies: A Few
Examples 239

A Look Below: Need for Combined
Computation/Storage   242
Parting Thoughts   243
Notes   243

CHAPTER 9   WHY INEVITABILITY IS . . . INEVITABLE   245

Driving Scale   247
Objections and Concerns   248
Overwhelming Rationality   253
A Natural Evolution   257
Parting Thoughts   259
Notes   260

APPENDIX   THE CLOUD COMPUTING
VENDOR LANDSCAPE   263

Infrastructure as a Service (IaaS)   264
Platforms as a Service (PaaS)   264
Software as a Service (SaaS)   265
Systems Integrators   265
Analysts and Services Providers   266
Parting Thoughts   266
Note   266

About the Authors   **267**

Index   **269**

Preface

What is cloud computing? Is this real, or simply another over-wrought marketing phenomena, which the thoughtful person should best simply let run its course? Suppose it is real—how important is this, what does it mean to our organization, what should we do, and how should we do it?

These questions and more are on the minds, or should be on the minds, of senior executives, leaders of many kinds and at many levels, and clear-thinking leaders-in-the-making at a wide range of organizations around the world.

As with any other area in which there is rapid innovation—and cloud computing is certainly such an area—there are many competing voices with a wide range of views, which can seem to be little more than a discordant cacophony. Fortunately, there are some valuable lessons that have already been learned; fundamental technologies, operational models, and business processes that have already been developed; real possibilities that have already been seen; these realities simply should not—no, *must* not—be ignored.

With all this in mind we set out to provide some basic understanding, clear guidance about the realities of cloud computing: what it is, why it has happened, and what best to do about it.

The term *cloud computing* is of relatively recent vintage. In fact, it was as recent as April 2008 when the nascent cloud community was roiled by a short-lived U.S. trademark on the term itself. The trademark was wisely abandoned quickly by the firm that had originally obtained it, thereby giving name to something which the participants all knew had become very real—not all at once, but gradually, in the convergence of a number of technical, business, even cultural, and sociological developments.

Yet those who had been working on some of the key technical developments had known for some time–five years, in some cases more–that there was something real here, something almost difficult to comprehend in the disruptive potential on the business of computing, something enormously exciting in the nearly breathtaking potential impact on the organizations dependent upon, enabled by, and all too often constrained by the then-present economics and capabilities of traditional computing technologies.

These are indeed exciting times in the computing world—cloud computing is, in fact, a real nexus, a moment when the endeavor of utilizing computing fundamentally changes. We have been in the thick of these developments since 2001, and through a fortuitous confluence of events were brought together to write this book.

That is the need and our intent—what about the book itself?

In many ways this is really "books within a book," and we believe a wide range of people with a wide range of backgrounds and interests will find it helpful.

The beginning of the book (Chapters 1 through 3) and the end (Chapters 8 and 9) are of general interest: While some technical perspective is inevitable, just skip whatever may be a bit too detailed. Take care to understand the main points, particularly of Chapters 1, 2, and 9. Chapters 4 through 6 will be most helpful for the more technology-savvy in a variety of roles, from strategic planner to IT professional. Chapter 7 falls somewhere in between, and should be read as your background suggests.

In any case, here are each of the chapters and a brief description:

Chapter 1, The Sound of Inevitability: This lays the historical context of the broad trends and developments that have led to cloud computing.

Chapter 2, Concepts, Terminology, and Standards: Names the basics, establishes a common language for what is what.

Chapter 3, Cloud Computing and Everything Else: More context, placing cloud computing in relation with everything from virtualization to service-oriented architecture (SOA).

Chapter 4, Strategic Implications of Cloud Computing: Why executives should care.

Chapter 5, Cloud Adoption Lifecycle: An adoption model for the enterprise, with special comments for the startup.

Chapter 6, Cloud Architecture, Modeling, and Design: Focus on creating cloud-enabled applications that work equally well on both private or public clouds; interoperable private and public clouds; and operational models that make use of the potential elasticity, scalability, reliability, and cost reductions.

Chapter 7, Where to Begin with Cloud Computing: Practical steps for planning, executing, and measuring incorporation of cloud computing in a wide variety of organizations.

Chapter 8, All Things Data: Explores how the inexorable drive toward "big data" is fundamentally changing nearly everything about how data is stored, found, and manipulated.

Chapter 9, Why Inevitability Is . . . Inevitable: The fundamental reasons why cloud computing is happening, will happen, and consequently is well worth understanding.

In addition there is a brief Appendix that describes the basic categories within the vendor community. Note that it is our intent to maintain a directory of sorts on www.execsguidetocloud.com with vendor descriptions, current cloud-related news, and so forth.

An effort like this does not happen without the help of many. To our customers who have continuously asked "why?"; our friends, competitors, and erstwhile compatriots throughout the industry; our friends and colleagues at both Appistry and AgilePath who are turning these ideas into practical realities; our editors Sheck Cho and Stacey Rivera and the rest of the team at Wiley; and of course to our families whose contributions are both sublime and essential; to all we acknowledge deep appreciation and offer our thanks for all that you have done to support, challenge, and call us to do better.

It is our sincere hope that this volume will help you gain a deeper understanding of what cloud computing is, why it is, and what you may reasonably do to make good use of what is a truly historic opportunity.

Bob Lozano
www.thoughtsoncomputing.com
www.execsguidetocloud.com
boblozano (twitter)

Eric Marks
emarks@agile-path.com
www.execsguidetocloud.com
ericmarks (twitter)

CHAPTER 1

The Sound of Inevitability

There have been very few fundamental changes in computing.

On the surface, that may sound like the statement of a madman, or perhaps at least someone from an alternate universe. Nonetheless, it is true.

Sure there have been, are, and will likely continue to be a nearly incomprehensible fire hose of particular changes, some rather flashy in and of themselves. Simple things like pocket-sized flash drives that store more than the corporate mainframes of 30 years ago, or perhaps ubiquitous mobile devices for everything from the mundanely practical—e-mail, calendars, and contacts—to the cheerfully sublime. Much more complex developments such as the open source movement; the advent of relational databases; and the rise (and fall) of whole operating systems and their surrounding ecosystems, even those whose perpetual dominance once seemed assured (how many desktop machines are running CP/M these days?). These have come and gone, perhaps lingering in some niche, forgotten by all but a few fanatical devotees.

But truly fundamental change—the tectonic shift that literally changes our landscape—happens only once in a long while, perhaps every ten or more years, even in the computing business. Fundamental change of this magnitude requires a number of smaller innovations to pile up until a true nexus is reached, and we all start marching down a different road.

Of course, as historians are fond of lecturing the rest of us mere mortals, these sort of fundamental changes are nearly impossible to recognize while we are in the middle of them, even as they loom imminently.

When researchers at the University of Pennsylvania were feverishly working on ENIAC—generally recognized as the first programmable, general-purpose electronic computer—as the future of the world hung in the balance in the midst of World War II, do you think they envisioned computers embedded in nearly everything, from greeting cards to automobiles, from microwaves to MRIs? When researchers at the University of California, Los Angeles, and elsewhere in the midst of the Cold War strove to make computer networks more resilient in the face of nuclear attack,[1] do you think any of them envisioned the Internet as we see it today? Likewise, when Tim Berners-Lee and other researchers at CERN were trying to come up with an easy way to create and display content over this new, literally nuclear-grade network, do you think they envisioned the impact on everyday life (both personal and professional) their new creation would have, or even the simple breadth and depth of stuff—from the sublime to the silly—that would be available on this new, supercharged "Internet" ? One estimate is that there are more than 500 exabytes—that's 500 *billion* gigabytes—in this "digital universe," and that this will double every 18 months.[2]

The simple truth is that very few, if any, of the people involved in these developments had much of an idea of the consequences of their creations, of the impact on our personal lives, our culture, even the society in which we live—from how we interact with our families to how we conduct business.

Whether you are "technologically modest," or are either by age or temperament not ashamed to let it be known, at least in certain circles, that you are a bit of a geek . . . either way, it is pretty much a given that developments in computing are having a big impact on our society, and more to the point, an even bigger impact on how we conduct our business.

And bigger changes—tectonic shift–scale changes—will have at least commensurate impact on our lives in every dimension, including the fields of commerce. One example, perhaps a seemingly simple one, yet central to many of the changes now underway, will suffice to illustrate this point.

Consider for a moment newspapers. We now face the very real prospect—actually the near-certainty—of at least one (and probably many) major metropolitan area in the United States without a traditional (local, general purpose, print, widely circulated) newspaper. While this eventuality may be stayed—perhaps for quite some time—via government intervention, the fact that this will eventually occur is not in doubt. In a culture still echoing with such reporteresque icons as Clark Kent, or at least the more prosaic Bernstein and Woodward, this was once unthinkable. Now it is simply inevitable.

There was a time when the technology of newspapers—cheap newsprint (paper), high volume printing presses, delivery networks including everything from trucks to kids on bicycles—was the only reasonable means for mass distribution of information. In fact, with help from some of the newer technologies there was even a new national newspaper (*USA Today*) founded in the United States as late as 1982. But with the advent of alternative delivery channels—first radio, then broadcast cable, and satellite television—increasing amounts of pressure were put on the newspapers.

The immediacy of the newer channels led to the widespread death of afternoon newspapers in most markets; anything delivered to the dinner table in a physical paper was hopelessly out of date with the evening news on television or radio. The morning papers had the advantage of broad coverage collected while most people slept, and as a result have held on longer.

However, at the same time intrinsic limitations of the newer technologies made them better for certain types of information, though not as useful for others. For example, a two-minute video from a war zone could convey the brutal reality of combat far more effectively than reams of newsprint, but did little to describe the complex strategic elements—political, economic, cultural—of the conflict itself. As a result, a certain stasis had been reached in which newspapers carved out what appeared to be a sustainable role in the delivery of news.

Then came the Internet.

In particular, the effectively free and ubiquitous—and yes, near-instantaneous—delivery of all sorts of information mortally wounded the newspaper business. As the first round of the web ecosystem grew, the only remaining stronghold of the traditional newspapers—their ad-based revenue model—was made largely irrelevant. eBay, Craigslist, and freecycle (among others) replaced the classifieds, and online ads took out most of what was left.

Some newspapers will undoubtedly manage the transition in some manner or another, perhaps even emerging as something fairly recognizable—particularly national/international properties such as the *Wall Street Journal* and the previously mentioned *USA Today*—and perhaps even financially sound.

But those that do will likely largely do so without their original distribution technologies, and more important, many will not make the transition at all.

All of this upheaval in news delivery—the enormous changes that have already occurred and that which is yet to come—have been enabled by developments in computing technologies, with the widespread adoption of everything from the Internet to the iPhone. It is probably worth remembering that all of this has occurred largely without cloud computing, and as a result we are probably less than 10% of the way through this transition in news delivery, and this is only one industry. One industry, one example, with entire economies yet to transform.

Even so, some things have not changed much, even in the delivery of news. The computing infrastructures range from the stodgy (server, even mainframe-based systems within many newspapers) to circa-2009 state of the art (which we might as well start referring to as "legacy web," web 2.0, old-school web, something like that). By and large these systems still cost too much to acquire, do not adapt to changes in demand nearly easily enough, are not reliable enough, and remain way too complex and costly to operate. Even the few systems that do not suffer from all of these problems are not ideal, to say the least: Some are proprietary, and most are either too complex to create new application software, or simply do not scale well enough, at least for the sort of software that researchers are hard at work developing. In particular, with the first generation of electronic news infrastructures focused on just *delivering* the news, the next generation will be focused on sifting through all of that content, looking for just the right stuff.

All of that sifting and sorting and searching will take orders of magnitude more computing capacity than we have anywhere today. How will we pay for hundreds and thousands, perhaps even tens of thousands *times* more servers and storage than we have today—almost unimaginable quantities of computing? How will we operate them? Write new software for them? It is fair to wonder how we will even power all that gear. Assuming that all of these concerns are resolved, then, we will face a larger question still, one which we presume has many answers: What sort of business models are enabled by all of this, and how do we get there?

Before we leave this example, it is probably worth considering our present circumstances just a bit more. In particular, most of the history of both economics and engineering can be understood by thinking about managing *scarcity*. In other words, how do I get the most done with the least stuff, or within certain limits? For example, that underlying drive to dealing with scarcity, at its core, drives the startup team to work harder and pay less, the Fortune 500 enterprise to optimize manufacturing processes, and entire nations to set energy policies. Allocating scarcity is just Economics 101. Of course, it is also Engineering 101. Dealing with scarcity causes communications engineers to develop better video compression schemes, improve CPU designs to get more done in the same amount of time, and even rethink server packaging to reduce power consumption and labor costs.

While scarcity may be the nemesis of some, it is quite literally a prime mover behind the developments that have together come to be known as cloud computing. What does this mean, and how can it be possible?

A Persistent Vision

Better, faster, cheaper is often heard in technology circles. More than a policy, more than a philosophy, this is literally a way of life within technology communities. In an ideal world imagine that:

Computing—computation, storage, communication—is relatively free, scales up or down as needed, scales as much as needed, operates itself, and always works.

To one degree or another, this is the persistent vision that drives many of those who are developing cloud computing. Is all of this presently possible? Of course not; yet we are inexorably on this path.

Achieving this vision is, of course, a complex endeavor with far more to it than may meet the eye at first glance. That is why there is the rest of this book, for starters!

Before we go further let us elaborate a bit on the dimensions of this vision.

Engineers and mathematicians talk about something being "within epsilon of zero." This is a term that comes from calculus. It simply means the process of approaching a particular limit, from wherever you started to the limit itself. In the case of the cost of computing infrastructure, that limit is zero. For most of computing history the costs of infrastructure have dominated decisions about what to deploy when: How much will those servers cost? How about that storage farm? That network? Now, however, we can start thinking about those costs being "within epsilon of zero"; that is, over time the computing infrastructure comes closer and closer to being free. That leaves other costs as the new, more significant considerations—software licensing, data acquisition, for just two examples—and this will be examined more closely later in the book.

A Little History

In one sense the evolution of computing has been one long blur, with change piling on change, products that are "long in the tooth" in less than a year and virtually classic soon after, and with new concepts—Moore's Law, for example—created simply so that we can describe, understand, and effectively institutionalize this relentless rate of change.

But there are times when these changes pile up in such number, in particular combinations of new capabilities and logical consequences, that the whole industry does head off in a new direction—when the very conversations, the underlying concepts, even the possibilities themselves change.

To help understand the import of our current transition into a computing world dominated by cloud computing, think a bit about where we have been, where we are now (at least just slightly before exactly right now), and both how and why we have travelled these paths. While there are clearly many ways that the history of computing can be written, this one will only focus on the big changes—the nexi[3] themselves—where the very possibilities change.

Three Ages of Computing

While there many ways to get a handle on the evolution of computing, in order to gain an initial understanding just where cloud computing fits, of just how significant and, yes, disruptive it is and will be, it is sufficient to consider the broad sweep of computing history.

First Age

Think about the role of computing within the typical organization prior to the widespread adoption of the Internet. The focus was on automating particular operations, creating supporting business processes, and of course, always improving efficiency.

Notice that the focus was *within* individual organizations, by and large. Yes there were purpose-built networks for interacting between organizations, some of them even fairly large and important (stock trading and manufacturer-specific EDI [electronic data interchange] networks are two notable examples), and even for certain organizations to interact with their customers (e.g., credit card authorization networks), but each of these tended to have a very specific, rather narrow focus. Even more important, these examples were relatively few and far between, and very difficult to achieve.

This was the first age of computing, in which organizations looked internally for the big wins. For the most part the edges of each organization remained the same as they had always been.

At the beginning of the first age the focus was on big infrastructure—mainframes, big point-to-point networks, centralized databases, and big batch jobs. Toward the end, terminals evolved into personal computers, networks went from hierarchical (with the mainframes at the center of each network) to decentralized, with a broader, generally more numerous collection of servers and storage scattered throughout an organization. While batch work still existed, many programs became interactive through this first age, eventually gaining much more visual interfaces along the way.

Infrastructure tended to be associated with particular applications—a practice since pejoratively known as "application silos"—and important applications generally demanded enterprise-grade (read: expensive) infrastructure—mainframes or big servers, and so forth.

Application architectures tended to follow the same evolutionary path, with earlier applications being generally centralized, large and heavy, while client-server and distributed application architectures became mainstream toward the end.

This period also saw the rise of databases, along with the beginnings of specialized storage infrastructure upon which those databases relied.

Technologies such as parallel computing, artificial intelligence, and even semantic processing remained exotic tools that were employed in only the most demanding problems, where "cost was no object" (at least in theory), where the goal was simply to solve ever-bigger, ever-thornier problems—places like the nuclear weapons laboratories, national intelligence agencies, scientific research institutions, and the like.

Despite the rapid, consistent improvements in individual hardware and software technologies throughout this period, the limitations and complaints remained nearly constant. In particular, no matter how much was poured into the IT budget, the foul nemesis of "application backlog" was heard in the hallways of nearly every enterprise. Who did not constantly complain about how much IT was costing?

Still, it was at least (generally speaking) possible to automate crucial operations within a company, and as a result overall corporate efficiency steadily increased. More autos were made with less labor, more packages delivered with the same number of employees, higher revenues per store per employee, and so forth.

This period covered about four decades, from the roots of enterprise computing in the 1950s until the rise of the Internet in the mid-1990s. As with all major shifts in a society, its culture and technology, the roots of the end of the first age of computing were sown years before the second age began.

Second Age

The second age of computing is really the story of the rise of the Internet—Sun, Cisco, Mosaic (which became Netscape), web 1.0, eBay, Yahoo, baby.com, and the first Internet Bubble—all of it, good and bad, all of the tumultuous commotion of the first Internet land rush.

While many advances contributed to the beginning of the second age, the two most crucial were the development of the Internet itself, and the development and near-ubiquity of easy-to-use, visually attractive devices that could be used by nearly everyone.

The story of the development of the Internet is well known[4]— starting from a research question (Can we build a more resilient network, one that can survive a nuclear attack?), to a more loosely coupled set of higher level communications protocols (e.g., ftp for file transfers, smtp for e-mail, http for web content) built on top of this newly resilient foundation, then to a whole ecosystem of new software. From browsers to web servers, among many others, the Internet quickly went from "who cares?" to "must have!". By the early 1990s this new, sort of crazy idea began to dominate even mainstream business thought, to the point that normally sane, rational people predicted such improbably outcomes as the elimination of all brick-and-mortar stores, the irrelevance of a nation's manufacturing base, and in some cases the irrelevance of nations themselves.

This in turn led to truly historic business hysteria: the Internet Bubble. (Truth be told, if not for macro-level economic problems that started in late 2008 the onset of cloud computing may have triggered Internet Bubble 2.0.)

But as the dust settled and all calmed down, it was clear that the world had shifted. Any enterprise intending to prosper now had to consider how best to reach their customers and their ecosystem of suppliers, and where to look for their newest competitors, all in the face of the newest reality—ubiquitous connectivity.

Likewise, the ubiquity of visually rich devices—at first stationary, then evolving to include the "handheld slabs of glass" (iPhone, android phones, Palm pre, and their successors) made it possible for the non-geek to care. While command lines and text terminals were enough for many of the early adopters, the simple reality is that audience is, by definition, limited.

There were people—including one of the authors—who went from cards, to command line, to modern bit-mapped displays (along with a mouse, laser printer, and local area network, all part of the experimental Alto workstations from Xerox PARC[5]), all well within the span of a single year—1979. At the beginning of that year most work was done on a mainframe via cards, printers, and batch jobs; halfway through 1979 work moved to interactive command-line access via dumb terminals; and by the end of the year you could sit in front of a Xerox Altos, mesmerized by mice, bit-mapped displays, and early networked games (Mazewars[6] being a great example).

While both of these trace their earliest roots—at least in forms that we would largely recognize today—to the mid-1970s, they each took 15 to 20 years to gestate sufficiently to have broad impact.

Overall, the biggest technical contribution of the second age was perhaps the network itself. Forced to deal with the possibility of massive network failures caused by a nuclear attack, researchers endowed their invention with the ability to self-organize, to seek out alternate routes for traffic, to adapt to all sorts of unforeseen circumstances.

In doing so (perhaps with only partial intent) these researchers removed the single point of failure that was typical of mainframe-inspired networks: and as a consequence in one fell swoop they removed the biggest technological barrier to scaling–the mainframe-centric network itself. Even more telling, foreshadowing changes that would usher in the third age-when they enabled the networks to take care of themselves-these researchers also removed the biggest obstacle to growth—they made these new networks *much* easier to operate.

It is hard to overestimate the importance of two fundamental realities: (1) with the Internet it was now true that everyone was connected to everyone else, anytime, anywhere; and (2) with the ubiquity of visually attractive devices, the data and services available over that pervasive network could actually be used by mere mortals.

Typical technologies included the J2EE application servers (often in clusters) along with relational databases, themselves often in clusters. Developers and researchers everywhere strove to stretch, push, pull, morph—everything but blowing them up and starting over—to make these application architectures more flexible, scalable, more resilient to failure, and so forth, but were mostly unsuccessful, or at least not successful enough.

There were plenty of innovations in software architectures, ranging from improved data techniques to the first forays into what became service-oriented architectures in the early part of the new millennia.

But what had not changed? Far too much remained as it always had, as things turned out. For starters, infrastructure remained expensive, chunky, siloed, and by modern standards phenomenally overengineered (after all, the infrastructure really should not fail), and consequently even more expensive. Great strides were being made in distributed software architectures, but (outside of the foundational TCP/IP networks themselves) most applications and infrastructure software remained difficult to configure, complex to create, and brittle when faced with failure. As a result, operations remained enormously difficult and therefore both costly and error prone, which in the final analysis was the cruelest constant reality of all.

Before we continue in this narrative, let us take a step back to consider two more constants in computing—the drive for ever-increasing scale and the drive for ever-lower expenditures (i.e., the "drive for cheap").

Drive for Scale   Remember back to the middle of the first age, in the 1970s and 1980s—most computing was done on relatively mundane, large-scale individual computers, or perhaps in small clusters of relatively big machines. Even then, for the researchers, scientists, or perhaps intelligence agencies who were simply trying to solve the biggest problems possible, this was never enough; for that matter, nothing was ever enough, no matter how big and fast. Those folks were the ones who were exploring the edges of parallel computing and distributed architectures, who were thinking of highly pipelined supercomputers and vector processors.

Yet in the mid-1980s another thread of investigation took root—inspired by biological systems themselves—which started by combining large numbers of relatively slow computers, sometimes loosely coupled via a local area network (these came to be often known as grids) and sometimes linked internally via specialized connections (such as the exotic Connection Machine 1, produced by Thinking Machines, Inc., which was the effort to commercialize the doctoral work of Daniel Hillis). In all cases these alternative architectures were difficult to develop software for, cranky to operate, and enormously expensive. Even though most of those efforts eventually evaporated, they did at least make one very important contribution: They showed that it was indeed possible, particularly for certain applications, to build very large computing facilities out of very modest components.

This drive for scale went mainstream along with the Internet. This was true in many dimensions, but for one easy example just think of the indexing problem itself—whereas an early (circa 1994) Yahoo index might have had less than a hundred, or at most a few hundred entries, and could be manually created, by the beginning of 1995 the number of web sites was doubling every 53 days[7] and was passing anyone's ability to manually index. This growth then created the need for computing infrastructures that could scale at the same rates or faster, as well as application and data storage architectures that could also scale apace.

Yet there was one fly in the ointment that occurred about this same time—the silicon companies (Intel, competitors, and friends) began to reach their practical limit for scaling individual execution units (which came to be known as "cores"). In fact, this problem had been looming for some time, but the processor designers tended to solve the problem the way they had always done: Throw more hardware at it and hope it would go away. In late 2004 Intel announced that they were largely abandoning their push to increase the "clock speed" of individual processing elements, and going forward would instead be, increasing the number of individual processing units (or cores). While, at least in theory, this drive for increased core counts can deliver the same raw computing capacity, in practice it is much more difficult to write application software that can make use of all of these cores.

This is, in essence, the "parallelization problem," which in many ways is the same no matter whether you are writing software for multiple cores within a single piece of silicon, multiple cores on multiple processors within a single computing system, or multiple cores on multiple processors on multiple computing systems within a single grid/cluster/fabric/cloud.

Sound complex? To be honest, it is—successfully writing a parallelizable application can be enormously complex, difficult to do well, even more difficult to do reliably, and more difficult still to make it also easy to operate. In other words, the silicon and systems designers had punted, shifting the burden for scaling to the application software and operational communities.

Drive for Cheap   Of course one drive that remains true in every age and in every domain is the drive to reduce costs—cost to acquire, cost to deploy, cost to operate, cost here, cost there, cost anywhere—just reduce them all.

In the midst of the rubble of the first Internet Bubble (bursting), many different groups began to wonder just how to make use of these increasingly capable commodity computers for problems that we really cared about—mission-critical problems, the ones that "absolutely, positively, have to work."[8]

For example, the roots of Appistry (a company founded by one of the authors) lie in just such a question. When building a digital recording studio out of purely commodity parts (no label, cheapest fastest stuff that money could buy), after running benchmarks the obvious question came up: Why are we not using cheap stuff like this (meaning the plain label, pure commodity computing parts) for problems that "we really care about"?

The answers to that question—how to ensure that commodity infrastructure could be ultimately reliable, easy to operate, easy to bring software into and so on—led to multiple patents, products, and companies, and is a question whose answers are definitely worthwhile.

The economics of utilizing commodity components are compelling, if—and only if—you can safely answer those key questions. The economies of scale with commodity infrastructure, such as general-purpose processors, are simply overwhelming when compared to specialty designs. It is common for a collection of commodity computers to deliver the same capacity for less than 10% of the cost—sometimes far less than 10%—of enterprise-grade servers and mainframes.

It is no longer a question of "is this possible," but rather "how, when, and where."

That same question—How can we use commodity infrastructure for problems that we care about?—is being asked and answered in various ways by forward-thinking technologists and executives everywhere in the relentless pursuit for "cheaper, faster, better," and is integral in the transitions to cloud.

Third Age

Now let us resume our narrative. Early in the second age Yahoo had made a name for itself by "indexing the Internet," which for some time was mostly manually done. While this was sufficient for a while, it soon became apparent that manually built indices could never keep up with the growth of the Internet itself.

Several other indexing efforts began, including AltaVista, Google, and others, but it was Google that brought everything together. While a full understanding of why Google became so dominant–at least as of this writing-is beyond the scope of this book, several key factors can be easily understood.

- First, the collection of data about the current state of the Internet, and the processing of that data had to be as absolutely automated as possible.

- In order to save as much money as possible, the infrastructure would be constructed out of commodity components, out of "cheap stuff that breaks."
- Data storage needed to be done in a simple, yet fairly reliable manner to facilitate scaling (the Google File System, or GFS—notice the lack of a traditional database, but more on that later).
- New types of application development architecture(s) would be required, which came to include the so-called map-reduce family (which inspired open source descendants such as Hadoop) among others.
- Operations needed to be as automatic and dependable as possible.
- Outages in the application were tolerable; after all this was search, and who would miss a few results if an outage occurred?

So almost before anyone really knew what was happening, in order to scale a basic search facility and do so cheaply, Google had created much of what we could probably first recognize as a cloud.

Another interesting case is Amazon. In the first six or seven years Amazon largely built its computing infrastructure the traditional way, out of big, heavy servers, with traditional relational databases scattered liberally throughout. That was fine in the early days, and definitely fine during the first couple of years after the Internet Bubble burst (particularly since much high-end hardware could be had for pennies on the dollar after the first bubble), but as commerce on the Internet began to gain some real momentum it became abundantly clear that the Amazon computing architecture(s) had to change.

At the same time, in order to build customer and vendor stickiness Amazon had begun exposing individual services, even select customer data as callable services—one of the key application lessons that is leading to the third age—and so had accelerated decomposing many of their applications into dozens, or sometimes hundreds, of individually callable services.

About that time (2001–2003) Amazon began to adopt many of the same principles as Google had done early on, but then they took things a step further. Instead of simply offering entire services such as search, e-mail, maps, photo, and so forth with various services exposed for calling from outside, in 2006 Amazon began to offer basic computing resources: computing, storage, and network bandwidth in highly flexible, easily provisioned, services, all of which could be paid for "by the drink."

Others offered public cloud services that made certain unique contributions, including Salesforce.com, which was probably the first public cloud service that was targeted at the enterprise customer and required those customers to store very sensitive data outside of their own facilities. While many thought that sale was not doable, that no enterprise large or small would risk their customer data on something so unproven, the allure of an easy, pay as you go CRM (customer relationship management) implementation led to the rise of Salesforce.com (and competitors, in the sincerest form of flattery), emphatically proving otherwise, that the enterprise customer could trust these services. That their initial rise to meaningful market share and then eventual dominance came largely at the expense of the traditional, install-in-your-own-shop application with an overwrought, often painful, and unintentionally costly implementation was simply a bonus.

While each of these examples have their roots firmly in the middle of the second age, either their original or subsequent decisions played crucial roles in bringing together the beginning of the third age, the age of cloud computing.

It is during this era that that persistent vision that we discussed earlier can finally begin to become true:

Computing—computation, storage, communication—is relatively free, scales up or down as needed, scales as much as needed, operates itself, and always works.

With that in mind, let us step back and take a look at some of the particular developments that are enabling this persistent vision to begin to become reality.

Broad Enablers

Over the course of the 1980s and 1990s there were key advances that came together to enable the transition to the cloud computing era—the third age. We are at the cusp of this transition as we complete the first decade of the new millennium. While not a comprehensive list, these are some of the more notable enablers:

- **Commodity Hardware.** In the three basic areas of computing components—chips (processors, memory, etc.), storage (mostly disc drives), and network (both within a datacenter, wide area, and wireless)—there have been large strides made in the capabilities of what is by historical standards throw-away equipment. For example, a client of one of the authors was able to match a competitor's industry-leading, mainframe-based performance in processing high-volume customer transaction with less than a dozen cheap commodity boxes sitting on a repurposed kitchen rack. Total bill? Less than $10,000. Yes it works, and it works very well. The key, of course, was in how the applications were constructed and how that set of machines is reliably managed. In any case, there will be more on this example as well as others later in the book.

- **Network Speed.** While network performance has not increased at the same rate as either processor or storage performance (which will lead to interesting problems as clouds develop—we will cover the details of this in depth in Chapter 8, All Things Data), huge strides have been made in both the connections within a datacenter and those outside.

  For example, by the time you are reading this a "gigE" network card (for use by a commodity computer within a data-center) will be less than $10 each in small quantities. To put that in perspective, that is *about 400% faster than the internal bus connections*[9] (the key internal connectivity within server computers) of the typical big servers of the early 1980s. Also as you are reading this, a 10 Mbps wired connection for the home or office will average less than $50 per month in the United States, and even less than that in many parts of the world. Mainstream mobile wireless (for those ubiquitous "slab of glass" mobile devices that make accessing all these services so pleasant) speeds will be closer to 7 Mbps, at the cost of only a modest part of the typical monthly cell phone budget. The point is simple: Whether within the datacenter, at fixed locations throughout the world, or on mobile devices, cheap, fast, reliable, and ubiquitous network connections are a fact of life.

- **Virtualization.** Virtualization started as a way to share the use of very expensive mainframes among otherwise incompatible operating systems, then flowered in the later similar trend to consolidate large numbers of small servers (each typically dedicated to one or two specific applications). It is the ability to operate particular resources (such as computers, networks, and so forth) largely independent of the physical infrastructure upon which they are deployed. This can be a tremendous boon for operations.

For example, the initial configuration of the operating system for a server, along with the applications to run on that server can take hours, if not days. With virtualization that initial work is done once and the results put on the shelf, to be deployed onto physical hardware when needed. This process, sometimes referred to as *hydration*, can be done in as little as a few seconds to minutes and repeated as often as needed, thereby enabling the possibility of easily deploying basic software to large numbers of computers.

- **Application Architectures.** Beginning with the development of *object-oriented* languages and tools in the 1980s and 1990s, and continuing on through the beginning of web services and service-oriented architectures during this decade, software architectures have made many strides toward the eternal goal of software reusability, itself driven by the desire to make it easier to construct software. A key characteristic of typical cloud applications has been the fine-grained components, with an exposed application programming interface (API) or interface (i.e., the ability to make use of that portion of an application from nearly anywhere on the Internet—any place that makes sense, and probably even a few places that are just for show!).

  This ability to mix and match relatively independent software services is crucial in making software more useful. For many, this has been the practical realization of service-oriented architectures (SOA), an interesting topic that we will explore in more detail later the book. (A more detailed discussion of the relationship between SOA and Cloud, and industry adoption trends for both, is explored in detail in Chapter 5.)

  In addition, there have been significant advances in creating more resilient, self-organizing application platforms that are inherently at home on top of the very fluid, commoditized infrastructure typical in cloud computing.

  Finally, the need to become more adept at parallelization in order to effectively use multi-core processors is beginning to have an impact.

- **Data Storage Architectures.** The first two ages of computing were very much dominated (for very good reasons) by the database systems—relational databases such as Oracle, MySQL, SQLServer, Postgress, and others. Entire (data management) organizations exist in most enterprises to manage the structure of this relational data within these repositories; with strict rules about how such data is accessed, updated, and so forth. Unfortunately, what we have learned from abundant experience is that at some point the block to scaling any given application will nearly always be the relational database itself.

  As a result the whole approach to reliably storing, processing, and managing data at large scale is being rethought, resulting in a number of innovative, novel technologies that show significant promise.

  We are also beginning to see some significant improvements in the underlying storage infrastructure itself, both in composition and operations. In any case, this whole area will be explored in much more depth in Chapter 8, All Things Data.

- **Pervasive High Quality Access.** The reality—quality, variety, quantity—of high quality, visually attractive, widely available devices has had a tremendous impact on the development of cloud computing. Typical devices include fixed desktops with one or more flat panels; laptops and netbooks of every size, price range, and performance; ubiquitous, sometimes specialized, and nearly always relatively inexpensive handheld devices such as the iPhone and its growing range of competitors (such as the rapidly-expanding range of devices running the Android operating system from Google). Perhaps most importantly, these devices share in common a wide range of wireless high-speed Internet access.

  Taking all this into account, this plethora of high quality, pervasive, always-connected devices has greatly increased the number of customers for services and content—the data and applications sold on the cloud—and has also increased each customer's appetite for even more services and data.

  Consider one small example. In March 2008 Apple announced that they would create a marketplace from which third-party developers could sell applications to owners of an iPhone. Despite a tremendous amount of uncertainty—

including many who thought that the whole concept would simply fizzle out for any of a number of reasons—within the first nine months Apple was able to sell[10] more than one billion individual applications; the second billion came in about six months; the third in just over three months. From zero to a billion in less than a year, then six months, then three, then . . . well, regardless of what is next, that is a nearly incomprehensible rate of growth, a reality worth pondering for a moment.

- **Culture.** We have become conditioned by the expectation (quite often the reality as well) that everything is available all the time—that Google and others will be able to tell you where any place is, and that you can then reach your friends (no matter the time or place) to tell them about it. Perhaps all that seems too obvious to think about much anymore, but take a moment and ponder what this assumption, this daily reality, has wrought on society. While an in-depth study of this phenomenon is outside the scope of this book, it is such an important factor that it must be considered.

    After all, in some sense culture is a measure of how members of a society interact with each other, and the transition to the era of cloud computing is bringing incalculable changes to this very arena.

    That in our culture—for that matter, nearly any culture around the world today—this means of communication is simply a given. The fact that we all take it for granted is a profound enabler for future services, for future proliferation of cloud-based services.

    For example, consider that even such a venerable, ancient institution as the Catholic Church has launched a number of initiatives in the social media (including Facebook, Twitter, YouTube, and more), and the present Pope has even encouraged young people to "evangelize the Gospel into these new societies" and "into this new continent" (speaking of the communities that are formed in the various social networks), and that this is "a very high priority."

    Ponder this carefully: If a 2,000-year-old institution that has rarely been accused of haste can understand the fundamental nature of these changes and act on them, can any organization afford to do less?

After all, this is what our cultures now expect; this is what people demand; this is how people interact.

To recap, there have been several key factors that have enabled the development of cloud computing at this time, in this place. Now let us turn our attention to what some of these early clouds have contributed to our understanding of cloud computing, of just what is possible.

Big Contributions

While most of these enablers came about for different reasons, it has really been the combination of "all of the above" that enabled cloud computing to get started. Once started, of course, the pace of innovation began to increase significantly, and that increase in the rate of change is itself continuing to increase—that whole "critical mass" notion all over again.

For example, once actual clouds began to be deployed, utilized, liked, and then as a result scaled up even more, then the early ideas about cloud-optimal application architectures needed to be advanced even further. Likewise, the very need to scale has pushed the innovative data models even further, which enables more scale.

Yet in addition to this self-fulfilling innovation there have been a few, perhaps unexpected "bonus" advances. In particular:

- **Operational Models.** In order to deal with the scale there has been some significant development of novel operational models, with a degree of automation far beyond any prior.
- **Flexibility.** From the beginning these infrastructures needed to be able to scale up easily; then it became clear that they also need to be able to scale down just as easily. This led to automated mechanisms for requesting more and releasing unused infrastructure, and in some cases going further and simply allowing policy-driven, automated scale changes with no human intervention. These capabilities are wrapped in APIs and available via the web, of course.
- **Consistent Infrastructure.** In order to facilitate the scale, flexibility, and ease of operations most clouds have a relatively small number of physical building blocks from which they are constructed. Rather than the hundreds of unique servers,

versions of servers, and configurations of versions of servers that populate the typical, pre-cloud datacenter, even the largest cloud computing datacenter may have no more than a handful, perhaps as few as three or four different possibilities.
- **Packaging and Construction.** With consistency a given, the next step is to consider more efficient, higher density packaging and datacenter construction. Innovations in this area include everything from the very cheap—naked computer motherboards mounted open air (no cases) on sheets of plywood, all arranged in stacks and rows—to the more costly (though highly engineered for space and cooling efficiency)—stackable, semi-trailer sized containers stuffed full of the actual computing infrastructure. There are now entire datacenters designed to accept a number of these preconfigured, stackable containers, with hardly a month or two passing before someone presents yet a more efficient, even more radical, highly scalable modular datacenter.

All of these advances work with each other, in turn depending on another and then enabling yet another. The interactions are fascinating and useful, and will be explored in more detail in Chapter 2, Concepts, Terminology, and Standards, and again in Chapter 8, All Things Data, and Chapter 9, Why Inevitability Is . . . Inevitable.

Limitations

Of course, with all of the excitement there remain substantive limitations. In particular, much of the early thought leadership (such as in *The Big Switch*, a seminal cloud computing book by Nicholas Carr[11]), or in the ideas contained in "Redshift Computing," a set of concepts put forth by Greg Papadopolous, then Chief Technology Officer of Sun (prior to the acquisition of Sun by Oracle), who claimed that all computing would eventually go into a small number of extremely large public clouds. Papadopolous went so far as to initially predict that eventually there will only be, in essence, five computers!

Upon calming down a bit and thinking through the implications a little more clearly, it began to become clear that while public clouds of various types will play very important roles as the cloud computing landscape develops, they will not work alone. Rather, the public clouds will interoperate and work interchangeably (where appropriate) with private clouds built and operated on the same cloud computing principles. Some organizations will create their own clouds for any of a number of reasons including control, privacy, security, and reliability, among others, or perhaps do so for data issues—data retention, reliability, and access to computing resources (in order to enable even larger scales, better efficiencies, etc.).

The realization of these concerns with the early Utopian vision of a small number of purely public clouds—and nothing else—is leading to the development of a much richer, more textured cloud computing landscape, with variations that can address these and other considerations as necessary, sharing common foundations yet differing where necessary.

The best part? Each organization has a wide range of choices from which to choose, with the ability to pick and choose as each need dictates.

I Want One of Those

As a result of all this—the promise of reduced costs, easier scale, greater flexibility, reduced deployment cycles and more, much more—over the past couple of years it has become very common, almost a litany, across many organizations to say in one form or another, that "We want what Google and Amazon have, except that we want it inside our organization, while at the same time interoperating and in other ways working very closely with those very public clouds, and we want to be able to use any of these clouds when WE choose, as best suits OUR needs."

Back to the Future?

A few years ago a friend of ours was given a tour of a large, technology-dependent Fortune 500 company that was trying to win her business. She was taken to what was an extremely large (for those days) datacenter, with row after row of large "excelsior class" mainframes (a figure of speech for very large and costly stuff, but it works, particularly here).

The salesperson, obviously proud of the datacenter pointed to all of this "big iron" and went on and on about how they could meet her needs, no matter what. They even were double-especially proud of the empty floor space in the datacenter, with tape outlines stretching as far as the eye could see marking the places where future, planned excelsior-class mainframes would be delivered early and often to handle growth.

"See, we can handle any need you might have."

Our friend was, on the inside, simply appalled. Turns out that she already had a taste of what cloud computing could be, so all she could see as she looked out across that floor was an enormous amount of fixed costs, with high operational costs at least partially driven by the legions of highly skilled technicians hovering about each precious mainframe, all these costs growing inexorably over time with no end in sight, and very little ability to actually scale up fast if her business did anything like what she was hoping.

Sensing her distraction, the salesperson reiterated that "they could handle growth with this gargantuan facility, that this Fortune 500 organization was most definitely futureproof."

No, our still-polite friend thought, I am just not looking at the future . . . this is a monument to the past.

It is just a matter of time.

Notes

1. Leiner, Cerf, et al., A Brief History of the Internet, last revised December 10, 2003; Internet Society: www.isoc.org/internet/history/brief.shtml
2. IDC Digital Universe White Paper, sponsored by EMC, May 2009.
3. Nexi is a slightly stylized plural of nexus—those crucial points where everything converges and fundamental change occurs.
4. A good starting place to find more is the "Histories of the Internet" section of the Internet Society site (www.isoc.org), where you will find several excellent histories.
5. Xerox Palo Alto Research Center, research lab made famous by luminaries such as Alan Kay and John Warnock (Adobe) as the home of such innovations as the bit-mapped display, highly visual user interfaces for normal computing, mice, local area networks, WISIWYG editing, Smalltalk, and more—all routinely used everyday now.
6. See A 30 Year Mazewar Retrospective at www.digibarn.com/collections/games/xerox-maze-war/index.html.
7. Kill the 53 Day Meme, Jakob Nielsen's Alertbox for September, 1995.
8. Inspired by and with apologies to that famous FedEx tagline "When it absolutely, positively, has to be there . . . "
9. A Vax 11/780 had 1200 nanosecond memory, with a synchronous 32-bit bus.
10. Note that this number includes free as well as paid applications, some of which are either ad-supported or involve generating revenue through some other means.
11. Norton, 2008.

2

Concepts, Terminology, and Standards

Some revel in the controversies, others decry the commotion as so much wasted energy—but no matter what you think about the seemingly endless discussions about what is and is not cloud computing, what to call the constituent components, what terms may be adopted from what has gone before, and what needs something new . . . well, these discussions have served a very useful purpose.

In particular, this is how the industry has been coming to grips with what is at its core fundamentally new terrain.

Still, some of us have had some fun with the whole thing. One of our favorite contributions comes from Sam Charrington and Noreen Barczweski, colleagues and frequent cloud computing pundits, who captured the spirit of the debate in this (only somewhat) tongue in cheek rhyme:

The Blind Men and the Cloud

It was six men of Info Tech
To learning much inclined,
Who went to see the Cloud
(Though all of them were blind),
That each by observation
Might satisfy his mind

The First approached the Cloud,
So sure that he was boasting

"I know exactly what this is . . .
This Cloud is simply Hosting."

The Second grasped within the Cloud,
Saying, "No it's obvious to me,
This Cloud is grid computing . . .
Servers working together in harmony!"

The Third, in need of an answer,
Cried, "Ho! I know its source of power
It's a utility computing solution
Which charges by the hour."

The Fourth reached out to touch it,
It was there, but it was not
"Virtualization," said he.
"That's precisely what we've got!"

The Fifth, so sure the rest were wrong
Declared "It's you fools,
Applications with no installation
It's breaking all the rules!"

The Sixth (whose name was Benioff),
Felt the future he did know,
He made haste in boldly stating,
"This*IS* Web 3.0."

And so these men of Info Tech
Disputed loud and long,
Each in his own opinion
Exceeding stiff and strong,
Though each was partly in the right,
And all were partly wrong!

Sam Charrington & Noreen Barczweski
© *2009, Appistry, Inc.*[1]

While poking and prodding a bit here and there, Sam and Noreen were making a serious point—for many folks, what precisely constitutes cloud computing depends on where they come from, and what sort of concerns—primarily, but not exclusively technical—occupy them.

Keeping that in mind, what we will do in this chapter is lay down a few of the more significant cloud computing concepts—building on the growing industry consensus, where it applies—and illustrate the most essential characteristics.

Basic Concepts: The Big Stuff

For many their first exposure to cloud computing comes from using a service from Google, Amazon, or the like, and so on first thought a definition like this one[2] might seem sufficient:

> **cloud computing** Cloud computing is on-demand access to virtualized IT resources that are housed outside of your own data center, shared by others, simple to use, paid for via subscription, and accessed over the Web.

While this does reflect a common experience, in reality it is a fairly limiting definition. For example, what about the requirement that everything is provided "as a service over the Internet?"

That might seem attractive at first, yet it does not allow for the reality that there are many applications—for sound, unemotional, pragmatic considerations—that will require a private deployment (off the Internet).

In any case, let us keep thinking.

A team at the National Institute of Standards and Technology (NIST) has been doing some very good work to bring some order to these discussions. Here is their working definition:[3]

> Cloud computing is a model for enabling convenient, on-demand network access to a shared pool of configurable computing resources (e.g., networks, servers, storage, applications, and services) that can be rapidly provisioned and released with minimal management effort or service provider interaction. This cloud model promotes availability and is composed of five essential characteristics, three delivery models, and four deployment models.

This definition is more precise, definitely more technical, yet still missing some of the practical realities that are crucial to the reality of cloud computing. For example, take a look at the largest, most successful cloud deployments and (among many other things) two more characteristics are immediately obvious: (1) almost everything is built out of commodity stuff, and (2) there are only a few basic building blocks (no matter what the scale).

To help bring about consensus in the industry, though, we have generally followed the organizational structure of the NIST effort in painting the picture.

A Definition

Therefore,

> Cloud computing is a type of computing that provides simple, on-demand access to pools of highly elastic computing resources. These resources are provided as a service over a network (often the Internet), and are now possible due to a series of innovations across computing technologies, operations, and business models. Cloud enables the consumers of the technology to think of computing as effectively limitless, of minimal cost, and reliable, as well as not be concerned about how it is constructed, how it works, who operates it, or where it is located.

or even more succinctly:

> Cloud computing is a style of computing where computing resources and are easy to obtain and access, simple to use, cheap, and just work.

It is this last definition that most clearly articulates what anyone outside of computing really needs to know when trying to understand what to make of cloud, and how it may impact their own operations. To gain perspective on these questions, simply compare and contrast this view with the present state of affairs.

With these as working definitions, let us look deeper and define the next layer of detail: the essential and nonessential characteristics, the big chunks (architectural layers), and where all of this will exist (deployment models). We will then examine the role of commodity, datacenter innovation, the "quest for green," and a few other interesting cloud concepts; then we will finish the chapter by considering standards and the state of the industry consensus.

Essential Characteristics

Both in theory and in practice cloud computing has become relatively consistent in a remarkably brief period of time. When looking at clouds, we define these seven essential characteristics.

Scalable (Aggregate)   While many characteristics come to mind when discussing cloud, probably the first one to affix firmly in the mind is the relative lack of concern about whether a facility can scale to handle any particular demand—the implicit assumption is that it can always scale as needed, at least to meet demand as a whole.

Note that the scalability of individual applications is not an absolute requirement—there are clouds that consist of a large number of relatively modest applications, and consequently still need to scale in the aggregate. In fact, this is commonly the case in many enterprises, certainly in the earlier stages of the adoption cycle.

Elastic   One of the biggest criticisms of traditional information technology (IT) infrastructures is how hard it is to scale resources—either up or down—in the face of a change in demand for an application. Both problems lead to over-allocation of resources—generally resulting in low utilization of total resources—in order to deal with peak loads.

By way of reference, a conventional, non-virtualized datacenter might typically run at 10% utilizations; with modest improvements it could reach 18%; heavy conventional virtualization (often called server consolidation) can result in increased utilizations to 25% or so; aggressive application of the best in class techniques might get to 35%; while Google averages 38%[4] adoption of certain advances in cloud application platforms (e.g., the Platform as a Service [PaaS] gains the ability to instruct the infrastructure to power down when not utilized, and so forth) that can lead to utilizations exceeding 90%.

In order to achieve these higher utilizations (greater than 50%), it is crucial that the cloud be *elastic*—that is, it must be able to easily scale up or down automatically, with no effort required by the operational personnel at time of need, and preferably minimal to no effort by the application developers in advance.

Note that in the best cases this level of flexibility is provided for each and every bit of work done in the cloud—typically measured in small fractions of a second.

Self-Service   Perhaps no other characteristic of cloud computing has captured the imagination of anyone who has ever tried to deploy a new software application sooner than anticipated, prepare for a planned increase in demand, or cope with a sudden influx of demand while using a traditional IT model than has self-service.

The process for adding capacity in the traditional model typically involves budgeting, acquisitions, facilities planning, staffing, training, and more, with lead times often running into the months or even years.

In contrast, a self-service capability enables the owner of an application to obtain the necessary computing resources—or at least the potential to use certain computing resources—with a simple request, no more than a few minutes before the need.

This type of capability is often implemented in web portals, and stems from the capability that the first public clouds provided: Acquiring infrastructure was no more difficult than ordering a book from Amazon.

While closely related to elasticity, self-service differs in both timeframe—minutes, hours, and even days versus fractions of a second—and intent—primarily about preparing for a range of capacities versus responding to the needs at any particular point in time.

Ubiquitous Access (Services and More)   Another characteristic essentially inherited as a byproduct of cloud's "web heritage" is that of *ubiquitous access*—all capabilities can be accessed from anywhere using any device (at least to the capabilities of that device) or application.

Prior to the Internet, about the only universally accessible, technology-enabled service was the phone system, and that was so only with difficulty.

With the advent of the Internet anywhere, any time, any device access went from novelty to expectation seemingly overnight. Traditional systems were typically wrapped with a web wrapper to make it accessible to either other software (also known as "service oriented") or to a person. Mobile applications typically combined both methods.

One interesting byproduct of ubiquitous, service-oriented/web access to all applications has been the ability for almost anyone to easily create new, ad-hoc applications—colloquially known as "mash-ups"—that mix and match individual applications, data, and services from anywhere, often in very unintended ways.

Long taken for granted in the web world, and long desired in the enterprise,[5] the advent of cloud computing is making this a reality inside and outside the enterprise.

Complete Virtualization: Acts as One   Much of the history of computing has involved discussion of infrastructure—servers, mainframes, SANs (storage area networks), NAS (network attached-storage), and so forth, as well as the software applications running on top of the infrastructure.

Over the past 10 to 20 years a variety of forms of virtualization have worked to decouple individual applications from particular pieces of infrastructure. This has been most successful with processors, less so with networks and storage, and least of all with applications.

What has been achieved has had significant impact—simplifying operations (at least initially) and increasing flexibility, availability, and utilization.

Eventually widespread adoption of virtualization actually complicated operations immensely—this is the so-called "vm (virtual machine) sprawl" problem that can be the bane of many IT operations groups—so something more was needed.

That something more is found in some of the more advanced cloud technology stacks, namely the ability for the infrastructure components to act like one, both for the operational groups and the software developers.

In other words, no matter how large a particular cloud has to scale, it remains as simple to operate and as easy to develop applications for as if it were only a single server.

This is what we mean by *complete virtualization.*

Note that in combination with ubiquitous access, this can lead to a real sense of location flexibility.[6]

Relative Consistency   As a practical matter, mostly due to operational complexity, even the earliest clouds have been built out of a relatively small number of unique components. Even relatively advanced IT operations that rely on conventional virtualization may have hundreds and even thousands of unique infrastructure building blocks (i.e., the servers, operating systems, storage, network components etc.) that must be deployable, and will be found somewhere in that datacenter.

In contrast, the same capacity can easily be provided with a handful of unique building blocks—perhaps two or three server types, one or two network switches, and so forth.

This leads to greatly increased economies of scale, simplified operations, and typically significantly reduced costs.

It is the computing equivalent of the well-known Southwest Airline decision to standardize on a single plane in its fleet and structure its entire operations around that decision. While a radical departure from conventional thinking, that decision was key to much of Southwest's success for many years.[7]

In any case, the decision to build a cloud out of a relatively small number of standardized building blocks has even more advantages here than it did for an airline, and even fewer limitations.

Commodity   While there are those who argue that a cloud can be composed of any type of infrastructure, from commodity to mainframes (and in a certain, less complete, and much less effective sense they are correct), most purpose-built clouds are constructed from what are traditionally thought of as *commodity components*, at least relatively speaking.

The economics are simply too compelling—because of economies of scale in manufacturing, the cost for each unit of capacity (be it computing, storage, or network) is radically less expensive (often less than ten percent of the cost) than that same capacity bought in a higher-end, "enterprise-grade" version of the same product.

While the enterprise-grade products will likely have a place for certain, very specialized (or perhaps legacy) applications for some time to come, for most cloud-based applications—particularly for those that also exhibit the optional (see the next section) characteristic of inherent reliability—commodity components will do just fine, while providing their own unique benefits.

It is worth remembering that this price differential has existed for some time, yet operational complexities and the difficulties in constructing software applications to run on a commodity infrastructure have usually made such a move infeasible.

However, once cost and scaling considerations drove widespread adoption of commodity for some clouds, then technological innovations made it practical (in most cases) for even the most demanding applications.

Other Common (though Nonessential) Characteristics

While the previous characteristics are essential to any cloud computing effort, the following characteristics are optional, at least at this point in time. It is fairly clear that each of these will probably become standard for most clouds over the next few years, if not sooner.

Measured Service (By the Drink)   Nearly all public clouds have always had the ability to bill for precisely the amount of resources consumed, with no prior commitment. While many shared enterprise facilities have had measurement/billing systems that enabled varying costs, those have typically been used simply to enable internal charge-back allocations within an enterprise. Since most clouds are generally more elastic, then the measured service needed is necessarily more precise.

Multiple Tenants   The presence of multiple tenants in the same cloud is certainly the case for nearly all public clouds—it is a simple matter of economics. While it is very likely that there will always be the need for a single-tenant cloud (e.g., imagine a national security organization) it is also clear that for many applications, deployment into a multi-tenant cloud will be satisfactory, presuming cost and other advantages.

This will become increasingly true as the enabling cloud platforms and the supporting operational models become more sophisticated. In addition, the simple passage of time and the accumulation of successes will also increase comfort levels for multi-tenant deployments.

Multiple Applications   Nearly all clouds are inherently multi-applications (i.e., they run multiple individual software applications on the same infrastructure). However, there are certain high-value applications for which a dedicated cloud makes sense.

It is interesting to note that the lower deployment and operational costs of cloud actually make it more (not less) palatable to consider a dedicated deployment. While dedicated deployments should be carefully regulated, it's good to have the practical option.

Scalable (Individual Applications)   While all clouds need to have the innate ability to easily scale as a whole, the ability to enable individual applications to achieve "web scale" may clearly be reserved for those circumstances for which it is required.

As a practical matter this leads to an adoption model where an organization can adopt cloud and start with applications "as is" (except that they are now running on a cloud), then make individual applications more "cloud native" (and hence more scalable) as needs dictate, and both time and budget permit.

Having said that, many organizations were initially driven to develop and/or adopt cloud computing by the need to scale an individual application—be it search for Google, e-commerce for Amazon, or delivery optimizations for Federal Express.[8]

Reliable   At first glance this may seem a pipe dream, perhaps a capability best left for those demanding "corner cases"—those difficult, high-cost, stringent applications that attract only the most daring. However, there are two rather surprising aspects of discussing (high) reliability with cloud-based software.

First, applications that are able to ensure their own reliable operation may easily be deployed on lower cost, full-commodity infrastructure—in other words, it will not matter if the underlying components fail. Therefore, building reliability into the applications will actually enable an organization to *lower* their costs.

Second, because of the larger number of components that are used to build a cloud infrastructure (versus a traditional IT infrastructure), it is actually possible for clever cloud software to develop a higher level of reliability than was ever possible in the early days of high-reliability systems, in the days of Tandem and so forth[9].

While this type of capability is not yet common in cloud computing, with the advent of more sophisticated cloud application platforms it will become possible to routinely ensure reliability for nearly all applications, no matter how aggressively the underlying infrastructure is commoditized.

Major Layers

Computer architects like to talk about "layers"[10] of an architecture, which correspond (in a certain sense) to the layers of a physical building. For cloud computing we define three major layers–the

Exhibit 2.1   Cloud Technology Stack

cloud infrastructure (commonly known as *Infrastructure as a Service*, or *IaaS*), *cloud application platform* (commonly known as *Platform as a Service*, or *PaaS*), and *cloud application* (commonly known as *Software as a Service*, or *SaaS*) layers[11]—moving from the most foundational to the top. Taken together, these define—at the broadest level—the cloud computing "technology stack."

While we are not here to explore and debate the merits of this stack in any detail, it is important to understand at a high level the major layers. See Exhibit 2.1 for a visual sense of this stack.

Note that this is a high-level view of the technology stack—in Chapter 4, Cloud Adoption Lifecycle, through Chapter 7, where to Begin with Cloud Computing, a more detailed model is developed and used. Chapter 6 details a Cloud Computing Reference Model with an expanded view of the layers of a Cloud Technology stack.

Infrastructure as a Service (IaaS)

This layer contains all of the physical and virtual resources used to construct the cloud, and most closely corresponds to what exists in the more advanced traditional IT operations.

Resources are provided and managed in fairly chunky units—whole (physical or virtual) servers, storage pools, and so on—and are generally unaware of what applications are running on them.

There are many innovations in dealing with the complexities of deployment and operations of this layer, yet even these new capabilities will have their limitations (mostly due to their lack of knowledge of what is running on top of them).

Platform as a Service (PaaS)

The PaaS layer is a relatively recent addition. Assuming that some cloud infrastructure layer will provide resources (computers, storage, and network) on which to run, the platform is responsible for organizing and operating all of these resources. In addition, the PaaS is responsible for providing complete virtualization of the infrastructure (i.e., for making all of these resources appear to be as simple as a single server).

How well that is done will greatly influence the complexity, cost, and effectiveness of both the operations and any efforts to construct (in whole or in part) software applications. In addition, it is at this layer where it is most logical to easily ensure reliability for both cloud applications and storage.

In Chapter 6, cloud platforms are further broken down into two layers—the Cloud Operating System and Cloud Platform tiers. Taken together these two layers include both pre-integrated platforms offered only as a service, as well as the middleware tools and technologies that enable platforms to be constructed out of any combination of infrastructures—physical or virtual, private or public, and so forth—virtualized, and then easily delivered as an interface-accessible cloud capability. For more details on this categorization, see Chapter 6.

Software as a Service (SaaS)

The cloud applications/SaaS are at the top of the stack, and when all is said and done are the reason why any cloud is built in the first place. That is, it's the applications that are precisely what anyone outside of the cloud technology and operations groups requires.

Modern cloud applications are often heavily influenced by and incorporate web technologies. It is worth noting that many of these techniques actually shift certain responsibilities to the storage facilities (e.g., databases, etc.), which has some interesting implications (see Chapter 8, All Things Data, for a fuller discussion).

In addition, bringing existing conventional applications into a cloud is made much simpler by a good cloud application platform, as is the task of constructing fully native cloud applications (either from an existing, conventional application, or from a blank slate).

Where They Live (Deployment Models)

Now that we have covered the broad outlines of the cloud technology stack, let us turn our attention to the basic forms in which it is/will be deployed. While this is an area of rapid innovation—rapid even by the standards of the cloud computing world—we can already see the basic options.

Private Cloud

For some time there were many who denied that such a concept as a private cloud was even possible—they claimed that it was oxymoronic—and indeed, there remain a diminishing few who still maintain that this is the case.

But most now recognize that there are many situations where for strategic, operational, or perhaps simply cultural reasons an organization may choose to build and operate their own, private cloud.

These private clouds can be built and operated as just what their name implies: a fully functional cloud that is owned, operated, and presumably restricted to a particular organization. In fact, there are an increasing number of software and service offerings designed to facilitate just this—essentially "private clouds in a box."

Depending on operational/security considerations, private clouds may be interconnected with public clouds [see the "Vertical Clouds (aka Community Clouds)" section later in this chapter].

A special case is the *virtual private cloud*, which is any private cloud that is provisioned and operated by an outsourcing/hosting provider. For some these offer the best of both worlds—the control, security, and privacy of a private cloud with the ease of deployment and operations typical in public clouds.

Public Cloud

The first clouds of any kind were mostly public clouds, e.g., Google, Amazon, and Salesforce are a few notable examples. These are multi-tenant clouds that have tended to focus on particular layers. For example, Google and Salesforce have tended to focus (at least in their public offerings) on cloud application offerings, while Amazon has tended to focus on the infrastructure layer. In addition, both Amazon and Google have recently entered the platform markets as well.

In any case, these can also be thought of as horizontal clouds, in that they are relatively broad-based offerings of a particular capability, be it infrastructure, a data service, search, or some other service.

These are an important and rapidly growing cloud sector, the source of much innovation, but will not consume all of computing.[12] That is simply irrational exuberance, which overlooks some very practical realities.

Vertical Clouds (aka Community Clouds)

An interesting recent development is the emergence of a specialized form of public cloud known as a vertical cloud, sometimes known as a community cloud. These are public clouds organized around a group of competing/cooperating businesses in a particular vertical market, such as financial services.

Able to provide industry-specific capabilities (such as governance, auditing, and security) these can be thought of as a sort of shopping mall for cloud services, virtually (and perhaps physically) co-located to help all achieve a critical mass for customers interested in that vertical.

For example, a financial services vertical cloud could bring together cloud-based services that provide everything a retail broker would need to service their customers—from specialized data feeds to account maintenance to reporting services and more—enabling those brokers to pick and choose among service providers, easily pulling together their own unique, customized offerings for their own customers; while still knowing that all of their industry-specific security and auditing requirements are met.

Hybrid Clouds

As the name implies, a hybrid cloud is a combination of any/all of the other types of clouds. In practice, this is what the most robust enterprise cloud approaches will utilize. While it is possible to dogmatically stick to *only* private, *only* public, or *only* vertical clouds, the real question is simply: why?

There is a class of modern platforms emerging that enable an organization to effectively create their own cloud out of a combination of particular private, public, and vertical clouds, yet manage this hybrid cloud as one, from one place, at the same time.

This approach enables an organization to use the best tool for each job, while containing the increase in complexity.

For these reasons it is likely that most enterprises will take, by design or by circumstance, a hybrid cloud approach.

Geographic Location

At first blush it may seem that with cloud computing, we no longer have to consider geographic location; after all, when is the last time that you thought about where your search is performed, for example?

While it is true that (due to the ubiquitous access nature of cloud computing, itself inherited from the Internet on which it is based) cloud-based services can be thought of in a certain sense without regard to their location, this is only a first step.

Nothing in cloud computing has any potential to repeal the laws of physics—the speed of light remains the speed of light—so consequently delays in transmitting data (known in geek speak as *latency*) can become a real problem in delivering a quality service.

That is why a sophisticated cloud strategy takes into account physical location, and provides controllable, relatively transparent mechanisms for staging data closer to where it is needed.

In any case, the bottom line is that while in one sense cloud-based services are inherently global, in another sense the best will know how to make informed decisions to minimize the negative impacts of geographic distance.

Datacenter Innovation

As a direct result of several cloud characteristics—relative uniformity, commoditization, aggregate scale, and complete virtualization—there has been a very high degree of innovation in the physical construction and packaging of datacenters, with undoubtedly much more to come.

Containerized Datacenters

Traditional datacenters have had a relatively high degree of customization, with particular servers, mainframes, and so forth requiring careful planning, provisioning of power, cooling and network access, then individual installation and operations.

Over time there has been a slow drift toward standardizing the choices and thereby simplifying the physical processes.

The aggressive consistency of a cloud infrastructure layer has opened up the possibility of a fully containerized datacenter, in which prepackaged containers—similar to shipping containers, except already full of a consistent set of servers, storage, and network components—are delivered into a large, warehouse-like facility and connected to standardized power, cooling, and network connections.

This enables some real gains from standardized components, at least for a given datacenter. Unfortunately, there are not yet any standards for the containers themselves, so each deployment is relatively unique.

Low-Density Datacenters

Most containerized datacenters have been optimized for a developed civil infrastructure, in which space is a relatively dominant consideration. Consequently, the goal has generally been to increase density. Unfortunately, with increased density comes increased heat, which then becomes perhaps the dominant engineering consideration—to the point where many datacenters are located near bodies of water, similar to power plants. In fact, some proposals have gone so far as to propose datacenters on ships, though these have some other significant limitations.

However, in economies where space is relatively plentiful, particularly with respect to reliable power—typical of much of the developing world, for example—a diametrically opposite approach will likely make the most sense: the low-density datacenter.

In this approach equipment is actually spaced far enough apart to allow for air cooling. While this will consume more space, in some climates it may be sufficient to essentially build a modest roof with open fencing around the perimeters (plus sufficient physical security, of course).

Note that this will actually be much more effective for clouds that provide reliability in software above the infrastructure—in a sense, this is the ultimate in commoditization.

The Quest for Green

Whether in the industrialized or developing world, the reality is that for economic, political, and sociological reasons it makes sense to minimize the environmental impact of any computing deployment.

Due to all of the characteristics mentioned previously, cloud computing is uniquely suited to enable significant advances.

In particular, complete virtualization enables the applications to be indifferent to the type of infrastructure upon which they run; that infrastructure can then be optimized for the most capacity for any given power or other resource consumption; and the inherent elasticity of cloud enables infrastructure to be run at much higher utilization levels.

All of this makes it practical to greatly improve the amount of computing capacity provided at any given level of environmental impact, a process that is in reality only just beginning.

Standards

The standards picture in cloud computing is decidedly mixed. On the positive side there are a number of standards-based web technologies that form many of the everyday software components used to build cloud applications.

In addition, there are a number of de facto standards (i.e., practices, application program interfaces (APIs), and technologies) that have proven successful for a market leader, and therefore by default form a sort of standard. For example, over the past few years many web-based services provided a standardized means by which other applications could make use of them that was based on a common, easily-used style called a ReST interface (Representational State Transfer—see Chapter 3, Cloud Computing and Everything Else, for more information). As these services evolved into cloud-based services the ReST interfaces naturally remained, and because they were so easy to use, actually spread through the cloud infrastructures. As a result, ReST-style interfaces have now become the de facto standard for cloud-based applications, platforms, and infrastructures.

However, there are few formal, cloud-specific standards in anything beyond the earliest stages of discussion. Examples here include the Cloud Computing Interoperability Forum (CCIF), NIST, and several others.

In practice, the lack of established, formal standards is not a barrier to adoption, at least not at this stage of the industry. However, as standards generally facilitate the interchangeability of suppliers, and therefore reduce the risk for customers and consequently facilitate overall industry adoption and growth, at some point it will be necessary to develop formal, widely-accepted standards. That is why initial discussions have started in several circles.

While a more in-depth discussion of cloud computing standards—de facto, developing, or simply missing—is included in Chapter 6, at this point it should suffice simply to remember that the de facto standards will do for now, industry-wide standards will eventually develop, and in the meantime it's up to each organization to make use of technologies such as cloud platforms (PaaS) that will enable them to make use of any standards as they develop.

Much Sound and Fury . . .

As discussed earlier there have been seemingly endless debates on exactly what is and is not a cloud, whether such ideas as a private cloud could ever make sense or was, as some allege, simply a hopeless oxymoron, and so forth.

There were even some—Nicholas Carr and Greg Papadapolous among others—who argued that this was mostly moot, since all private datacenters would eventually disappear, and all public clouds would consolidate until there were, essentially, only a few big computers (each actually a cloud itself) on which all of the computing needs of all residents and organizations on the planet were met.

Still, much of this ideological debate really misses the point.

That is, it is not unsubstantiated, unpersuasive ideological statements that will win these arguments; rather, organizations will use whatever works best for them.

In other words, the approach that is truly the best will eventually win out.

Parting Thoughts

Setting aside a few emotion-laden, caffeine-exacerbated debates, what remains to keep in mind?

Cloud computing:

- Has come together relatively quickly
- Offers a new technological, operational, and business model approach
- Radically increases scalability, elasticity, and more
- Dramatically reduces deployment and operational costs

Taken together, this paints a fundamentally different picture in every dimension. Consider the very audacity of anyone from the computing industry even semi-seriously claiming that any computing resource could be thought of as "easy to obtain, cheap, easily accessible, and just works."

Audacious, perhaps . . . yet most definitely true. Yes, this is a new age in computing. One that is not only possible, but here today.

Notes

1. With apologies to John Godfrey Saxe. This was first presented at the 2008 Next Generation Datacenter Conference, then appeared in a popular blog post: www.appistry.com/blogs/sam/the-blind-men-and-cloud.
2. Foley, "A Definition of Cloud Computing," *Information Week*, September 26, 2008.
3. Mell and Grance, "Draft Working Definition of Cloud Computing" V14, US National Institute of Standards, June 2009.
4. "Clearing the Air on Cloud Computing," McKinsey & Company, March 2009.
5. For a number of years there has been a push within the enterprise for service-oriented architectures (SOA). In many ways SOA evolved into an important enabler for cloud computing—while some of the particular technologies and standards are different, the basic approaches remain very useful. This will be explored in more detail in Chapter 3, Cloud Computing and Everything Else.
6. Some claim actual *location independence*, but this is unrealistic as it ignores the technical realities that stem from the laws of physics. The delays that stem from distance will always lead to a need to consider location, at least for many applications.
7. That Southwest faces challenges is primarily due to other factors, including some that derive from its very success. Of course, a full discussion of their circumstances is outside the scope of this book.
8. Charrington, "Cloud Computing for Government Featuring Federal Express," CloudPulse Blog, August 12, 2009.
9. Tandem "Non Stop" Computers were the most widely used and arguably the most well-known of a small group of technology providers who's entire focus was ultra-high reliability–the so-called "five nines" and beyond–computing systems. These systems often duplicated every piece of hardware and even many software components, and found wide usage in certain financial service applications (like stock-trading platforms) and other similar areas. Such reliability came at a very high price, and as a result these types of technologies never approached mainstream acceptance.
10. These correspond to what the NIST team calls their "deployment models."
11. Note that *Infrastructure as a Service, IaaS,* and simply *infrastructure* are used interchangeably to refer to the bottom tier of the cloud technology stack; *Platform as a Service, PaaS, cloud application platform,* and simply *platform* are used

interchangeably for the middle tier; in a similar vein *Software as a Service, SaaS, cloud application,* and sometimes simply *application* are generally equivalent for the top tier.

12. Nicholas Carr in *The Big Switch* (Norton, 2008) and Greg Papadapolous (Chief Technology Officer of Sun prior to the acquisition of Sun by Oracle) in various talks have each famously argued that all computing will eventually consolidate into a small handful of computers/clouds. This is better as a conversation-starter than a reality, and will be examined in more detail in Chapter 9, Why Inevitability Is . . . Inevitable.

3

Cloud Computing and Everything Else

As with any fundamentally new innovation cloud computing does not come into a controlled laboratory environment—rather, this is the real world, a complicated amalgam of decent systems that work, slightly out of date facilities that cost too much to run, are hard to expand, and costly to modify, and those archaic old legacy monstrosities for which we've lost the source code, all run by teams of folks armed with duct tape that just pray that they can coax it to work each month and not cause too much pain . . . or as Clint Eastwood would say, "the good, the bad, and the ugly."

That is what we already have in place—so where does cloud computing fit in?

In this chapter we will seek to understand the relationships between cloud computing and all the other stuff in and around the technology infrastructure of the enterprise (i.e., service-oriented architecture [SOA], web services, grid computing, clusters, etc.). You can read this chapter in just about any order, all at once or in bite-sized chunks.

The Neighborhood

In this first section we will focus on tangible and abstract entities, those existing architectures, software, and physical components that either have been or are currently common in the enterprise technology infrastructure.

Service-Oriented Architectures

In the earliest days of computing, application software was often built in a large, complex, tightly integrated fashion, often with circuitous internal structures. Since these applications were relatively difficult to maintain and even harder to evolve, during the 1980s and 1990s the industry increasingly adopted "object-oriented" techniques.

In object-oriented software development each application—while still quite large itself—is built from a relatively large number of small components, with each component formally defined. This tended to significantly help by narrowing the functionality of each individual component, making each component easier to maintain and evolve, and when done well, these benefits extended to the entire application. In fact, an entire market of software development tooling developed, as did many development methodologies.

In essence, what made this evolution work was that many of the unnecessary dependencies between objects were removed from within the application. Still, this was not enough—first, the individual objects still tended to be too dependent on each other (too "tightly coupled"); second, it was still difficult to make use of useful functionality within an application without involving nearly the entire application; finally, even applications that had been built entirely in the object-oriented style were not necessarily easy to distribute across multiple machines within an enterprise, much less across the Internet.

So at the beginning of the new millennium the industry began to take the next step in this drive toward independence between software components, and this next step came to be known as service-oriented architectures (SOA).

In the SOA approach, the key structure is the "service" (i.e., a bit of application software that can do something useful (service implementation), has a formal mechanism that specifies how to invoke the service (service interface, e.g. WSDL or REST) and which can be invoked across a network whether across a network within an enterprise or across the Internet does not). In the SOA paradigm, a service contract specifies both the service interface, as described above, as well as the contractual terms of the consumer-provider relationship, the quality of service committed to by the provider and expected by the consumer, and the detailed service level agreement (SLA) requirements for security, uptime, availability, response time, et cetera. The concept of a contract and SLAs are directly relevant in the context of cloud computing.

There are many different approaches for defining these individual services, for discovering where they may be found within a network, and for invoking them. Some of these are more formal, others less so; some tightly controlled, others more inherently flexible. Regardless of which precise form of service-oriented architecture one chooses, the main point is that individual services are generally more independent from one another than before (more "loosely coupled" in geek speak).

It is worth noting that, by design, the specification for a service does not say much about the sort of computer on which that service runs, nor how much a particular instance of a service is capable of scaling (i.e., how much work it can handle). As long at the service provider can meet the terms of the service contract, and the specified quality of service (QoS), and other requirements of the SLA, the service consumer will be satisfied. This was done in the name of increasing independence, but led to an interesting problem, which we like to think of as the "unintentionally mission critical" service.

Too Much of a Good Thing   The idea of "unintentionally mission critical" can best be understood by way of example.

Suppose that an application developer at Amazon (in the early days, of course, when services were still running on more traditional infrastructures) was assigned to create the facility for handling digital music sales. As part of that effort, the developer decided to implement a service that did a particularly good job of detecting and avoiding credit card fraud.

So they dutifully build and deploy the fraud detection service, planning for the capacity anticipated for the new digital music store. All is well until the results are in, and word circulates amongst the owners of the other commerce facilities that this particular fraud detection algorithm is superior to their own.

What happens next is interesting.

Since the details about the fraud detection service are not visible to the calling applications, and since *how* to invoke the service is both well understood and works well across the internal network, each of the other owners will tend to do the obvious: They will begin using the new, superior fraud detection service, even though this was not taken into account in the initial creation and deployment of that new service. This seems rational, and since the SOA makes the actual software integration trivial, then this is what will tend to happen.

However, no matter how cleanly the SOA defined the relationships between the services and the responsibilities of each one, the service itself still has to be built and physically run somewhere. If this is done with one of the dominant enterprise software architectures prior to cloud computing, then this will simply lead to capacity problems (at best), or near-chaos at worst. As much as estimating capacity for business applications is more art than science, estimating capacity requirements for SOA services, especially a large quantity of services, is even more challenging.

While it is true that careful SOA governance can avoid (or at least reduce) the possibility of chaos, services built and deployed on traditional architectures will, of course, retain all of the scalability, reliability, and flexibility of the architectures on which they reside.

A Perfect Fit   This is where cloud computing and SOA come together. In short, services defined within an SOA are best deployed within a cloud (public, private, or hybrid), and in doing so will gain all of the advantages of cloud-based software. Thus, with a cloud as the hosting environment for SOA services the SOA paradigm can better deal with unanticipated demand for services, and better support many SLAs for multiple service consumers in a more elegant fashion. Conversely, while it is not strictly necessary to define cloud applications in terms of services (within a SOA), experience has shown us that cloud applications are at their best when defined this way—so much so that many see the two as inseparable.[1]

This perfect fit is explored in much more detail in Chapter 4, Strategic Implications of Cloud Computing, and Chapter 5, Cloud Adoption Lifecycle.

Web Services

For many the term "web services" is entirely synonymous with SOA, but for this discussion we are going to highlight the internet-breeding of web services.

In particular, even as the transition to object-oriented software design was underway, efforts continued to enable objects to be distributed across many machines.[2] These efforts led rather naturally to hints of distributing basic services across the Internet. For example, in 1996 Marc Andreesen (at that point a newly minted entrepreneur and co-founder of Netscape, a seminal purveyor of Internet technologies) wrote a note entitled "IIOP and the Distributed Objects Model" which posited this very idea: basic services in a sense "published" across the fledgling Internet, available to all to use as they saw fit.

As this idea began to take shape, there were many voices calling for formal standards, which were just plain common sense—if this would be how companies interacted in the future, there had to be a lingua franca acceptable to all. After all, it was the creation of TCP/IP in the 1970s and a handful of protocols in the 1980s and early 1990s (http, html, etc.) that had led to the Internet itself. With that in mind a vigorous effort was undertaken by many to define formal web services standards, which came to be known as the WS-* family of protocols.

The WS-* family of protocols came to be known as that because the definitions themselves proliferated rapidly ("*" being the technical symbol for "wildcard," meaning anything could go there). WS-MetadataExchange, WS-Coordination, WS-I, WS-CAF, WS-Atomic-Transactions, WS-ReliableMessaging, WS-Basic Security Profile, WS-DL, WS-BusinessActivity, WS-MakeConnection, WS-Star, WS-Reliability, WS-Security, WS-TX, SOAP, WS-Policy, WS-Addressing, WS-Trust, WS-Transfer—these were only a few of the standards defined. Many efforts were made to make sense of all this, leading to complex poster-sized maps, and so forth.[3]

These maps look interesting to be sure, but upon closer examination they are rather sobering: dozens upon dozens of boxes, each representing at least one WS-* standard, each with its own detailed definition of how to use it, when to use what, how they interacted with each other and the outside world, and so forth.

The unfortunate reality is that while the WS-* world was technically correct in a certain sense, it introduced a level of complexity that was difficult for nearly anyone to really understand well, leading to a learning curve that started way up in the . . . well, way up in the clouds. This led to a real barrier to entry that significantly inhibited adoption. There were many other issues as well,[4] but those are outside of the scope of this discussion.

In search of a simpler, easier to use approach to web services the industry developed a relatively simple extension to basic web

protocols known as ReST[5]—a development "style" –that is part philosophy, part technology, part discipline. ReST was proposed in
2000, and ReST-style web services began appearing around 2002.
Part and parcel with the web, ReST was indeed simpler to use and
understand (for a number of reasons, including the simple fact that
there were a lot less standards, and therefore less to learn before a
developer could get started), promoted greater independence between individual services, and generally encouraged experimentation and flexibility.

With all that in mind, it should come as no surprise that ReST–
style web services quickly came to dominate web services. In fact, as
early as April 2003 it was reported that (speaking of what developers
were actually using) "Amazon has both SOAP and ReST interfaces
to their web services, and 85% of their usage is of the ReST interface."[6] That early momentum continues to this day, to the point
where ReST is likely to become the de facto standard (or at least
"dominant style"[7]) for web services.

So then, web services in this sense are part of the DNA of cloud
computing—this is simply how native cloud applications tend to be
thought about, built, and accessed, whether or not there is a comprehensive SOA-anything in place. While it is possible to run an application in a cloud without making portions available via one or
more ReST-style web services, it just is not done that often . . . and
that is a good thing.

Web 2.0

The first 20 or so years of the Internet (before 2000) were mostly a
struggle simply to connect—to develop the basic plumbing and infrastructure to allow the Internet to even exist. As the early Internet
began to take shape the very hint of the possibilities led to the first
Internet Bubble and its demise in 2000—famously foreshadowed as
"irrational exuberance" by then U.S. Federal Reserve Chairman
Alan Greenspan.

It is ironic to look back now and consider the impact of the
bursting of that Internet Bubble. Many considered the Internet itself a bust, hype whose heyday had come and gone, a sort of market
and technology best remembered over drinks, if at all. Yet the reality
was quite the opposite: While the financial calamity for many had

been real, the simple truth was that the Internet had barely begun taking its first "baby steps."

At some point around 2003 to 2004 enough web-based services (that had no equivalent outside of the Internet) existed—Google, Amazon, blogs of all kinds, Yahoo, Wikipedia, MySpace, eBay, and so forth—that there was a qualitatively different feel to the Internet, more possibilities for both personal and business use, more to what it all meant. Note that it was also during this period that Salesforce.com began to gain some serious traction (credibility and market acceptance), the first Software as a Service (SaaS) offering specifically aimed at enterprise customers to reach milestone.

So gradually the term "web 2.0" came into use, which while pushed and pulled by many in one direction or another, in time came to refer to this new phase of the Internet.[8] There were certain characteristics that were common to many of these new services. In particular, many of these services had a:

- Natural sense of scale
- Certain flexibility/dynamicism
- Universal "anywhere" accessibility
- Ability to mix and match one service with another by anyone
- Fostered collaboration

Some were stronger in one characteristic or another, but over time most services either tended to adopt all of these characteristics or they disappeared.

The ability to mix and match one service with the other was enabled by the wrapping of these services with a ReST interface, also known as an application programming interface (API), and this turned out to be a key development. Sometimes the "mixing and matching" is done in client-based applications (often resident within a browser), sometimes in traditional server-based applications, or sometimes in applications themselves resident with a web services provider. While it is not the only way to create these composite applications, the ad-hoc approach came to be known as a "mash-up."[9]

In addition, there were two other characteristics that ironically owed much of their existence to the financial challenges resulting from the bursting of the Internet Bubble.

First, the best of these services had an aggressive sense of commodity for the infrastructure. For example, Google was famous for building racks of very cheap boxes rather than simply using the traditional sturdy servers. Combined with the need for flexibility and scale, this encouraged the development of new types of application architectures, operations, and so forth.

Second, the need for business models that could financially support the growth of these services was acute, and as much as any technical contribution, the development of a viable advertising supported business model fueled the explosive growth of Google, which of course proliferated rapidly. Eventually this mixed with subscription models, leading to such hybrids as the "freemium" model (i.e., a free, advertising supported basic service to promote easy adoption, combined with subscription-supported premium offerings).

It is clear that much of what transpired in web 2.0 was a natural progenitor of cloud computing. While modern cloud computing includes much more, nearly all of web 2.0 can now reasonably be understood as cloud-based.

Agile Development

During the middle 1990s there were a number of efforts to begin developing software development methodologies that were more efficient ("lighter weight") and more effective (making it more likely that the software would do what was needed and do it well), yet retained strong management controls and accountability. Over time these came to be known as "agile development methodologies," or simply "agile development."

One of the hallmarks of most agile development methodologies is the idea that development is done in relatively short chunks known as "iterations," typically on the order of two or three weeks. A key reason for this is to enable adaptation to changing conditions, to knowledge gained about requirements and surrounding systems, and so forth.

This type of rapid iteration, with relatively fine-grained corrections in direction, makes good use of the idea of data and services being exposed via web services, and also tends to further encourage the growth of these services and APIs.

In many ways agile development is a far more natural fit with the malleable nature of web services, so while not required to either create or make use of web services, agile development tools and methodologies are used in the creation of and consumption of most web services.

As a consequence, it is only natural to make use of agile development tools and methodologies when creating, maintaining, operating, and supporting cloud-based applications, platforms, and infrastructures, whether those are in a public, private, or hybrid cloud.

Application Servers

Toward the end of the 1990s the drive toward building out web-enabled applications created a need for a set of common services that would ease the task of the application developers. These rapidly developed into numerous products and a few standards: By 1999 there were more than 30 startups offering products in this area—and within a couple of years this consolidated into a mature market with a handful of dominant players.[10] In fact, this domination was so complete that as one of the authors raised money for a startup[11] in 2003 and 2004 it was common wisdom that the world of software development was now complete—it would be impossible to convince any enterprise to consider any approach other than the big application servers for any enterprise application.

An interesting thing happened in the short transition from innovation to: In the rush to add features and capabilities, a growing contingent were dissatisfied with the relative "weight" (performance penalty and effort needed by a developer) and complexity of the then-modern application servers. This led to the development of frameworks[12] that could enable a developer to pay less attention to the requirements of each application server, to effectively decouple the applications from the application servers themselves, as well as attempt to simplify life for developers.

As these frameworks gained popularity it became more common for applications that had previously been built and deployed on classic applications platforms to make use of smaller, relatively lightweight app servers such as Tomcat,[13] Jetty, and others. In fact, by late 2007 Tomcat was being used by 64% of enterprise Java developers.[14]

Besides the relatively heavy performance and development taxes imposed by the classic application server, there was an even more fundamental problem—a dissonance of assumptions. The classic application server was intended to run on an enterprise cluster, a relatively small number (2 to 4, sometimes up to 8) of relatively costly, high performance servers. This was the world of the typical large Unix server. This led to certain architectural and design decisions that did not adapt well to a world of large numbers of relatively cheap, small, lightweight commodity computers. Many attempts have been made to make that transition, but at this point there is broad consensus that such efforts will not be sufficiently productive.

Taken together, these trends are leading to the gradual emergence of the cloud application platform (aka Platform as a Service)—the true successor to the classic application server. Combining lightweight application containers (language- and sometimes problem-specific), a variety of storage, messaging, and other useful core facilities, along with self-operational capabilities, all of which are intended for the large number of small computers (physical or virtual) that are typical of cloud infrastructures, these cloud application platforms are advancing rapidly.

Messaging and Transactional Middleware

Message-queuing middleware (such as an enterprise service bus) has traditionally been one of the key approaches in providing the glue that holds many enterprise applications together, the foundation upon which disparate applications have been integrated. They have provided some elements of reliability across distributed systems, among other technical contributions.

The transition to cloud computing will generally reduce the need for traditional messaging middleware for two reasons. First, one of the roles of a cloud platform is to radically reduce the complexity of the infrastructure, at least in its appearance to the developer. Consequently there are fewer individual components to coordinate for the messaging layer. In other words, if a messaging layer is used to communicate between systems it will have quite a bit less to do. As you can see in Exhibit 3.1, rather than relying on the messaging layer to communicate between individual servers (physical or virtual), it need only communicate between major services.

Second, the actual communication is increasingly occurring via web service invocation directly. One of the reasons that this is practical with web services that are deployed on cloud application

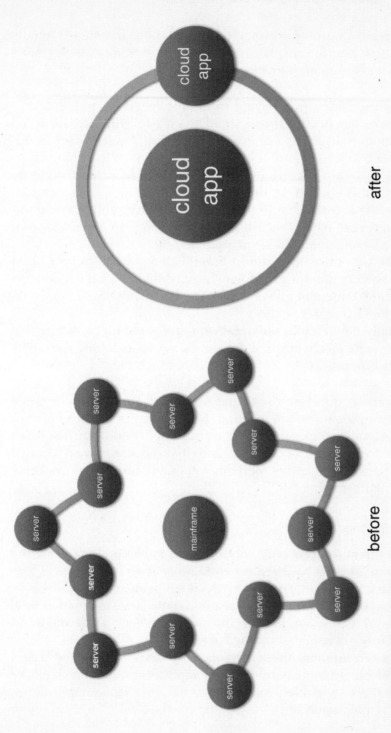

Exhibit 3.1 Overview

platforms is that they are much more adept at handling high-demand bursts, minimizing the need for another historically useful aspect of messaging middleware.

Easy on the State   In a related trend, for reliability and scale reasons there has been a broad trend toward relaxing transactional requirements in many applications, moving toward a set of approaches that implement "eventual consistency." That is, the applications maintain everything that is needed to ensure accurate results, but this may take time (seconds, minutes, or perhaps longer) for the accurate results to be reflected consistently throughout the enterprise. While this will not be applicable to every situation, "eventual consistency" is often quite helpful.

Note that this goes hand in hand with a general trend toward "stateless programming," in which individual operations are executed independent of one another. This is a requirement, for example, of ReST-style web services.

Finally, cloud application platforms are generally providing one or more state mechanisms of their own, as well as having the ability to easily host others.

All Together   It is safe to say that this is one area that will change the most in the transition to cloud. For a variety of reasons much of the need for both messaging and transactional middleware facilities (as now conceived) will decrease, and what remains may be handled by lighter-weight facilities, perhaps integrated into the cloud application platform directly.

Dynamic Languages

One of the more surprising developments in computing during the past 10 or 20 years has been renewed innovation in the area of programming languages. For many years it has been an a priori assumption that software would be written in a static language such as Java, C/C++, C#, and so on. But recently there has been a growing trend toward using dynamic/scripting languages.

In a certain sense these dynamic languages are part and parcel of the whole dynamic nature of web applications, which as we have discussed are themselves instrumental in native cloud applications. For example, much of the code that presents the "face" of a web service is written in Javascript, which despite its name is actually very much a dynamic language. Other dynamic languages common in web development are PHP, Perl, Ruby, and a whole litany of others.

While their heritage may be modest (dynamic languages used to be derided as unstructured, unmaintainable, not proper for "serious software"), dynamic languages are carving out significant roles in the cloud computing ecosystem. From their beginnings as scripting languages, dynamic languages have always been used to glue applications together; with the decomposition of applications into sets of web services, this becomes an increasingly significant role.

There has been and will continue to be significant innovation in this area for some time.

However, at the same time there are many situations for which a traditional static language remains preferable. For this reason most cloud application platforms just assume that software will be written in a variety of languages, and that all resident software should be able to reasonably interoperate. Look no farther than Google's entrant, Google App Engine: It was initially launched with support only for services written in Python, but over time support for Java-based services was added as well. Other offerings, such as the Appistry CloudIQ platform support services written in a wide variety of dynamic and static languages have also been added.

In short, dynamic languages match much of the intrinsic nature of cloud's roots, and as such have an important (though not exclusive) role to play in creating the services and applications native to cloud computing.

Databases, Data Warehouses, and Storage

It is in the business of storing and accessing data (particularly at scale) that the transition to cloud computing will have the largest impact . . . so much so that Chapter 8, All Things Data, of this book is dedicated to this topic. So for a more detailed sense of the changes that will occur, refer to that chapter. Here we will briefly cover the relationship of existing databases, data warehouses, and storage facilities to cloud computing.

The headline is simple: Most existing databases, data warehouses, and enterprise storage facilities can be utilized by a cloud-based application, provided that application is operating within a private cloud, or in a properly secure hybrid cloud. At a high level these applications will appear essentially the same as any other existing enterprise application to the database, data warehouse, or enterprise storage facility, which is very helpful in and of itself.

Having said that, there are several issues that will quickly become apparent. First, the computing capabilities in a private cloud will tend to pressure the storage infrastructure—first the networking interconnect, then the database/storage servers themselves—and this will lead quickly to performance and capacity limitations. This will be particularly true if the applications are relatively "cloud native."

Second, databases that are resident on large server clusters and mainframes will tend to have a large penalty for accessing the data outside of that cluster or mainframe.

Third, many existing databases are severely handicapped by having application logic embedded within the database itself (this was a big trend in the 1980s and 1990s). While this may have made sense at the time it was done (and was often done without real knowledge of the consequences), it can be a real impediment to scale, and therefore to meaningful accessibility to cloud-based applications.

All of these caveats lead to the discussion that is Chapter 8, All Things Data. So what is the bottom line? Regarding accessing existing databases, data warehouses, and enterprise storage facilities, cloud-based applications (particularly those in a private or hybrid cloud) are on an equal footing with other enterprise applications that are not resident on the database, data warehouse, or storage facility itself—no better or no worse—and that is a fine place to begin.

Mainframes, Clusters, Big Servers, and Legacy Applications

Let us go ahead and ask the question right now that many wonder about: Will cloud computing finally bring about the death of the mainframe? (Of course, by extension this could also be applied [with caveats] to the big servers, clusters of those servers, and the legacy applications that run on them all.)

Well, in a word the answer is: no.[15]

While this may seem counterintuitive, particularly when one considers all of the many advantages of cloud computing, there are two large issues that drive the stickiness of these mainframe and big servers.

First and foremost is the data resident on these machines, particularly that resident within a database of some kind. While this data can nearly always be migrated to a cloud-based facility, it is not always prudent to do so at this time.[16]

Second are the applications themselves. While these tend to closely follow the data, there are many practical limitations to migrating applications. The world of computing in the enterprise is replete with stories of applications for which no source exists; applications for which sources exist but the required supporting tools are no longer supported; and applications for which sources and supporting tools do and are supported, but for which no living person has any reasonable ability to understand enough about the application to even hope to modify, much less move the application. These stories are real; these applications exist.

Well then, what can we do?

For this there are two words: integration and interaction. First, either by using existing integration points or by creating new ones (preferably wrapped within a web service), the legacy application can be made available to the cloud-based applications within the enterprise as they are created. Second, those integration points can then be used to allow the newer cloud-based applications to naturally interact with the legacy applications, to include them in the evolving workflow. This will ease the introduction of and progressive transition to cloud-based applications.

As a practical matter this transition is not likely to have a specific horizon, though a particularly aggressive organization may choose to define a particular horizon (timeframe for retirement) for cost, competitive, or other strategic reasons. In addition, note that existence of a mainframe facility will tend to drive an enterprise toward the hybrid or private cloud options, though not necessarily so.

In any case, the reality is that each enterprise will migrate what makes sense as it makes sense. While some may choose to call their mainframes and big servers part of their private cloud, that does not really make sense as it tends to obscure the real issues involved and the real gains to be made by implementing such a cloud.

So the bottom line: mainframes, big servers, and legacy applications can cooperate and coexist with cloud-based applications, but are not otherwise themselves within the cloud directly.

Grid and High-Performance Computing

The drive for scale is very old in computing (i.e., there has long been a quest to do more). More data, more analysis, more often. These goals have ever been the elusive quarry of the computing industry and research scientists.

In the late 1970s and 1980s this led to rise of supercomputers and attached vector processors, with Cray being preeminent in the former and Floating Point Systems in the latter. During the late 1980s and early 1990s another persistent idea kept emerging: Can this be done with large numbers of cheaper, even commodity components?

Initially this led to a series of startups that built larger and larger servers with multiple relatively cheap processors–These included Sequent, Masspar, Thinking Machines, and others. This was the initial motivation for many entry level and mid-tier servers from many companies. Eventually even many large-scale cloud server providers claimed that they were using "commodity components" in some sense (but that claim tended to be undercut by expensive internal architecture, a discussion beyond the scope of this book).

In any case, the dream to build collections of large numbers of commodity computers into a usable facility to solve large problems finally took serious root in the late 1990s and the early part of the next decade.

Because of this history, these systems tended to be batch-oriented without much of a sense of either reliability or transactional integrity—these were after all generally large computer problems—and also complex for both developers and operational people. All of these considerations were generally acceptable for several reasons: First, it was fine for the problems in question; and second, the national laboratories, research institutions, and universities generally had the personnel to deal with the complexity.

Since many of the infrastructures were either relatively rare or expensive, over time there was a drive to create grids in which excess capacity could be shared (with the name itself coming from the idea of power grids, which are often used as a metaphor for public clouds). Unfortunately while that seemed attractive at first, the grid concept usually exacerbated the inherent operational complexity and time predictability of these systems. As a result, these have tended to only be useful for long-term scientific research questions, such as searching for cures for cancer or intelligent life beyond earth.[17]

With the rise of cloud computing some of these efforts are naturally focused on making themselves "cloud friendly," and are in various stages of progress in that effort. As a practical matter, some of the programming models and APIs[18] may make that transition for the specialized research problems that they address well, but most of the others will tend to be supplanted by cloud-based technologies.

Virtualization/Server Consolidation

There are many forms of virtualization, yet all forms share a common characteristic: They provide some level of insulation, of independence, of . . . well, virtualization between a physical set of resources (such as a server, or a network, or a storage array) and the ordinary consumers of those resources.

For example, in server virtualization many operating systems can each run on a single physical server at the same time, each thinking that a physical machine entirely to itself. They can each go about their business blissfully unaware that other operating systems are each going about their business, with none interfering with another, even though none of the operating systems (and the applications that run upon them) were designed to cooperate with each other.

In this way an enterprise can, for example, take many small physical servers (typically scattered both physically as well as organizationally, almost always running at low utilization rates) and consolidate them onto a smaller number of servers, usually centrally located and managed. This is called server consolidation, and has been helpful in battling server sprawl, a bane for many an enterprise. Server sprawl is discussed in more detail later in this section.

Cost savings vary, of course, but can be meaningful (on the order of 20% to 50%) when compared to non-consolidated infrastructure. Some of these savings come from reduction in capital and operational expenses that can accrue due to the reduction in numbers of servers, and some come simply from the reduction in labor costs. Note that these reductions are partially reduced by the costs of the virtualization technology as well as its impact on the computing infrastructure, and the tendency to acquire larger servers to support consolidation.

As with anything there are limits to how much this helps. While no change is needed either to the operating systems or the applications that run upon the virtualized servers, the virtualization layer does nothing to help the applications either—they remain precisely as they were, no better and no worse. If the applications already had scalability and reliability problems before, then they still have those same scalability and reliability problems after.[19]

The same can be said of the early forms of application virtualization, in which an application can be easily moved about from one server to another (either physical or a virtual server instance, a ''slice'' of a physical server). While this adds a bit of flexibility, it does not help much when a spike in demand requires an application to scale . . . and scale . . . and scale, nor does it help, for example, when infrastructure failures cause the application itself to fail and work in progress is lost.

There is also another problem that often begins to plague an enterprise that has heavily invested in server virtualization: a phenomenon known as *server sprawl*. Like kudzu, that noxious weed that grows more than 30cm each day,[20] server sprawl can quickly dominate the operational landscape of an enterprise by adding significant operational complexity. Added complexity nearly always mean added expense and reduced reliability and availability (from an increase in the number of errors). Ironically this problem stems in part from the ease in which the server virtualization layer enables users to create new server instances (much easier than going through an acquisition process and standing up a new server!), and partly from the inability of many applications to safely coexist with each other on the same server (this is itself a form of dependency).

So how does all this relate to cloud computing?

Imagine an enterprise that has invested heavily in virtualization of every traditional form, and has developed both the technological expertise and the operational knowledge to use all that technology. They are able to move applications around the physical infrastructure easily, and are able to provide a measure of elasticity (the flexibility to scale up and down with changes in demand) for the best applications.

By taking a couple of key steps they will be able to create a private cloud, itself easily expandable to a hybrid cloud (thus gaining the option of utilizing public cloud resources as well). In particular, if the enterprise takes these steps:

- Implement a cloud application platform (aka PaaS). This enables all of the infrastructure (physical and virtual) to appear to be a single, albeit exceedingly high capacity and reliable server/mainframe; to operate itself, adapt to failures and changing load; and to be provisioned either by an application or simply by a web request (self-service capabilities).
- (Optionally) select one or more public cloud providers.
- Gradually shift the physical infrastructure to a larger number of smaller, cheaper, essentially disposable servers with fewer variations–in other words, stick with one or two simple, cheap, commodity "servers."
- Simplify and adapt supporting business and operational policies.

With these steps, the enterprise will have made the transition and will be able to gain the cost, elasticity, scalability, reliability, and other benefits of a cloud-computing technical infrastructure.

This is a high-level view. For more detail on moving an existing IT environment to a private/hybrid cloud, see Chapter 5, Cloud Adoption Lifecycle, and Chapter 7, Where to Begin with Cloud Computing.

There is an interesting caveat to this example. In yet another ironic twist, when an enterprise decides to take the steps to go from virtualization to a private cloud, the original server virtualization technologies become unnecessary over time. It is true that they may continue to be used and add some value (providing an additional sense of isolation between the cloud application platform and the physical commodity servers), but it is also true that the much greater sense of virtualization (all of the underlying physical and virtual server instances look and act like one single ginormous [extraordinarily large] server/mainframe, albeit the most reliable one ever seen) completely supersedes the earlier server and application virtualization layers. Consequently, the enterprise is free to do without those earlier layers as well, freeing those investments for redeployment, and increasing the efficiency of the infrastructure investment.

Datacenters

Is cloud computing the harbinger of the end of the enterprise datacenter?

Among the most ardent proponents of public cloud computing, the answer to this question is a foregone conclusion: "yes/of course/absolutely/etc."[21] The thinking generally runs along these lines: In the transition to a cloud-based infrastructure, the economies of scale and expertise derived by the largest providers will dwarf those of even the largest enterprise, making the transition inevitable and making those who resist seem like modern-day Luddites.

However, while public clouds will have a significant role for most enterprises, they are unlikely to completely dominate for several reasons:

- It will become easier to build private, community/vertical, and hybrid clouds. This is primarily due to the advent of PaaS, pre-packaged commodity hardware (including racks, pods, and containers), and so forth. This will become even easier as more applications become more "cloud native."
- Security, continuity, control, and other business requirements may dictate other than public clouds in particular circumstances.
- Location, location, location. Latency—the amount of time it takes for data to travel from where it is to where it needs to be consumed—will become an extraordinarily significant consideration, particularly as technical infrastructures transition to cloud (since it will become progressively easier to geographically disperse infrastructure).
- Culture. There are particular organizational cultures which will favor more direct control of infrastructure for the foreseeable future. Right, wrong, or indifferent, this is simply a fact.

Rather than have a non-productive argument bordering on the dogmatic, we suggest that since the new class of cloud application platforms will make this discussion essentially moot, a more productive approach is to simply realize that each organization will do as it sees fit, and deal with it.

In any case, we believe that a mix along these lines is more likely over the next few years:

- Startups have already almost entirely made the transition, and at least initially nearly always begin on a public cloud of some sort.
- Small to medium businesses will gradually make the transition to a mostly public cloud infrastructure. While in a sense they have the most to gain, small to medium businesses are also the most dependent on applications and technology providers to enable the transition.
- Large enterprises will tend towards hybrid clouds, utilizing public, private, and community/vertical clouds as appropriate.
- Public clouds will begin to play a significant role in the enterprise landscape and that role will expand.
- Civilian government agencies will transition relatively aggressively to public cloud providers.
- Defense and intelligence government agencies will tend to private cloud almost entirely, though at those scales the secure community/vertical clouds will effectively be their own public clouds.

In other words, as all of the cloud choices mature (albeit with different characteristics) then it is only natural that organizations will do what is in their own best interest.

Datacenters will continue to exist, though over time the private clouds will increasingly resemble their public counterparts: Simplified but at larger scale, with more consistent, modular, even containerized commodity components tied together with functional cloud application platforms that will enable greater interoperability and therefore choice.

Managed Services

This industry originated from very simple beginnings, as an option for locating physical infrastructure someplace other than a facility already owned by the enterprise. Over time what have now come to be known as managed service providers began moving up the stack, and now offer a wide variety of operations, provisioning, network, and other services, all primarily targeted at enterprises of various forms. As such, many of the offerings also reflect the limitations of the current, dominant enterprise IT ethos: difficulty in scaling of both individual applications as well as aggregate capacity, sluggish response to change, uneven reliability, smothering complexity, and so forth.

As you might expect that is beginning to change, with the transformation beginning to a new "cloud ethos for the enterprise," one driven by the notion of self-service—that is, capacity available on demand, at the request of the customer, flexibly moving up and down.

This is naturally beginning with the infrastructure (Infrastructure as a Service [IaaS]), and will gradually move up the stack. Next stop will be the platform (PaaS).

This evolution has and will continue to loosely track the evolution of the enterprise datacenter, with the general opportunity to provide the whole spectrum of enterprise-friendly clouds—private, public, vertical/community, and hybrid.

Parting Thoughts

In this chapter we have touched only on the highlights, of course. A full accounting of the existing information technology landscape and the effect of cloud computing upon it would require an entire volume of its own, or perhaps several. Still, it is our hope that this overview has given you a sense of the transformation in progress, and at the same time highlighted some of the more important aspects.

In the Darwinian *Evolution of Species* sense, this is the new, superior species, the pervasive mammals—as opposed to the lumbering stegosaurus and kin that are unable to adapt to a landscape that has changed unalterably.

Some of the existing players in the landscape will adapt, some will thrive, others will struggle but remain (perhaps in a diminished role), yet none can remain as they were before.

This change is underway at this very moment—and that is good news, very good indeed.

Notes

1. Many will agree that at least web services, if not a full service-oriented architecture, are part and parcel with cloud-computing applications.
2. Such as Common Object Request Broker Architecture (CORBA).
3. As an example see the "Web Services Standards Overview" poster created by innoQ, www.innoq.com/soa/ws-standards/poster/
4. For example, all of these standards created a number of dependencies between components, which tended to make applications less flexible and more brittle (error prone) than necessary. This is the exact opposite of the broad trend toward less dependence.
5. Representational State Transfer, an architectural style first proposed by Roy Thomas Fielding in his PhD dissertation "Architectural Styles and the Design of Network-Based Software Architectures," University of California Irvine, 2000.
6. Tim O'Reilly reporting on a conversation with Jeff Barr, Chief Web Services Evangelist, Amazon in his blog post REST vs. SOAP at Amazon, www.oreilly-net.com/pub/wlg/3005
7. While the WS-* protocols and SOAP really are a set of standards, ReST is really more of an "architectural style" that makes uses of existing web standards in a particular way. Having said that, for most common web services it really comes down to choosing WS-* and SOAP versus ReST—it is in this sense that some people talk about "de facto standards" . . . that is, in the sense that "ReST is what most folks are actually using for their web services."
8. Some point to the first O'Reilly "web 2.0" conference held in October 2004 as the beginning of widespread acceptance of that term. For an excellent summary of first year web 2.0 thinking see What is web 2.0, Tim O'Reilly, September 30, 2005, http://oreilly.com/web2/archive/what-is-web-20.html
9. "Mash-up" emphasizes the experimental nature, as well as the fact that many of the combinations were not anticipated by the creators of each individual service.
10. Websphere from IBM, Weblogic from BEA (now part of Oracle Corp.), and JBoss (now part of RedHat); the Net servers from Microsoft.
11. Appistry, whose mission is to create cloud application platforms (aka Platforms as a Service, or PaaS), the successor to the classic application server.
12. These included Spring and Guice, among others.
13. Apache Tomcat, an open source, lightweight web server.
14. S. Pinchikula, "Tomcat Used By 64% of Java Developers," InfoQ, December 3, 2007.
15. At least not in the near to mid term—operational inertia is a strong factor, as are cultural norms within the enterprise.
16. See Chapter 9 for a more in-depth discussion of the considerations.
17. Examples include the search for a cure for cancer at the World Community Grid (www.worldcommunitygrid.com) and the Search for Extraterrestrial Intelligence project (known as SETI@home, http://setiathome.berkeley.edu/)
18. Such as the Nimbus effort from the Globus Alliance, http://globus.org/

19. *Reliability* is often confused with *availability*, particularly by vendors who are not truly reliable. While swapping a virtual machine to a new physical machine when the original physical machine breaks may provide great *availability* (and may be sufficient for some applications), it does not help with the work that was lost when the first physical machine failed—that would require *reliability*, which would ensure that work in progress at the time of failure is automatically completed elsewhere.

20. McClain, "The Green Plague Moves North," *OutdoorIllinois*, Vol VIII No 2, February 2000.

21. Two prominent examples come to mind. In *The Big Switch* (Norton, 2008), Nicholas Carr makes this point emphatically from a macro-forces perspective; and in his "Red Shift" work Greg Papadapoulos (Chief Technology Officer of Sun at the time) went so far as to say that this consolidation would continue until only five computers remain in the world.

CHAPTER 4

Strategic Implications of Cloud Computing

With the hype of cloud computing dominating the current information technology (IT) landscape, much as service-oriented architecture (SOA) did six years ago, we should stop and take a breath and remember the reasons why SOA was positioned as a critical business and IT initiative then. The promise of SOA came from the desire to enable business agility and flexibility, and at the same time achieve reduced application maintenance costs and faster time-to-market, drive savings and cost avoidance through service reuse, and cut into the 20–30% integration burden most companies spend today. These are typical SOA value drivers, and they still remain valid. However, based on the overhyping of SOA, the challenge to live up to those overinflated expectations has been enormous. SOA has not failed as a business, IT, and architectural strategy, but it has failed to live up to the claims and expectations that were hyped. Could any technology live up to those expectations?

However, take a look at the "typical" benefits of cloud computing, and you begin to feel as if you have seen part of this movie before. Many of the target benefits of cloud computing are the same ones we began our SOA initiatives to achieve: agility, flexibility, faster time-to-market, and cost savings. Fortunately as we have seen in Chapter 1, The Sound of Inevitability, the forces that drive this transition run very deep indeed and demand to be understood.

In this chapter, we develop and explore the strategic implications of cloud computing and what this significant business and technology trend means to a business executive. There are many strategic, financial, and operational implications of cloud computing that must be understood as this trend becomes a mainstream component of the chief information officer's (CIO's) toolkit. We will address them here.

A Survey of Cloud Implications

The economic meltdown of 2008–2009 caused significant uncertainty in the business world, and had an especially poignant impact in IT investments that were more discretionary. This intense economic downturn dampened many firms' appetites for complex transformational initiatives, such as SOA, in favor of more concrete, bottom-line-oriented initiatives, which means cloud computing to many IT executives.

Much of the limited discretionary spending has been sprinkled over a few opportunities, but it was not enough to have a significant impact on business or IT operations. Discretionary spending tends to be focused on strategic investments, research and development, and IT innovation initiatives. However, as we all have seen, an economic blip usually crushes all discretionary budgets across the board, including IT discretionary budgets. Therefore, all non–business sponsored IT initiatives tend to be pruned back or cancelled, and IT innovation ceases until the next economic upturn. IT innovation and transformation efforts include initiatives such as SOA (if not sponsored by the business), and other technology explorations and research and development efforts, such as understanding effective utilization of cloud computing, mobile applications, web 2.0, social networks and related technology trends. Without business sponsorship, these initiatives will have no support in a difficult economy.

However, technologies with high potential for rapid return on investment will start or continue to be pursued. Cloud computing falls into this category. The combination of business value potential, industry buzz, and a sour economy have made cloud computing a very relevant focus for business and IT executives. Cloud computing offers a very potent combination of business agility, rapid time to market, and IT cost savings that can be realized quickly for aspects of your business. That is why cloud computing is compelling to business and IT executives. The troubled economy has reprioritized IT initiatives, and cloud rose to the top of the stack. Cloud offers an opportunity to deliver tangible, hard dollar savings to an organization by reducing IT operations costs and personnel costs associated with internally owned datacenters.

Strategic Business and Financial Implications

The challenging economy made the cloud computing conversation especially relevant. The business and financial potential of cloud makes it a special trend for us to embrace. We will delve deeper into the full range of business and financial benefits later. The strategic business and financial implications of cloud are the focus of this section.

First and foremost, with cloud computing, we have another avenue for realizing business agility, the Holy Grail of all business strategies. As with all technology trends, business agility is probably the most frequently mentioned goal of business and technology executives when they describe their strategies, and yet it remains the least realized in terms of execution. We could even go so far as to say that a clearly articulated business or technology strategy that can deliver on that promise, that is clearly articulated, and has been incorporated into daily operations can seem as elusive as any mythological beast. Fortunately, this opportunity truly is different.

Cloud computing offers business agility in a simple, clearly understandable model: For a new startup or for emergent business requirements of established enterprises, cloud computing allows an organization to implement a rapid time-to-market model by securely accessing a ready-to-use IT infrastructure environment, hosted and managed by a trusted third party, with right-sized, scalable computing, network and storage capability, that we pay for only as we use it and based on how much of it we use. Hmmm, let me think about this a while . . . . NOT!!!

We do not have to build or expand our data center (no construction of buildings, raised floor, energy and cooling equipment, building automation and monitoring equipment, and no staff); we do not have to buy any hardware, software, or network infrastructure (no dealing with the procurement hassles we are so accustomed to, especially with the inevitable delays in IT acquisition); we can rapidly implement a new business model or start a new company to address a new market need far faster than we normally could have; and we do not have to continue to pay for the cloud infrastructure and resources if we discontinue the project or if the company fails. From a business and IT executive's perspective, what is not to like about this business vignette?

There are countless new startup firms that have leveraged cloud computing models to obtain their IT infrastructure as a service, therefore enabling them to focus their limited funds and resource bandwidth on their unique technology and business model innovation. Resource constraints are liberating in this sense, since they force new startups to leverage ready-to-use cloud resources as opposed to building a data center.

These types of scenarios, of course, raise a number of business and financial implications that must be explored further.

Convert Fixed Costs to Variable Costs

First, cloud computing offers a business executive the opportunity to convert what have traditionally been significant fixed costs of owning and operating a data center into a variable cost, paid only by the volume of IT resources that are actually used. Data center costs are paid up front, but are capital from an accounting perspective, where the physical assets are depreciated over their useful lives. Thus, data centers are fixed costs in that the expenses paid monthly will be relatively fixed compared to business volume.

Fixed costs are expenses that stay relatively constant regardless of the level of sales. For example, the cost of renting a corporate headquarters is likely to be a constant amount (say, $100,000 per month) regardless of how much revenue the company generates. Data centers, and the computing resources, cooling and energy management equipment, and supporting building automation and physical security equipment contained therein, are considered fixed costs, are treated as capital expenses in accounting terms, and are depreciated over their useful lives per generally accepted accounting principles (GAAP) rules. For the purposes of quarterly or annual accounting, the monthly expense for data centers will be a fixed cost, or the same quantity of expense, regardless of how effectively it contributes to or supports revenue volume. So, if sales are down, you still have to pay the same fixed costs. If your sales are up, you have the same fixed expense obligations.

Variable costs, however, vary with the amount of output or sales that is generated. Examples of common variable costs include raw materials, packaging, and labor directly involved in a company's manufacturing process. These costs vary with the amount of output and/or sales volume a company generates. More sales, more variable costs, but they are aligned with sales and output volume. Less sales or output, the less your variable costs will be. Cloud computing models, based on the pay-as-you-go model offered via utility computing benefits, means that the expenses associated with cloud-provided resources, e.g. IT infrastructure, platforms as a service (Paas), software as a service (SaaS), vary more directly with your output or sales volume, and you can add or reduce capacity based on sales volume or output volume. Thus, cloud computing expenses to a cloud consumer are a variable cost instead of a fixed cost. From a cash flow and financial perspective, converting fixed costs into variable costs is far better for the enterprise. Cloud computing is especially attractive in enabling this fixed cost to variable cost conversion benefit.

Cloud Delivers Superior Return on Assets

Cloud computing potential to deliver a superior return on assets (ROA) to the enterprise than the ROA of an organization that owns and operates its own data centers. ROA is an indicator of how profitable a company is relative to its total assets. ROA tells you what the company can do with what it has (i.e., how many dollars of earnings they derive from each dollar of assets they control). Companies that require large initial investments in physical assets will generally have lower return on assets.

$$\text{ROA} = (\text{Net Income} - \text{Interest Expense} - \text{Interest Tax Savings})/\text{Average Total Assets}$$

Consider two internet startups, each with a $20 million tranche of venture capital. StartCo1 invests in a small data center, computing infrastructure, staffing, power and cooling equipment, which costs $5 million. Instead leverages a third-party cloud for its IT infrastructure, costing it $750,000 annually. Each has $3 million in revenue in year one, with a net income of (–$2 million. The calculations for ROA for each of these startups are below. For the purposes of this ROA example, we assume interest expenses and interest tax savings are zero.

StartCo1 ROA calculation = ($ − 2,000,000/$5,000,000) = −4
StartCo2 ROA calculation − ($ − 2,000,000/$750,000) = 0

A higher ROA value indicates superior return on assets. Thus, the calculation above illustrates that StartCo1, with a ROA of −4.0 or minus four, has a poor ROA relative to StartCo2, with a ROA of 0.0, or zero.

The ROA calculation provides insights into how efficient business management is at using its assets to generate earnings. ROA is calculated by dividing a company's annual earnings by its total assets, and is displayed as a percentage. Data centers and IT infrastructure are treated as a firm's assets, and thus will impact the ROA calculation. Under a cloud strategy, the data centers are owned and operated by an external third party, while the revenue generated from a cloud-based business model is yours. Thus, the ROA calculation clearly confers a benefit to the enterprise leveraging a cloud model.

Cloud computing helps reduce IT costs by offloading data centers, IT operations staff, and related costs to third-party cloud providers. While a small percentage of overall corporate expenses, this still contributes to a better allocation of capital toward strategic business and IT requirements. However, as we will see, there are a range of compelling business, information technology, and strategic benefits of cloud computing. Adoption of cloud computing is not a one size fits all proposition. Rather, cloud will offer different value propositions based on your particular business requirements and technology foundation, and the specific types of cloud resources your firm requires. Cloud is much more than outsourcing all or portions of your IT infrastructure to a third party cloud service provider.

Business Agility and Faster Time to Market

Cloud computing offers a new pathway to business agility and faster time to market by offering ready-to-consume cloud-enabled resources, such as IT infrastructure, software platforms and business applications, that can be accessed and operated in support of a new business requirement far faster than acquiring, installing, configuring and operating these IT resources on your own. For the business executive, cloud means the ability to quickly get a new business model to market without the typical IT procurement delays, infrastructure engineering and configuration management needs, and software configuration and maintenance requirements. Instead, the business defines its computing, storage, network, platform and application resource requirements; goes to a third-party cloud provider; and obtains the necessary resources with a credit card transaction. The resources will be available within hours, as opposed to weeks and months.

There are many scenarios where cloud makes perfect sense for a business executive. Often, new business model concepts are tested and piloted on a limited basis in order to wring out the kinks and nuances of a new business model or limited aspects of a new business strategy. Many times, speed to market is a major driver of a new business model innovation, and along with that comes security and intellectual property protection. The longer you wait to launch, the sooner critical trade secrets can fall into the hands of your competition. For a business executive, cloud provides a means to conduct limited scope business-model experiments to pilot a new service or product, quickly and securely, without having to conduct normal IT acquisition of hardware, software, and network infrastructure. As the business model innovation proceeds, and if it is successful, cloud offers a scalable on-demand model to add new capacity precisely as it is needed, no more and no less. If the business model pilot is cancelled, the cloud capacity is relinquished, and you stop paying for the cloud resources immediately. If you had acquired the IT infrastructure to support the new business model construct, you would still be paying for it, and you would still have the capacity—probably unused capacity—going forward. Excess capacity is waste, both in hard dollar terms, physical computing and storage terms, and in manpower and IT human resources terms.

The business agility and rapid time-to-market value of cloud is particularly attractive as a means to respond to new markets quickly, to innovate and test new business model concepts quickly, and to offer new startups a rapid model to go to market without up-front costs and time delays in acquiring and operating IT infrastructure. These are all reasons why a business executive should care about cloud. The strategic implications are clear.

Information Technology Benefits of Cloud Computing

The IT benefits of cloud computing are significant as well—at first blush, however, IT executives will blanch at the idea of more outsourcing of IT capabilities, in this case IT infrastructure to cloud providers. However, that perspective is a very narrow one, and does not consider the strategic value of clouds in the strategic context of the overall business enterprise. Cloud offers a way to increase IT resource and capacity utilization, which are historically very low in privately-operated datacenters of large enterprises, usually in the low to mid teens (15%). Often, the dramatic underutilization of datacenter resources—especially computing, storage and network resources—are caused by stovepiped system-based acquisition of dedicated IT infrastructure, scoped for peak loads anticipated under best case estimates for a new business application. There are two fundamental problems with this model: (1) a business application project team usually acquires its own dedicated IT resources, which are explicitly not meant to be shared with other business applications or by other business units; and (2) the estimated peak utilization of the computing, storage and network resources is almost always too optimistic, meaning that too much capacity is acquired and installed, and most of the available capacity is never utilized.

These two factors are why virtualization technologies have become mainstream today. At least by leveraging virtualization concepts, an enterprise can acquire less computing hardware initially (usually inexpensive commodity blades), virtualize these computing resources for the initial application requirement, and still leverage the remaining excess capacity for other computing needs by others in the enterprise. Cloud applied in this model offers clear IT savings in optimizing infrastructure spending across multiple application project requirements, rather than acquiring dedicated servers and storage for application stovepipes that are inherently not intended nor designed to be shared and leveraged by others.

While the IT cost savings are clear in the scenario above, there are broader IT implications with cloud computing, as described in the list below:

- **Optimize IT Costs.** Cloud can reduce a portion of IT operations costs. Through judicious leveraging of cloud service providers to offload portions of IT infrastructure costs, a combination of IT savings and business enablement can be achieved. Cloud should not be pursued strictly as a cost-savings initiative, although cost is most certainly a core driver of the cloud push today. Cloud savings must be balanced by some degree of business enablement or business assurance in order to justify pursuing a cloud strategy.

- **Time Compression of Go to Market Models.** Cloud offers time compression of time-to-market for key business initiatives. We feel this is a key driver for adoption of cloud computing en masse. Time compression of time-to-market is critical for new business initiatives where a novel innovation must be launched quickly, without long lead times, in order to capitalize on its market potential. Cloud offers an ideal business capability platform to market in a dramatically time-compressed fashion. Time-compression helps avoid intellectual property leakage, competitive advantage erosion, and loss of market potential through product launch delays due to IT acquisition delays, internal organizational friction, and related factors.

- **Inexpensive Access to New Business Applications.** Cloud offers the ability of the IT organization to evaluate, access and provide business applications to its business customers quickly and inexpensively via the Software as a Service (SaaS) Cloud pattern. Cloud-enabled SaaS-based applications have low startup costs, low monthly access fees, and eliminate the need to acquire and install hardware, software, network and storage capacity typically required for the very same application on an enterprise license basis.

- **Reduced Maintenance of IT Infrastructure and Applications.** Another IT benefit of cloud involves the reduced maintenance for applications and platforms (SaaS and PaaS, Platform as a Service) that are accessed via the cloud on behalf of the IT organization's business customers.

- **Business Alignment of IT resources.** Cloud supports better alignment of IT resources to business needs by focusing these valuable enterprise assets on competitive advantage and strategic initiatives rather than commodity IT requirements.

- **IT Resources Deployed in Support of Competitive Advantage.** Furthermore, an appropriate cloud strategy will leverage cloud as a competitive advantage enabler, which means that resources focused on pursuing cloud for competitive advantage purposes will have clear alignment to the needs of the business.

Also, the strategic implications of cloud for the CIO rest in the ability of the IT organization to offer cloud capabilities to its business customers and truly be a force for faster time-to-market for new business applications. The IT organization should develop either an internal private cloud that can be applied to multiple business scenarios, or develop the relationships with multiple external cloud service providers to be able to quickly provision cloud resources to enable specific business application requirements. Developing internal, private cloud capabilities is a significant research and development effort, and must be pursued with care and with the full support of business leadership to invest in such an internal project. However, the private cloud offers immediate cost savings through server consolidation, staff realignment, and better asset utilization.

In the public third-party cloud scenario, the IT organization must still perform research and development in order to understand the types of cloud providers and their capabilities, and to develop key relationships with a few trusted cloud providers to which they will offload portions of their IT infrastructure over time.

In all of these scenarios, the IT organization can leverage cloud computing to drive cost and resource optimization internally to the IT function, increase business support by introducing cloud-enabled business capabilities to the business, and support competitive advantage by leveraging various cloud patterns to best support the strategic direction of the business.

Business Benefits of Cloud Computing

Cloud computing offers significant benefits for the enterprise in addition to agility. The additional benefits from cloud computing include:

- **Reduced/Optimized IT Cost.** Cloud computing offers a way to reduce IT infrastructure costs through a combination of capital expense avoidance, pay-as-you-go capacity, better utilization of virtualized commodity computing capacity, and reduced operational costs by requiring fewer internal IT resources to focus on commodity infrastructure needs.

Furthermore, cloud patterns that focus on PaaS, SaaS, and using Cloud operating systems platforms as replacements for conventional application server and middleware needs will realize great potential for IT cost savings. Overall, the accumulated cost savings from cloud can become significant, especially for firms that avoided investing in data centers and related IT fixed costs to begin with. As larger enterprises begin to transition larger portions of their enterprises to cloud, there will be a dramatic decrease in IT costs, with a corresponding increase in business agility and rapid time-to-market.

- **Better Asset Utilization (Infrastructure).** Cloud computing leverages infrastructure virtualization approaches that dramatically improve server utilization, from the 10% current average to −50–65% server utilization, and in some cases even higher. The same asset utilization improvement opportunity applies to storage virtualization as well. Better asset utilization reduces IT costs by reducing fixed cost overhead, maintenance costs, and IT operations staff required to run and manage a datacenter. Recall that return on assets, or ROA, is an indicator of superior use of assets to drive business value.

- **Better Asset Utilization (People and Skills).** Cloud computing allows you essentially to outsource your IT infrastructure, platform middleware, and application infrastructure, depending on your cloud needs, to a third-party firm. This means you can focus your precious IT staff on more strategic and innovative enterprise requirements. This is a far better use of corporate people skills and knowledge, and offers a greater return on your people assets.

- **Pay-as-You-Go Model.** A key feature of cloud computing is its on-demand utility nature, whereby computing, storage capacity, or application resources are consumed only when needed, and you pay only for what you use when you use it. If you no longer need the cloud-enabled resources, the capacity is released back to the cloud pool for others to draw from. This helps align computing and storage demand with business needs, and unused capacity will not sit idle as a capital expense, paid for whether it is utilized or not.

- **Convert Fixed Costs into Variable Costs.** A related and powerful benefit from cloud computing is the ability to convert what were formerly fixed costs into variable costs, which are only paid by actual usage based on internal business demand. This is a powerful concept that has significant financial and operations benefits for IT and business executives.

- **Bypass Slow IT Acquisition Processes.** Cloud computing models offer a means to quickly add operational IT infrastructure in hours/days, versus weeks/months, by enabling innovation projects to bypass often slow and arduous IT acquisition and procurement processes and quickly put into production new business capabilities. This rapid time-to-market model will be one of the major reasons companies will quickly adopt cloud computing. Corporate acquisition processes are so laborious and slow that any approach that enables low cost IT infrastructure services in an accelerated time frame will be warmly embraced. Eventually, IT acquisition processes will be "cloud-enabled," meaning that they will provide acquisition processes and governance to explicitly support cloud computing resource acquisition models.

- **Easy Onramp to IT Infrastructure for Startups or Innovative Business Ventures.** For startup firms that do not have the capital to acquire IT infrastructure to enable their business models, the benefits are similar: less capital expense up front, and easy onboarding into an already-operational IT infrastructure, which lets the startup focus on its unique differentiated business model. For larger enterprises launching new innovation projects, cloud computing allows a very rapid time-to-market to test new business models, and avoids the need to acquire, install, configure, operate, and maintain dedicated IT infrastructure.

- **Innovation Enabler.** Cloud offers a way to create more innovation both within the business and within IT organizations. With pre-integrated IT infrastructure, cloud-enabled platforms, and business applications available in modular, pay-as-you-go pricing models, cloud invites organizations to leverage various cloud deployments on behalf of new business concepts, IT research and development, product and process innovation, and more.

- **Market Response Tactic.** Cloud can become an integral element of an organization's market response process. As an organization monitors the market, its customers, and its competitors, cloud computing can become part of the overall response framework to address emergent competitive threats, emergent customer needs, and spot markets in different geographies. Cloud can become a standard tactic to respond to these emergent competitive circumstances, in addition to being a preemptive platform for attacking the competition.

- **Procurement Accelerator.** Cloud offers a way for business and IT leaders to quickly gain access to various cloud-enabled resources—IT infrastructure, platforms, business applications, and others—already installed, configured and ready to consume—simply with a credit card transaction. The procurement avoidance and/or procurement acceleration benefits of cloud are, in our opinion, one of the major reasons cloud will become a force for good in large enterprises. One of the most often cited challenges in large organizations is the IT procurement process, which almost always imposes serious delays upon projects due to the slow acquisition and procurement processes necessary to acquire IT infrastructure. We urge IT organizations to embrace cloud service providers to help accelerate the procurement process, as opposed to going around your internal procurement process. We all know of instances where project teams have avoided internal procurement processes precisely due to their slowness. Cloud offers a way for procurement to become part of the solution. Cloud solutions can provide standardized IT infrastructure rapidly within your enterprise (within certain procurement thresholds to avoid abuse).

- **Business Experimentation Enabler.** Cloud offers a platform for business experimentation, risk mitigation, and innovation enablement. The cost equation of conducting business model exploration changes dramatically when fixed IT costs and IT support costs are a much lower proportion of the overall costs for business model innovation. Again, many forms of cloud-enabled resources fit this model, from infrastructure as a service (IaaS), to pure-play cloud enablement platforms or operating systems, to platforms as a service (PaaS) to software as a service (SaaS). Regardless of the specific combinations of cloud-enabled resources you are exploiting, they become part of an overall approach to business experimentation and innovation that becomes possible via the cloud.

Cloud computing, as we have shown, offers a range of business benefits. Regardless of the value you hope to realize from cloud computing, you must nevertheless focus your efforts on business opportunities where cloud computing makes sense for you, where risk can be mitigated and/or controlled, and where you can really deliver business value through the adoption of cloud-enabled resources.

Cloud-Based Business Models

A cloud-based business model is a new business model that is entirely envisioned, enabled, and realized based on a cloud-computing capability. A cloud-based business model is thoroughly realized by leveraging cloud computing concepts, technology, and revenue models to execute the envisioned business-model concept. Cloud-based business models may apply equally to both cloud consumers and cloud providers. A *cloud provider business model* is based on the development of cloud enablement technologies and solutions. It includes the following solutions:

- A *cloud service* provides the network and computing infrastructure upon which cloud platforms and cloud solutions operate. *Service providers and cloud solution providers* are similar in that they both develop *and provide cloud enablement services and solutions to prospective cloud consumers to address* their respective business needs. CSPs include organizations that operate cloud-enabled data centers, which provide preconfigured cloud deployments to end-customers to address their cloud needs.
- A *cloud platform service provider* (CPSP, e.g., Amazon.com, Google.com, Salesforce.com, and others) provide cloud-based platforms, hosted in a cloud-enabled infrastructure and cloud operating system environment, such that developers can access the platform, develop a new business application, and then host that application on the cloud-based platform. Cloud platform service providers are unique in that they have developed a complete application platform, hosted in a cloud, which enables rapid application development on that platform, while providing an "as a Service" deployment and hosting framework for the applications to be provided "as a

Service" through that platform, which is in turn hosted on a cloud.

- A *cloud technology provider (CTP)* develops the tools and technologies that enable cloud to be established and provided to consumers of cloud-enabled resources. Cloud technology providers provide the foundational enablement technology for cloud computing. Cloud technology providers offer the range of tools, technologies, middleware and Cloud operating system solutions that are needed to enable private clouds, public clouds and hybrid clouds. CTPs provide the basic tools that help end-users leverage cloud internally to an enterprise, as well as enable, cloud service providers and cloud platform service providers to deliver cloud-based solutions. VMware is an example of a cloud technology provider, as is Appistry, 3tera, Eucalyptus and a host of others.

- A *cloud solution provider* develops entire suites of cloud capabilities to provide to a broad market of cloud consumers. Amazon is a cloud solution provider in this taxonomy. System integrators are cloud solution providers, or will become cloud solution providers, in this parlance.

- A *cloud consumer business model* is an enterprise that strategically applies cloud computing concepts to a significant portion of its business, or to a completely stand-alone business unit, in order to build in the inherent competitive advantages of cloud computing.

Cloud-Enabled Business Models

A cloud-enabled business model is a business that leverages cloud computing to enable specific aspects of its business model to gain competitive advantage. This is particularly applicable to end-user enterprises that apply cloud to their IT operations, or to new business units that with new business models or new business processes.

A cloud-enabled business model differs in that the adopting organization is leveraging cloud on a narrowly defined and bounded portion of its enterprise, and only insofar as cloud helps it drive out costs or achieve time-to-market for a small segment of its operations. In a cloud-enabled business model, cloud merely augments the primary business model concept already committed to by the adopting enterprise. A cloud-enabled business model is superior to one that is not cloud-enabled, but is less sophisticated than a cloud-based business model, which is a cloud pure play in terms of strategy definition, envisioning, and execution.

A cloud-enabled business model "layers" cloud computing approaches onto its legacy business model to drive enhanced competitive advantage, but again, the incremental competitive advantage is a value overlay to the current business model concept. For example, a manufacturing enterprise under competitive pressure from China may leverage cloud to drive incremental costs out of it current domestic headquarters and administrative operations thereby lowering its IT costs. In addition, the same enterprise might also leverage a cloud infrastructure to establish a new overseas manufacturing site, leveraging contract manufacturing from several outsourced manufacturers but implementing its international hub quickly through cloud enablement provided by third-party cloud providers.

In both scenarios, the core business model is manufacturing of goods, leveraging domestic and offshore manufacturing capabilities. However, cloud-enabling this manufacturing business model may provide the incremental margin necessary for profit, or to support research and development of new products to be manufactured in the future.

The following are some examples of cloud-enabled business models where aspects of a business might be transitioned into a cloud deployment to drive value for an existing enterprise:

- **Cloud-Enabled Supply Chain.** A cloud-enabled supply chain is a scenario where a large manufacturing enterprise elects to push demand management, inventory management, and supplier management into a cloud such that the information and data can be globally managed virtually worldwide, while ensuring authoritative, real-time reporting of stock levels, raw materials, work in process, and finished goods inventory. The value of supply chain management in the cloud is being able to manage massive amounts of data, in real time, from global suppliers, manufacturing partners, and distribution and warehouse management partners on the end-to-end supply chain.
- **Cloud-Enabled Sales and Marketing.** Cloud-enabled sales and marketing can benefit by aggregating lead generation, web

site contacts and customer inquiries into a globally-deployed cloud to develop a worldwide view of business development efforts, marketing program effectiveness, and customer feedback and interactions from global web site activities, help desk and customer support contacts, all from call centers integrated into the same cloud. A cloud-enabled sales and marketing operation can enable similar real-time operational pictures of customer data to help react and respond to market signals.

- **Cloud-Enabled New Business Unit.** A cloud-enabled business can be entirely bootstrapped on a cloud-based platform to test a new business model or expand an existing business into a new geography without acquiring dedicated IT infrastructure to support a highly prospective business venture. The risk profile of starting new business ventures changes if it is not necessary to acquire, implement, and maintain an IT datacenter to support the new business. An organization can quickly onboard its new business operations onto a cloud deployment, managed by a cloud service provider, which can be quickly ramped up based on actual business demand from the new business, or ramped down if the business experiment does not succeed. This application of cloud computing will encourage more risk-taking with new business models, and should spur a burst of new business innovation as a result of a much lower risk profile for new business experimentation enabled by cloud computing.

- **Cloud-Enabled Call Centers.** In many ways this is a natural fit with the recent evolution of associated call-center technologies, such as Voice over Internet Protocol (VoIP), which is intrinsically cloud resonant. A truly cloud-enabled call center could be fully distributed and incremental, able to expand or contract as demand warrants, in increments as small as one agent at a time. In this manner this could enable call centers to become even more responsive and efficient, in that infrastructure costs can more precisely scale proportionate with labor costs.

We have offered a few examples of cloud-enabled business models here. This is a small list, but your imagination is the only barrier to imagining the ways in which an existing enterprise can leverage cloud computing models to enable portions of a current business model to drive competitive advantage. As cloud matures, we expect to see many variations of these concepts based on hybrid clouds that blend the best aspects of private clouds applied internally to an enterprise, while leveraging the raw potential of public clouds for access to new markets, new distribution channels, and new products and services.

Strategic Implications of Cloud Computing

Asymmetric Competition

A critical strategic implication of cloud computing is that it will enable a host of new asymmetric competitors to enter various existing markets without an installed base of rigid IT infrastructure and legacy applications that anchor them to their accumulated past investments. These new competitors will not have an installed base of legacy applications, nor will they have fixed costs invested in physical data centers and related IT infrastructure. In fact, these new asymmetric cloud-based competitors will not even approach business problems the same way as their more established competitors. This is the real threat: the mindset of a cloud-based asymmetric competitor. Asymmetric competitors do not view IT infrastructure and data centers as necessary because they have never had them, nor have they ever needed them. IT infrastructure does not convey competitive advantage to them, so they simply do not acquire it. Moreover, they do not want it, as it limits agility and flexibility of the business model more than anything else. The next generation of cloud-based asymmetric competitors view IT infrastructure with disdain and suspicion. They want nothing to do with any physical assets that will hold their business models back.

Rather, these asymmetric competitors will compete on business model differentiation and speed, and instead of building infrastructure when they are larger more mature enterprises, they will continue to leverage the variable cost model of cloud to extend the inherent advantage of agility, capacity alignment, and fixed cost avoidance to outpace their competition. Cloud offers new rules of competitive differentiation, and these nimble new asymmetric competitors will press the advantage.

Furthermore, asymmetric competitors know of no other operating model than a cloud computing paradigm. Therefore, they will accumulate expertise and skills at leveraging cloud-based business models, and thus will outpace their entrenched traditional rivals on a knowledge and experience basis with cloud. Their cloud-based competitive advantage will rapidly accrue based on accumulated knowledge through more cycles of learning of their cloud-enabled business model. A cloud-based business model can learn and adapt faster than a typical IT-infrastructure based business model, which is one reason why cloud-based businesses will run roughshod over their traditional competitors.

Legacy business models suffer from installed base and aging IT infrastructures. Such legacy business anchors are impairing many firms and preventing them from innovating their IT capabilities to better support today's emerging business requirements. Ask any CIO, and they will concur that they spend 70–80% of their IT budget maintaining their current installed base and legacy applications, as opposed to being able to shed legacy applications and invest capital in new innovations on behalf of the business. Asymmetric competition is already occurring through the widespread adoption of cloud computing to create new, nimble cloud-based competitors. For mature enterprises, the need for agility becomes a critical requirement to counter the tactics of these new asymmetric competitors. However, the real battle is not protection of the current business model, but the development and innovation of new business models through the aggressive adoption of cloud computing. This is the new frontier where asymmetric competitors will be hard to match.

Speed of Competition

Another strategic implication of cloud computing is the speed of competition. In addition to enabling a new pack of asymmetric competitors, cloud enables a new pace of competition from current competitors as well. Cloud offers a new model to get to market with new solutions, services, and capabilities that can literally pop onto your radar and take market share before you can blink an eye. This is a unique feature of cloud-based business models and even cloud-enabled business models. As Stalk and Hout (in their book *Competing Against Time*[1]) advocate, cloud-based competitors have a clear advantage simply on the basis of speed, cycles of learning, and accelerating up the learning curve for new business model innovations.

Cloud-based competitors have many of the time-based advantages that are identified in Stalk and Hout's groundbreaking book, and will therefore be formidable to entrenched competitors in similar markets. Cloud-based competition will center on agility and speed, and both are related to having no internally-owned and operated IT infrastructure. Speed of competition is supported by a number of variations, which are explored in the sections below.

- **Speed to Market.** A cloud-based business model can bring a new product or service to market faster than its traditional competitors. The speed to market benefit of cloud computing is a key feature of this computing evolution, and will be a compelling reason why all organizations will explore cloud for aspects of their business models. Compressing relative time to market enables an organization to get to market with its products and services faster, which has direct implications for revenue generation, market share capture, and for their competitive position against other firms. As history clearly shows, first to market very often wins, and cloud enables that competitive advantage.
- **Speed of Innovation.** Cloud-based business models will enable rapid cycles of innovation for new business models, new products and services, and new business tactics that can leverage the speed and agility of cloud to gain competitive advantage over competitors. An organization's speed of innovation will increase dramatically based on its ability to leverage cloud-enabled research and development to innovate, experiment, and bring to market new concepts and ideas.
- **Speed of Learning.** Another critical dimension of cloud computing is the speed of learning enabled through cloud-based business models. Related to many of the other dimensions of speed and time-based competition, cloud-based business models will benefit from speed of knowledge and speed of learning, a dynamic that supports rapid change, evolution of business models, and a higher cadence or pace of innovation. For a new business, the speed of learning has everything to do with that organization's ability not only to survive but to thrive in any business environment.
- **Speed of Business Model Evolution.** The pinnacle of cloud-based competition is the speed and pace of business model

evolution and innovation that cloud enables. By simply focusing more personnel resources on its business model, an organization can rapidly evolve and adapt its business model concepts to better compete against its competitors. Cloud-based business models offer a superior business model evolution framework because of the absence of internal integration to an installed base of legacy systems, without the need to wait for the IT infrastructure to adapt in lockstep with your business model.

Infrastructure Avoidance: Today's Entrepreneurial Mindset

A critical cloud benefit that we must emphasize is the ability to bypass IT infrastructure investment and operations completely. Today's startups are averse to the entire concept of buying and maintaining IT infrastructure, data centers, server farms, and the like. Why waste money and effort on infrastructure when we can be focusing on a cool new innovation, a new technology or a completely new business model? This IT infrastructure avoidance mindset is the current reality of today's generation of entrepreneurs. In fact, if you acquire IT infrastructure you are considered an old school startup right away. It is neither "cool" nor "hip" to buy IT infrastructure.

Infrastructure avoidance allows the ultimate in flexible and agile business models. We must understand, however, the mindset of today's entrepreneurs in order to fully appreciate this dynamic. Today's entrepreneurs exhibit the following characteristics:

- **Web-Centric Culture.** Today's new entrepreneurs grew up on the web, the whole web, and nothing but the web. They live their lives on the web. They represent a culture that embraces all things web. They are digital natives. This generation of entrepreneurs will be extremely comfortable with cloud-based competition because they are comfortable with the web-based dimensions of cloud computing.
- **Remote Distributed Anonymous Collaborators (RDAC).** Today's generation of new competitors is extremely comfortable with remote collaboration, often anonymously, with peers and partners that they have never met. This generation of entrepreneurs can achieve their goals via a highly virtualized

web-enabled collaboration process with peers and partners with shared vision and goals. Because the network or community is defined and aligned with shared ideals, vision, and objectives, they can succeed by leveraging a remote anonymous collaboration model. This organizational construct is ideal as a precursor to cloud-based business models—a web-based collaboration business model can be migrated to a cloud-based execution model.

- **Web Application Ecosystems.** Today's entrepreneurs are intimate with "all things web", Google, Amazon, Facebook, Apple/iPhone, Android, pervasive mobile devices, and wireless communications—they grew up with these applications, models and computing paradigms, and care little about traditional computing models based on installed software on fat clients connected to a conventional datacenter. If the capability is not provided via the web and a browser, they do not want it.

- **Open Source and Everything Is Free.** This generation of new entrepreneurs wants software for free—in fact they want everything for free if they can get. Open source and free is always the first choice. If they cannot get their software for free, they will alternatively look to rent it as cheaply as possible over the web. They will almost always avoid buying physical assets or license software, as much to avoid having to manage installed base as to avoid paying for software tools they believe should be free for a common good. Open source web-based business models are what they know and want.

- **Mobile Devices and Untethered Telecommunications.** Today's entrepreneurs are most likely to skip a physical land line for their home telephone requirements, and instead rely on wireless communications. This generation eschews physical connections, physical infrastructure, and being physically tethered to anything. This further feeds the mindset that avoids infrastructure at all costs.

- **Distributed Collaboration.** Today's entrepreneurs are committed to highly distributed collaboration models, where their partners, peers, and colleagues are connected via the web into loosely coupled business processes in support of the shared vision of the business model. The physical distribution of the

team, the processes, and organization model make cloud-based competition models ideal for these new competitors.
- **Put It All on the Web.** They do not have the fear of the web that more traditional competitors display. In other words, while there are most certainly security and performance challenges of web-based business models and operations, today's young entrepreneurs do not view them with suspicion and dismay; they view them as the current reality and work around these obstacles to launch their business models in spite of them.

The entrepreneurial mindset of today will create a new generation of cloud-based business models that will soon be attacking legacy marketplaces and industries, as well as creating entirely new ones. The discussion above develops a profile of the likely cloud-based competitors that will become asymmetric competitors. These asymmetric competitors will be a force to reckon with, and cloud computing will be the fundamental technology foundation that they will be competing with. Combine the mindset of these new entrepreneurs with the technology approach of cloud computing, and there is real danger for naysayers along with tremendous opportunity for adopters of cloud.

Evolving from SOA into the Cloud

Up to now, this chapter has focused on some of the strategic, business, IT, and financial implications of cloud computing, and the characteristics of cloud-based competitors. In this section, we explore some cloud migration and adoption scenarios that have bearing on relative cloud success for organizations in their transition from the last major architecture paradigm, Service-Oriented Architecture, or SOA, to cloud computing. While SOA still is an emerging architectural and technology trend, it has become the de facto architectural paradigm for business applications and information technology capabilities today. Though some analysts self-servingly declare that SOA is "dead," the paradigm of services and service-enablement of capabilities associated with SOA—despite the baggage—will be the dominant architectural pattern for years to come. Cloud will benefit from the goodness of SOA both in the short term and in the long term.

Cloud computing, of course, benefits from SOA in significant ways. Cloud computing is directly related to the provisioning and consumption of IT capabilities as a service over the web. SOA enables cloud-based business models and cloud-enabled business models. Cloud builds on the shoulders of SOA. SOA, of course, built on previous technology and architecture advancements and innovations around web computing and massively distributed computing.

Many organizations have had success with their SOA initiatives, and thus are well postured to adopt cloud computing as a viable technology strategy. Cloud logically builds on SOA concepts of *services*, in particular shared SOA infrastructure services, core enterprise services, and the clean layered architectures that SOA represents. Those organizations that have embraced SOA will have an easier transition computing. However, many organizations that struggled with SOA have rapidly abandoned their failed SOA strategies and have instead focused their efforts on cloud computing with hopes of realizing many similar benefits. The question is, can those organizations realize their cloud goals building on a failed SOA strategy?

This section explores the relationships between SOA and cloud computing, and how one discipline builds on the other. SOA and cloud computing are interdependent initiatives, and if executed as related initiatives, offer an Agility Double Play. You can achieve agility and flexibility from SOA adoption, and additional enterprise agility from cloud computing. If an organization skips SOA and moves toward cloud computing, it will eventually have to revisit SOA and services concepts, as well as the architectural and organizational disciplines required to succeed with both. Our position is that you need SOA behavior with cloud computing. However, success with SOA, we suggest, means your organization is better positioned to succeed with cloud computing.

SOA Cloud Transitions: Jumping into Cloud Computing

The transition to cloud computing for many organizations is occurring now, beginning with education and awareness, evaluation of vendor platforms in relation to targeted benefits, and proof of concepts and pilot implementations. The hype cycle of cloud computing has begun, fueled by analyst hype, vendor claims, and end-user desires. The focus of this section is the adoption path to cloud computing from SOA. We have observed that many organizations are embracing cloud computing, and their launch pad into cloud computing is represented by five broad cloud computing transition pathways:

1. **Transition to Cloud Computing from a Successful SOA Initiative.** Your cloud computing initiative builds on SOA successes by leveraging SOA governance disciplines, shared infrastructure services, shared data services layers, well-defined and layered enterprise architectures, and, of course, applications composed of services, which should be more easily transitioned onto a cloud platform. This is a relatively easy cloud computing transition pattern, and offers a virtuous cycle of cumulative SOA benefits coupled with the incremental benefits of cloud computing. This is an Agility Double Play!

2. **Transition to Cloud Computing from an Immature SOA Initiative, with Preliminary Success.** Your cloud computing initiative begins from an immature and potentially successful SOA initiative, where cloud computing can leverage architectural discipline, build on already-implemented SOA shared infrastructure services and core enterprise services, and leverage SOA governance disciplines. This cloud transition pattern offers promise for both SOA and cloud computing success.

3. **Transition to Cloud Computing from an Immature SOA Initiative, Struggling to Achieve Success.** This cloud transition pattern essentially means the organization is frustrated with its SOA initiative, and believes that cloud computing can deliver IT value to the enterprise in a lower-risk, less business-engaged fashion. This transition pattern does not mean SOA will not succeed, just that the organization is struggling with typical SOA adoption challenges. Thus cloud computing offers another avenue to pursue that may not endure the organizational, behavioral, and cultural changes that SOA demands. The danger here is diverting critical IT resources and funding to cloud when SOA still requires sustained focus and effort. This is what we call

a "SOA red zone," where SOA adoption can be critically impaired during its normal SOA adoption lifecycle.[2] Our experience suggests that cloud will suffer from the very same behavioral, cultural, and incentive challenges that SOA did.

4. **Transition to Cloud Computing from a Failed SOA Initiative. Your** cloud computing initiative begins from a failed SOA strategy, and essentially your organization "cuts its losses" and walks away from the SOA concepts—infrastructure services, composition of applications from services, reuse and sharing of services, and so forth. SOA failure comes in many forms, but generally it indicates the organization did not have the appetite for SOA, SOA governance, sustained SOA investment, and the discipline required to realize the incremental and cumulative SOA benefits over time.

5. **Transition to Cloud Computing, Skipping SOA Altogether.** This cloud transition pattern essentially means an organization is a late adopter of SOA, or it never really gained traction with its SOA efforts, and instead has chosen to skip directly to a cloud computing paradigm. This cloud adoption pattern is centered on small and mid-sized businesses, where the accumulated combination of business and IT complexity, integration challenges, and duplicate application capabilities have not forced them to consider a SOA initiative. SOA initiatives are more popular with larger, more complex organizations that have accumulated complexity through mergers and acquisitions, as well as from natural organic growth where IT complexity and duplicate applications and capabilities evolved from organizational and structural choices, combined with decentralized IT oversight and weak governance. This cloud adoption pattern is very typical for new startups, or small businesses that never really needed to pursue an internal SOA strategy to attack the typical integration challenges of larger organizations.

The jumping off point into cloud computing from SOA is a natural extension in some ways, but, in other ways, it means bypassing the sometimes arduous effort represented by an enterprise SOA initiative. We will explore some of the implications of transitioning to cloud computing from various stages of SOA adoption.

Agility Double Play: SOA + Cloud Computing = More Agile Enterprise

The most compelling aspect of the cloud transition patterns above is the ability to drive enterprise agility truly from two perspectives in parallel. SOA combined with cloud computing offers an Agility Double Play, which combines the agility offered by a flexible, virtualized cloud environment with the business process and application composition agility offered by SOA through reusable, composable services.

SOA offers enterprise agility though composition of applications and orchestration of business processes based on consuming web services (or services) available in your enterprise or accessible through third-party service providers. SOA also supports IT flexibility by abstracting legacy systems and infrastructure from applications through a layered services architecture, which helps eliminate point-to-point interfaces and instead encourages access to service implementations via standards-based interfaces leveraging industry standards.

Cloud computing offers another level of enterprise agility through the rapid provisioning of new business applications into service by hosting them on a cloud-enabled platform, which eliminates the need to specify, order, acquire, install, configure, test, and manage the infrastructure (servers, storage, networks, security) to enable that business application. By leveraging a cloud computing paradigm, a business application can be quickly introduced without the cost, time, and effort required to buy, install, and configure dedicated infrastructure. This Agility Double Play of SOA combined with cloud computing combines many best-of-both-worlds scenarios into a very real and tangible value proposition that is too significant to ignore.

Exhibit 4.1 illustrates the power of the Agility Double Play.

Critical to the Agility Double Play is the parallel implementation of both SOA and cloud to enable your enterprise business objectives. You must understand that these are complementary efforts, and that in fact cloud explicitly relies on SOA and service enablement in order to provide its capabilities to a given enterprise.

Cloud Pulls SOA Initiatives Through   A clear industry pattern already underway is that cloud interest is pulling new SOA initiatives through. The economic pressures on many organizations triggered

SOA–Cloud Iteration

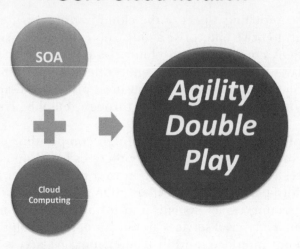

Exhibit 4.1   Agility Double Play

Source: AgilePath Corporation. Used with permission.

a spike of interest in cloud technology. The interest in cloud, unexpectedly, spurred renewed interest in SOA, or brought to the surface new demand for SOA that needed a cloud push to energize. Regardless, interest in cloud computing has triggered latent demand for SOA. The cloud pull of new SOA efforts, from one perspective, should not be a surprise. After all, cloud demands a certain technical and behavioral maturity such that an organization will be comfortable with service-enablement of capabilities and applications, and is also equally accustomed to consuming IT capabilities as services. The mindset of a service-oriented organization and culture is highly aligned with the nascent cloud computing paradigm.

Technically, cloud pulling SOA is due to the requirement for service-enabled capabilities in order to provide or consume them via a cloud-based paradigm.

Behaviorally, cloud pulling SOA through is the comfort level with acquiring critical IT capabilities as a service provided by others. The trust-based model of cloud is very much akin to the trust-based model of SOA and shared, reusable services provided by others.

Culturally, when a company is accustomed to providing and consuming resources from third parties, externally or internally, the organization will have a superior ability to absorb and adopt cloud-based business capabilities into its enterprise.

Putting these forces together, it is no surprise that interest in cloud computing is pulling SOA as a business model, an IT strategy, and an architectural paradigm into greater relevance for all organizations.

SOA Enables Cloud From business, IT, and architectural perspectives, SOA also enables cloud. SOA enables cloud because of the cultural and behavioral forces we identified previously—the mindset and culture of providing and consuming critical resources in a trust-based model from third parties.

SOA enables cloud from a business model perspective, where service orientation is all about making appropriate decisions about core and context capabilities, driven most often by transaction cost analysis and evaluation of economic trade-offs and relative cost-benefit analysis justifications for doing certain business functions internally versus having external service providers perform them on an organization's behalf. These are common decisions in the organization and structure of any business operation.

SOA enables cloud from an IT strategy perspective in that the information technology functions of an enterprise must provide a level of support to the business that is on par, minimally, with external service providers of the same IT capabilities. In this fashion, the IT organization must examine how it best supports the strategic business model and the tactical day-to-day operations of the business, and then make the same core and context decisions that are made by the business. Thus, SOA enables cloud from this perspective in driving a behavioral model of optimizing the IT enterprise based on service and cost decisions in support of the business.

SOA enables cloud, most assuredly, from an architectural and technical perspective. Service enablement of resources enables them to be logically understood and utilized in a granularity that is more intrinsically cloud-native. In addition, service enablement of resources establishes the logical boundaries and modes of interaction that best suit the cloud. Finally, service enablement may be used to ensure that interdependencies are maintained to ensure natural scalability and elasticity (see Exhibit 4.2). See Chapter 8, All Things Data, for more on this.

SOA–Cloud Iteration

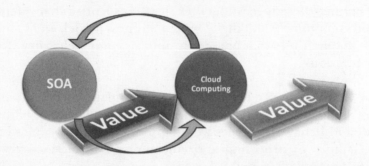

Iterating SOA and cloud can deliver successive waves or tiers of value to the Enterprise

Exhibit 4.2   SOA–Cloud Iteration
Source: AgilePath Corporation. Used with permission.

When to Do SOA versus Cloud?

A key topic that emerges from the Agility Double Play discussion and the transition from SOA to cloud is understanding when your business needs call for a SOA-based architectural model as opposed to, or in conjunction with, a cloud-based architectural model. The answer, ultimately, is that you will eventually be doing them both, simultaneously, with cloud being the master enterprise infrastructure and application hosting and deployment architecture, and SOA being the master application architecture.

In the short term, however, while cloud computing matures, there must be a reconciliation of SOA and cloud to one another based on industry reference models and reference architectures. Both of these approaches, however, must be mapped and aligned to a well-formulated and documented Enterprise Architecture for your organization. Furthermore, determining whether SOA or cloud is the master architecture for your business needs must be determined initially based on business goals and objectives. While there is overlap of the respective value propositions of

Contrasting SOA and Cloud Cont'd.

SOA	Cloud
• Increase business agility	• Rapid time to market for new capabilities
• Improve time to market	
• Achieve better business-IT alignment	• Acquisition end around
	• Competitive time compression
• Reduce IT costs	• Asymmetric competition
• Improve IT flexibility	• New start-ups LOATHE infrastructure
• Reduce integration costs	
• Reduce application maintenance costs	• Better asset utilization – hardware/infrastructure
• Achieve reuse	• Better asset utilization – people resources
	• Convert fixed costs to variable costs

Exhibit 4.3   SOA–Cloud Value Propositions

Source: AgilePath Corporation. Used with permission.

SOA and cloud, there are differences as well, as illustrated in Figure 4.3.

As shown, the business drivers for SOA and cloud are similar in some ways, yet different many others. Remember, SOA is fundamentally an application architecture construct predicated on reusable services, while cloud is in many ways much broader than SOA in its ability to support a wide range of business, technology and economic challenges.

Many organizations are headed down the SOA path, and are trying to determine how cloud either supports or augments their current SOA strategies, or how cloud should be pursued as a separate yet related IT initiative for their enterprise. For these organizations, they may consider leveraging cloud virtualization technologies and cloud platform middleware to provide the core enterprise services or SOA infrastructure services required of their SOA initiative. This approach offers a framework to cloud-enable the infrastructure services layer(s) of your SOA reference architecture, while maintaining the SOA–centric business and data services layers, as well as the ability to support process orchestration and application composition.

Thus, this approach effectively "inserts" cloud into your SOA reference architecture.

For organizations who are late adopters of SOA, but are early adopters of cloud, we suggest making cloud the master reference architecture, thereby leveraging cloud to enable your SOA strategy. Thus, rather than acquiring SOA infrastructure and middleware tools, you would deploy your services to a cloud-enabled platform that will host your services, provide the runtime container and/or application server functions, and support orchestration and composition of business applications built from your portfolio of services. The cloud platform you select could be a private cloud that you implement internally, or it could be a third party cloud platform offered as a service by a multitude of cloud service providers. This approach "inserts" SOA and services hosting/provisioning into a cloud reference architecture. The upside associated with this approach is that you can leverage a cloud-based SOA framework to ramp up or down capacity demand for services for which you are unsure of their true consumption demand within your enterprise or by your customers.

So, answering the question, "What is the master reference architecture?" is not quite as straightforward as it might seem. Building on the previous discussions, there are four main approaches to determining how SOA and Cloud can be reconciled, as described below.

- **Cloud as the SOA-enablement and services hosting/provisioning framework:** In this approach, cloud is leveraged as the master reference architecture, and thus provides the SOA platform and supporting middleware for services hosting, provisioning, management, and application composition. This approach will work especially well when there is organizational alignment and cooperation of the application architecture organization with the enterprise infrastructure/data center organization, and they are both aligned under a cloud strategy that will make this model a priority.
- **SOA with Cloud-enabled SOA Infrastructure:** In this approach, SOA remains the master reference architecture for applications and services, yet it recognizes the value that a cloud framework can bring for the SOA infrastructure and middleware tools. Thus, this approach seeks to enable SOA

through cloud-enablement of the SOA infrastructure, either with an internal cloud platform or leveraging a third party cloud service provider. This approach is already being pursued by many organizations today.

- **SOA and Cloud as Parallel Strategies:** This scenario involves pursing SOA and cloud as separate but parallel strategies, with SOA being executed by the Enterprise Applications organization, and cloud being executed by the IT Operations/Data Center organization. Often, in large enterprises, these functions reside in separate management domains, and are usually different skill sets. Application architecture is a separate discipline from the data center, infrastructure engineering and operations activities of an enterprise. Thus, enterprise applications, application architecture, and application development are often organized in a separate organizational structure from the activities focused on data center operations, infrastructure engineering, IT operations, and capacity management. This model will work as long as the touch points between SOA and cloud are defined and well understood, such that they are working together to optimize their alignment and support to business goals. Most likely, the strategies for each must be converged, and there must be appropriate enterprise architecture governance controls, supported by other IT governance constructs to ensure alignment and joint delivery of both SOA and cloud for the business.

- **Agility Double Play: SOA and Cloud Together:** Of course, we have been advocating for the Agility Double Play in this chapter, where SOA and cloud are pursued as part of a single enterprise strategy that leverages the benefits of both architectural approaches on behalf of the IT organization and the business. In the Agility Double Play, regardless of relative maturity of SOA and cloud strategies, they are converged under an umbrella strategy that incorporates both as key elements of a single business and IT strategy. In this model, there may be two focused working groups or teams pursuing the details of both SOA and cloud, but there will be an integrated team that brings them both together, architecturally, organizationally, and from an execution perspective, so that they can deliver the mutual benefits that SOA and cloud offer as a single, integrated strategy.

What Cloud Computing Does Not Do, but SOA Does (or Can)

SOA offers a range of business benefits that are unique to SOA, and that cloud computing cannot deliver. Thus these should not be treated as mutually exclusive initiatives but as complementary initiatives. Below are a few key SOA benefits that cloud computing cannot offer:

- **Support Faster Application Development via Compostion/Orchestration.** SOA offers the compelling ability to rapidly compose new business applications and orchestrate new or changed business processes based on consuming available web services. This is a unique value proposition of SOA initiatives. Cloud computing does not offer value in faster application development, but it does support faster time-to-market by eliminating the infrastructure procurement and provisioning aspects of new business applications, as well as access to platforms as a service (PaaS), which can help shorten time to market for new business applications.

- **Support Development and Reuse of Business Services.** While SOA initiatives are all about developing and consuming reusable, sharable reusable services, cloud computing is more about leveraging internal or externally hosted infrastructure services, platform services (PaaS), application services (SaaS). There is a common thread here, as SOA initiatives recognize the value in establishing a shared core enterprise services layer, and cloud computing is based on an internal or third-party shared infrastructure services, platform services, and application services. The fundamental difference between SOA and cloud is that SOA emphasized the development and reuse of data, business, and presentation services from an application architecture perspective.

- **Reduce Application Maintenance for Custom Applications.** SOA initiatives reduce application maintenance costs by leveraging pre-built pre-tested services to compose business applications, which directly reduces maintenance and development costs. In addition, revising or enhancing applications composed from services is much less costly than recoding software applications. Cloud can eliminate application maintenance by consuming SaaS-based business applications for appropriate business needs. Cloud can also reduce aspects of application maintenance by building custom applications from Platforms as a service (Paas) approaches, which eliminate the need to maintain the application platform and associated platform middleware required to support applications.

- **Reduce Integration Costs.** SOA dramatically reduces integration costs for an enterprise, which can range from 20 to 30% of a typical IT budget. Integration cost reductions come in the form of elimination of point-to-point interfaces, leveraging SOA tools such as enterprise service buses and related integration tools, and of course web services and XML approaches to building and integrating applications.
- **Support Application Portfolio Rationalization and Consolidation.** SOA initiatives facilitate sharing and reusing common services, which provide a means to consolidate and rationalize your legacy application portfolios. Cloud computing is focused more on simplifying and optimizing (and potentially outsourcing) the IT infrastructure layers of an enterprise architecture, while SOA tends to focus more on the application portfolios and application architecture layers of an enterprise architecture. SOA thus has more direct impact on rationalization of application portfolios, streamlining of business processes, and harmonization of data across your enterprise.

The main message here is that while cloud computing and SOA offer some related benefits, they are really complementary initiatives as opposed to mutually exclusive initiatives. We would argue that cloud computing will benefit significantly from SOA, and the behaviors of successful SOA initiatives are very transferrable to your incipient cloud computing initiative. If your enterprise pursues both initiatives, you can achieve the Agility Double Play.

SOA Failure and the Effects on Cloud Computing Success

SOA failure does not breed cloud computing success. However, SOA failure does not directly portend cloud computing failure either. They each require differing levels of engagement with business stakeholders and business process owners for success, while there is overlap in areas where both can be successful in a given enterprise. SOA success may well facilitate the transition into a successful cloud computing initiative by leveraging disciplines, capabilities, and knowledge acquired through your SOA initiatives.

SOA failure can be caused by a variety of reasons, some of which may impact an organization's ability to transition to cloud computing, and some of which do not. Below are some typical SOA challenges that may contribute to limited SOA success or outright failure:

- **SOA Governance Shortcomings.** SOA challenges or outright failures can in many instances be attributed to the failure to properly address the SOA governance requirements, not so much from a technical governance perspective but from an organizational, cultural, acquisition, funding, and service ownership perspective. As we have experienced, the governance requirements will evolve as SOA adoption progresses and matures, so the governance demands of SOA are persistent and long lasting. This is perhaps why SOA governance is so critical to SOA success.

- **Failure to Deliver End-User Value.** (e.g., faster time-to-market for business applications, reduced development cost). Often we see organizations spending too much time on service provider activities and SOA enablement technology implementations as opposed to working with business and end-user communities to apply SOA to their business problems quickly. The SOA benefits tend to get lost when the effort is focused on "doing SOA" versus "doing business via SOA-enablement of applications, data, business processes and IT infrastructure." There is a profound difference between the two. SOA success is most often realized by delivering rapid value to the business stakeholders of a given enterprise.

- **Too Much Focus on SOA Service Provider Capabilities, and Not Enough Time Delivering End-User Applications and Capabilities.** Related to the comments above, if you cannot successfully engage with the business leaders and business end-user community, you will struggle to maintain ongoing commitment to SOA unless you rapidly deliver business value to your customers.

- **Too Much Effort Trying to Explain What SOA Is versus Delivering Business Results through Services.** As we all know, the most successful SOA initiatives are embedded in the business such that we are not talking about SOA at all. The sooner we get the SOA conversation out of the way and focus on the business or mission objectives, the better off we all will be, and the more successful SOA will be.

Many SOA failures and SOA red zone struggles can be attributed to an internal, service provider focus as opposed to understanding how to engage with business stakeholders and apply SOA to their business challenges. Cloud, by virtue of its more targeted and narrower value proposition, may be able to avoid the overpromise and trough of disillusionment that SOA has suffered through.

SOA Patterns and Cloud Adoption Implications

There are a few cloud transition patterns from SOA that clearly augur well for a successful cloud computing initiative. We explore a few of these here, with the stipulation that this list is not exhaustive, nor is it intended to be.

SOA initiatives tend to cluster into five primary patterns: data-centric, process-centric, legacy-centric, consumer-centric and core enterprise services patterns. The core enterprise services pattern focuses on integrating a SOA enablement platform to provide core enterprise services such as security, messaging, mediation, routing, transformation and the like.

Success with any of these SOA patterns will bode well for cloud computing. However, some SOA patterns lend themselves particularly well to the transition to cloud computing. We will explore a few here:

- **SOA Infrastructure Services/Core Enterprise Services Pattern.** SOA initiatives often center on developing a robust, integrated SOA platform and infrastructure that delivers core enterprise services that are shared by business and mission applications. Cloud computing offers a similar infrastructure virtualization model. Thus a successful SOA infrastructure services effort will pave the way for a successful cloud computing infrastructure virtualization pattern, which is normally an industry starting point for many cloud computing initiatives. Of course, as discussed above, cloud service providers can offer the SOA platform for the hosting, management and provisioning of SOA infrastructure services, which represents the cloud-enablement of SOA.

- **SOA Data-Centric Pattern.** Many SOA initiatives focus on semantic integration, data accuracy, and data normalization around an enterprise data model. These efforts fall under the data-centric SOA pattern, which is typically implemented via a robust SOA data services layer. Successful data-centric SOA initiatives can lend themselves to cloud computing success through the data and storage cloud computing pattern, as well as through cloud-enablement of data services platforms and hosting of data services. Storage as a service and rapid sourcing, analysis, and dissemination of information from data are fairly common cloud computing patterns, although the storage cloud pattern is more common than the data cloud pattern to date.

- **Consumer-Centric SOA Pattern.** Presentation services and application composition frameworks are positioned in the consumer-centric SOA pattern, which enables end-user capabilities at the glass under a SOA paradigm. The corresponding cloud computing patterns include the Cloud platform pattern and is the application/platform cloud computing pattern, where applications and platforms are virtualized and provisioned via cloud middleware to enable application scalability, reliability, and remote user access via the web, and also where application platforms are similarly provisioned to users over the web. The application/platform cloud computing pattern is supported in many respects by the consumer-centric SOA pattern, although applications and platforms in cloud computing are provider-side features of cloud computing rather than service consumption activities represented by the consumer-centric SOA pattern.

- **SOA/Service-Virtualization Sub Pattern.** Enabling services virtualization is a SOA subpattern or best practice that helps ease the development of provisioning of services by providing SOA platform middleware functionality such that service developers do not have to focus on it. Service virtualization is based on loose coupling and abstraction concepts, but functionally allows services deployment to be simplified, and services development, testing, and provisioning to be standardized for distributed developer teams. SOA/service virtualization is a clear onramp to cloud computing, and is supported by the SOA/services cloud pattern.

- **SOA Governance (Plus Two) Pattern.** There are two additional dimensions to the four core SOA patterns: governance and security. These are sometimes called "Plus Two" SOA patterns. SOA success can almost always be associated with a solid SOA governance model, comprised in part of governance policies, processes, enablement technology, organizational models, and boards. Cloud computing governance is emergent, and its requirements and disciplines are not well defined yet. However, we expect that an organization that has implemented successful SOA governance can transition those experiences and best practices into the requirements of cloud computing governance to address issues of cloud security, cloud onboarding/offboarding, cloud management, monitoring, and operations, QoS, and SLA documentation and enforcement.

Certain SOA patterns we addressed in the list above provide a natural onramp to cloud computing, although there are differences in the deployment and support requirements for them. In this light, successful SOA initiatives can be directly supportive of an organization's transition to cloud computing. Again, we emphasize that these initiatives bring some overlapping and unique value propositions to the enterprise that pursues them both. For those that have not succeeded with SOA, we urge that you do not give up. Cloud computing and SOA are mutually interdependent, and success with one will enable success with the other. Success with both allows the Agility Double Play described previously.

Cloud Computing Adoption Obstacles

There are some obstacles with cloud computing, obstacles that can hinder an organization's adoption of cloud and slow the industry migration toward cloud-based business initiatives. Some of these are:

- **Security and Privacy Challenges.** The security of cloud, and associated privacy concerns, give many organizations pause as they think through their particular cloud computing concerns.

Security and privacy concerns include physical security and simple access to facilities and equipment, as well as logical security, industry compliance requirements, auditability, and more. There are also two perspectives: (1) where the security glass is half-full and (2) where it is half-empty. The glass half-full perspective believes that the cloud security concerns are manageable and in fact are better when handled by a third-party cloud service provider. The glass half-empty point of view views all security challenges as hurdles that are immovable and cannot be mitigated or overcome, regardless of the business profile that merits onboarding into a cloud. As with the security challenges that attended SOA and web services, the security architecture and models associated with cloud will similarly be stridently debated, and quietly overcome with security solutions as the industry evolves.

- **Governance, SLA, and QoS.** A critical set of potential cloud obstacles include governance, service level agreements (SLA), and overall quality of service (QoS) assurance. Much as governance dominates the SOA discussion in ensuring appropriate end-to-end governance across the IT and services lifecycle in support of SOA initiatives, governance for cloud must also include this.
- **Reliability and Trust.** Cloud outages are well documented and highly publicized, especially when the primary proponents of cloud computing, such as Amazon, Google, Rackspace, and others experience such challenges. If the cloud dial tone cannot be assured, such that cloud consumers know that their cloud-enabled resources will always be there for them, then cloud will be relegated to niche needs where network availability can be ensured. Cloud, like SOA, is a trust-based model where lack of trust will severely cripple cloud adoption by the masses.
- **Cloud integration and interoperability.** The integration and interoperability of private to private clouds, public to private clouds, public to public, and hybrids poses a great challenge in the absence of industry standards for APIs and cloud interfaces, interoperability standards, and related technical standards.
- **Cross-cloud composition, collaboration, and orchestration of applications.** The concept of composing distributed business applications across clouds, orchestrating business processes

from services hosted in different clouds, both private and public, and of integrating multiple hybrid clouds together into a seamless business application fabric is new. There will be progress on these fronts as industry standards emerge to address these potential needs.

Parting Thoughts: Things to Do Tomorrow

This chapter discussed ways in which SOA and cloud computing are interdependent and mutually reinforcing business initiatives for an enterprise. We suggested that SOA success can lead to cloud computing success based on the SOA patterns that have been pursued in the industry to date. While SOA and cloud offer some overlapping benefits to your enterprise, they each bring unique value as well. The following are some suggestions for you, and some things you should begin doing tomorrow:

- Develop a cloud computing strategy and roadmap, stating clearly what you hope to achieve through cloud computing, what business challenges cloud potentially applies to, and what business challenges are not in cloud's scope.
- Understand various cloud computing patterns and the implications of implementing cloud computing for target business requirements in your enterprise. Understand the relationship of SOA patterns to cloud computing patterns, and how they might reinforce one another.
- Be clear on the desired business and financial benefits you are seeking; operationalize the cloud and SOA tactics you will implement to achieve those value propositions.
- Understand that SOA and cloud computing, together, offer the Agility Double Play to your enterprise. SOA and cloud computing are not mutually exclusive efforts.
- SOA brings enterprise value that cloud computing efforts do not deliver. Be sure that the value you seek is being delivered by an appropriate paradigm—SOA and/or cloud computing.
- The Agility Double Play is achieved through a unique implementation of both SOA and cloud computing. Enterprise agility can come from iterative implementations of SOA and cloud computing, based on the various SOA patterns and cloud computing patterns we have documented.

- The cloud hype cycle[3] has already overshadowed SOA's hype cycle. Avoid the trough of disillusionment by being clear on the value you seek, and how you will attain it. The use of SOA and cloud computing patterns will help align your efforts to deliver the business results you hope to achieve.

The rapid rise of cloud computing is following the typical hype cycle of another technology trend. Many organizations are making the leap to cloud and bypassing their failed or stalled SOA efforts. Our observation is that many enterprises who struggled with their SOA adoption efforts may also struggle with their cloud computing adoption. While cloud computing offers benefits that SOA does not, SOA offers benefits that cloud computing cannot deliver. They are related, interdependent, and mutually reinforcing. SOA combined with cloud computing enables the Agility Double Play. Successful SOA adopters are better prepared for cloud computing success, while failed SOA adopters may struggle. However, both business initiatives will benefit from clarity around business goals, and the strategies applied to realize those business goals.

Notes

1. Stalk and Hout, *Competing Against Time: How Time-Based Competition is Reshaping Global Markets,* Free Press, 1990.
2. *Excelling in the SOA Red Zone,* AgilePath Corporation Whitepaper, 2009.
3. *Trough of disillusionment* and *hype cycle* are both terms popularized by Gartner (www.gartner.com).

Cloud Adoption Lifecycle

This chapter develops a Cloud Adoption Lifecycle Model that describes the major cloud adoption phases and necessary activities that an organization should proceed through on its way to realizing business value from a cloud initiative. These cloud adoption phases are realistic and represent tangible planning, architecture, deployment, and operational requirements we believe reflect the reality of this nascent information technology (IT) trend.

However, as with any emerging business and technology trend, some of the later maturity stages of the proposed Cloud Adoption Lifecycle are a bit more speculative. We simply do not know exactly how cloud will develop as a segment of the IT industry and as a business and technology trend. For example, the following questions emerge from what we offer as the latter Cloud Adoption Lifecycle stages:

- Will there be a cloud integration and interoperability stage where organizations are forced to contend with integration of disparate clouds across organizational boundaries? If so, will it be addressed early in the Cloud Adoption Lifecycle?
- Will there be the "usual" interoperability challenges with cloud that have accompanied all other technology and architectural shifts? Cloud, given its emergent nature, has few industry standards to help guide the vendors and end-user organizations.
- Will there be requirements for cross-cloud collaboration, where organizations will establish collaboration processes

leveraging data, applications, and infrastructure provisioned into private, public, and hybrid cloud deployments?

- Will organizations require the capability to perform cross-cloud composition and orchestration of distributed, cloud-enabled business applications and business processes that leverage and access cloud-enabled data and related capabilities within and across organizational boundaries?
- What path will cloud evolution eventually take as a technology trend? Will it materialize as the analysts and other pundits predict, or will it be derailed by an economic disruption akin to what we are experiencing currently?

The Cloud Adoption Lifecycle Model helps lay out a sequence of necessary steps to proceed through on the pathway to successful cloud computing adoption for your organization. The Cloud Adoption Lifecycle Model will help guide and shape how organizations begin thinking about cloud as it applies to their organizations. It creates a business-centric dialog and inquiry that maps and aligns cloud computing patterns and capabilities with explicitly defined business challenges and business needs, and transitions that initial business-technology alignment through the rest of the Cloud Adoption Lifecycle stages.

However, the Cloud Adoption Lifecycle must also be supported by a tool to facilitate cloud technology alignment to business drivers and business objectives. That tool is the Cloud Modeling Framework, which will help map and align various cloud technology patterns to the desired business goals. The relationship of these to cloud planning and execution tools is explained below, and both are developed further later in this chapter.

Cloud Adoption Lifecycle and Cloud Modeling Framework: Two Necessary Tools for Cloud Success

In order to plan and execute a cloud initiative, we suggest you will need two core tools to expedite your efforts: a *Cloud Adoption Lifecycle Model* and a *Cloud Modeling Framework*. The Cloud Adoption Lifecycle Model drives explicit business alignment between the emerging cloud technology and a set of desired business outcomes that will be realized through the appropriate exploitation of cloud. The Cloud Adoption Lifecycle Model is illustrated in Exhibit 5.1.

Cloud Computing Adoption Playbook™

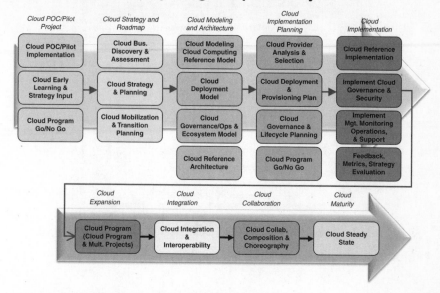

Exhibit 5.1   Cloud Adoption Lifecycle Model

Each of these Cloud Adoption Lifecycle stages will be explored in detail in this chapter. The Cloud Adoption Lifecycle Model is also supported by the Cloud Computing Reference Model (CC-RM). The Cloud Computing Reference Model develops the core cloud technology patterns that support major business drivers and challenges, thus enabling a tighter alignment of cloud solutions to business goals. There is no cloud reference modeling framework in the industry, so this section will break new ground. The Cloud Computing Reference Model is illustrated in Exhibit 5.2.

The details of the Cloud Computing Reference Model Framework, as implemented during the course of the Cloud Adoption Lifecycle Model, are detailed below. In addition, Chapter 6, Cloud Architecture, Modeling, and Design, will explore cloud computing architectures, which will further decompose the elements of the cloud computing reference model framework from a technology perspective.

Leveraging the Cloud Adoption Lifecycle Model and the Cloud Reference Model together will not only accelerate your cloud initiative, but they will also lead to higher fidelity of business drivers and

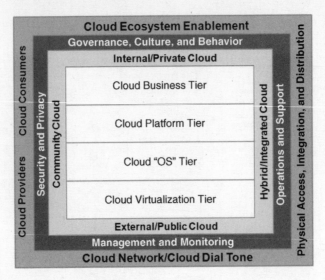

Exhibit 5.2   Cloud Modeling Framework

goals to the eventual cloud solutions that are deployed to meet those business goals.

In the remainder of this chapter, we will walk through the stages of the Cloud Adoption Lifecycle Model, and then delve into the Cloud Computing Reference Model as it enables and supports the Cloud Adoption Lifecycle.

Cloud Adoption Lifecycle

The Cloud Adoption Lifecycle Model presents an idealized set of steps we feel cloud adopters will progress through as they begin exploring cloud computing for their respective enterprises. The Cloud Adoption Lifecycle Model is not a maturity model, nor is it a strict recipe for cloud success. Rather, the Cloud Adoption Lifecycle Model represents a generalized framework upon which an organization can plan and execute its own cloud adoption process based on its particular needs.

This idealized Cloud Adoption Lifecycle follows five mainline stages of cloud adoption, as illustrated in Exhibit 5.1, as well as the anticipated cloud adoption stages farther out as cloud adoption matures.

The core mainline stages of the Cloud Adoption Lifecycle Model are:

- Cloud proof concept (POC)/pilot project stage
- Cloud strategy and roadmap
- Cloud modeling and architecture
- Cloud implementation planning
- Cloud implementation

The supporting Cloud Adoption Lifecycle Model stages, which build on your initial cloud implementation and are thus further up the maturity curve, are:

- Cloud expansion
- Cloud integration
- Cloud collaboration
- Cloud maturity

Each of these stages of the Cloud Adoption Lifecycle Model is explained in detail in the following sections. The Cloud Adoption Lifecycle Model offers a baseline from which you can determine your entry point into cloud computing, and the steps you should consider to support your adoption of cloud computing. At the end of this chapter, we will offer suggestions for using the Cloud Adoption Lifecycle Model.

Cloud Proof of Concept (POC)/Pilot Project

The goal of this cloud adoption lifecycle stage is knowledge and early learning about cloud technologies. This stage closes knowledge gaps, helps understand what you do and do not know about cloud, and prepares your enterprise for a more formalized planning and implementation process going forward. The following activities are included in the cloud proof of concept (POC)/pilot project adoption stage, and are explained in the paragraphs that follow:

- Cloud POC/pilot implementation.
- Cloud learning, evaluation, and cloud strategy input.
- Cloud program go/no go decisions.

Cloud POC/Pilot Implementation The cloud pilot implementation is a very important substage of the Cloud Adoption Lifecycle, and one that prepares the organization for dramatic cloud learning and hands on understanding of cloud's potential for your organization. Your cloud pilot implementation sows the seeds of cloud success. Before beginning your cloud pilot, you should have clear goals and metrics that will inform you whether the pilot was successful.

A cloud pilot should not be a technical proof of concept. Your cloud pilot should actually test a business scenario that you feel represents how cloud may be applied on a broader basis in your enterprise, albeit in a smaller, controlled scope. The following attributes of a cloud pilot should be considered:

- Has defined goals and objectives, with metrics to evaluate relative success or failure
- Is scoped narrowly enough, yet accomplishes defined business objectives
- Is planned as a business pilot versus a technology POC
- Can be performed within a well-defined budget and time duration
- Informs the organization with respect to business, technology, and operational lessons learned
- Supports the cloud evaluation criteria defined beforehand
- Informs the cloud strategy so that it can be validated, refined, and tuned based on pilot lessons learned
- Provides enough data to make an informed go/no go decision with respect to cloud

Your cloud pilot is a stepping stone into solving pressing business challenges via a well reasoned, technically sound cloud strategy. The cloud pilot should be executed with intent to gain early learning, basic cloud knowledge and hands-on experience, to inform your strategy based on this early learning to test potential cloud patterns, architecture, and deployment models, and to ensure you can realize the target business outcomes via your cloud strategy.

Cloud Early Learning and Strategy Input   A cloud POC or pilot project should enable your cloud team to gain valuable knowledge and early learning about cloud computing. POCs and pilots help you develop an understanding of what you do and, more importantly, what you do not know, in order to successfully implement cloud computing in your organization. In addition, you should be in a position to evaluate whether cloud is right for your enterprise, and to evaluate various industry solutions and approaches to cloud computing. Finally, your cloud POCs and pilots should generate a baseline of information that will become explicit inputs into your formal cloud strategy development process.

Based on the cloud pilot, and the criteria and metrics you defined to evaluate cloud pilot success, you should be in a position to answer the following questions:

- What have we learned from the cloud pilot that makes us confident we will be successful?
- Should we postpone developing our formal cloud strategy until the industry is more mature?
- Is cloud appropriate for the stated business, technical, and operational challenges we face?
- Have we performed a sufficient evaluation of cloud relative to our business and IT organization?
- Do we understand the risks as well as the business benefits cloud offers to us? Do the potential benefits outweigh the potential risks?
- Did the pilot sufficiently answer the business, technical, operational, and security issues we identified pre-pilot?
- Are we organizationally ready for cloud, given its immaturity and the associated risks? Can we overcome potential behavioral and cultural obstacles?
- Do we have the knowledge and experience to develop and successfully execute a business-aligned cloud strategy?

The cloud learning stage should be just that—an explicit exercise to review lessons learned from your cloud pilot project, to evaluate your cloud readiness as an organization—from both a business readiness and a technical readiness perspective. Often, organizational learning is not a directed activity as part of a formal strategic planning process. This is why you should build into your Cloud Adoption Lifecycle Model this process of learning, strategy evaluation, confirmation, and/or revision, and then a clear definition of the exit criteria to formally proceed into execution of your cloud strategy. The cloud go/no go decision process is discussed next.

Cloud Program Go/No Go Decision   At this point in the Cloud Adoption Lifecycle, your organization should be prepared to make decisions about whether or not cloud offers real business potential to your organization. Based on your cloud POC or pilot projects, you should now have a body of knowledge and data that allow you to make the appropriate choice as to whether cloud makes sense for your goals, and if so, exactly how and to what magnitude.

The following are sample exit criteria that may be considered as part of your cloud program go/no go decision calculus:

- Cloud offers potential to satisfy business requirements based on your cloud POC/pilot.
- Cloud has the potential to address our technical requirements based on our POC/pilot project.
- Cloud will satisfy operational requirements based on your cloud POC/pilot project.
- Cloud security considerations and risks are clearly understood and are not show stoppers.
- Cloud governance requirements can be met with current approaches and technical solutions.
- Cloud is affordable within some predictable range such that you can estimate the investment or costs, and the resultant savings or organizational benefit, and make planning decisions accordingly.
- Cloud is realistic given the organizational priorities.
- Cloud is realistic given your current technology staff levels and training.
- Our POC/pilot projects have provided sufficient knowledge and experience that we can develop a realistic cloud strategy and roadmap, and execute that cloud strategy with confidence.

The go/no go decision here is quite simple. Should your organization pursue a formal cloud computing program, you must allocate the requisite resources to support the level of cloud program your strategy calls for, and you will assign appropriate accountability for the cloud effort.

Cloud Strategy and Roadmap

The goal of this Cloud Adoption Lifecycle stage is to incorporate the lessons learned from your POC and pilots into a formal cloud strategy development process. The cloud strategy and roadmap stage establishes a formalized and actionable cloud strategy that will be executed to achieve stated business objectives.

The activities to be performed in the cloud strategy and road-map adoption stage are:

- Cloud business discovery and assessment
- Cloud strategy and roadmap
- Cloud mobilization and transition planning

Cloud Business Discovery and Assessment   The cloud business discovery and assessment activities are necessary to understand where your organization currently is with respect to cloud computing capabilities, how mature your cloud efforts are, and your overall organizational and IT readiness for cloud computing. Your cloud readiness can be determined by your general maturity and organizational readiness along three broad dimensions:

1. **IT Outsourcing Experience**
   - Have you had experience outsourcing all or portions of your IT capabilities to third-party service delivery organizations?
   - Have you managed these relationships successfully?
   - Did you establish SLAs and performance measures to monitor those relationships?
   - Have you migrated from one service provider/outsourcing partner to another successfully?
2. **IT Infrastructure Virtualization Experience**
   - Have you successfully explored various virtualization technologies?
   - Have you gained experience with various tools supporting the foundational competencies of today's cloud computing industry?
   - Are you prepared to build on your virtualization foundation to add higher order cloud capabilities?
3. **Service-Oriented Architecture (SOA) Maturity and Experience**
   - Have you achieved some level of success with SOA (e.g., SOA-enabling technology, infrastructure services, and related technologies)?

- Does your organization understand the basic concepts of service interfaces, implementations, and service level agreements (SLAs)?
- Have you developed the internal competencies to manage the relationships between service providers and service consumers?
- Have you developed the funding, incentives, and cultural and behavioral models necessary for SOA, which are also critical for becoming an internal cloud service provider?
- Have you implemented enterprise governance processes, policies, organizational models and enforcement technologies and tools to support IT and SOA governance? Can these be adapted to and extended to support your adoption of cloud computing?

Once you have determined your cloud readiness, you should consider the following cloud business discovery steps preparatory to developing your formal cloud strategy and roadmap:

- Assess external business environment
- Review business and IT strategy
- Assess cloud strategy, if one exists
- Perform cloud readiness assessment (see previous section)
- Determine cloud maturity
- Identify cloud business and technology drivers
- Identify cloud business imperatives, or the issues that must be resolved to be successful
- Identify potential cloud obstacles or barriers
- Define clear cloud goals and outcomes if you pursue a cloud strategy

You will most likely develop other criteria for your cloud business discovery and assessment needs. You can use these as a foundation to get started, and add others as you see fit.

Successful forays into cloud will depend on and leverage your IT organization's collective experience and comfort levels with these types of IT initiatives. The relative success you have had with each of these will have bearing on your ability to realize success through cloud.

Cloud Strategy and Planning   Cloud strategy and planning is essential to prepare your enterprise for cloud with a realistic and attainable cloud strategy that supports and is aligned with business and mission objectives. A viable cloud strategy should state in clear unambiguous terms what business problems a cloud approach will solve, how cloud will address those business and technology challenges, what actionable and measurable steps will be taken to implement cloud to realize those goals and objectives, and by when.

As with a SOA strategy, the emphasis should not be on the length of the strategy document but on how actionable, implementable, and operationalized the cloud strategy actually is. The following attributes should characterize your cloud strategy:

- **Actionable.** Cloud strategy clearly states what problems it addresses, how cloud will be leveraged to meet those challenges, and what actions will be taken to do so. A cloud strategy should not only be a call to action, but it should also specifically state what actions will be taken, by when, and to what effect as measured by some objective metric.

- **Implementable.** The cloud strategy can realistically be implemented, its impact can be tested and measured with appropriate instrumentation and proof, and it can be scaled in production operations to meet the business challenges it was targeted to address. Along with the actionable attribute, the cloud strategy must be sufficiently detailed and grounded in real world effects. You must be able to actually implement cloud and measure its impact on your operations, time-to-market, cost reductions, and so on.

- **Operationalized.** The cloud strategy is specific in its purpose, goals, and objectives, and the activities and initiatives contemplated in the cloud strategy are specified with the following level of detail:
  - *What will happen.* Cloud will improve time-to-market for new business requirements.
  - *By when.* We will have our first public cloud in place by *day, month, year.*
  - *As measured by the following metric.* We will launch business applications 50% faster by leveraging public clouds, and save 65% of the capital expenses associated with acquiring our own servers, storage, and IT infrastructure.

The biggest problem we see with strategic documents is a lack of operationalized clarity, with dates, metrics, and accountability for implementation. Make sure your cloud strategy is sufficiently detailed so that it is actionable, implementable, and operationalizable.

Use these guidelines to develop your cloud strategy and executable roadmap.

Cloud Mobilization and Transition Planning   Upon completion of your cloud strategy and roadmap, preparing for the transition to cloud is next. An organization cannot simply perform a cloud business discovery and readiness assessment, develop a cloud strategy and roadmap, and suddenly, as if by magic, begin operating a private, public, or hybrid cloud. First, your organization must go through a period of planning, followed by the ramping of your organization's knowledge, skills and capabilities, such that you will enable a smooth transition from your pre-cloud operating model to an implemented cloud operating model.

Cloud mobilization and planning is the phase in which you ramp your organizational capabilities and ensure your functional readiness to implement cloud in accordance with your stated cloud strategy and roadmap. The following activities should be part of your cloud mobilization and transition planning phase:

- **Conduct a Cloud Training and Awareness Program.** Conduct a broad-based cloud training, education, and awareness program to obtain general cloud skills and training, education for key executives and middle management, and provide comprehensive organizational awareness to explain what cloud is, what it means to your organization, and how your team can engage in its realization. This cloud ramp and transition activity will smooth the pathway to cloud success by ensuring consistent terminology, awareness of the cloud strategy, and accelerated buy-in to the cloud strategy by middle management.
- **Obtain Cloud Architecture, Technical, and Operations Skills.** Obtain technical, architectural, and operations skills through external consulting, technical training, prototypes, proof of concept implementations, and pilots. This cloud ramp and

transition phase is critical to ensure you have the necessary architectural, technical, and operational skills and capabilities to meet your strategic cloud objectives. As with SOA, cloud adopters will struggle if they do not have access to the appropriate skilled technicians, architects, and operations managers to facilitate the realization of cloud.

- **Cloud Transition Planning.** Develop a plan to transition from the cloud strategy phase into action. The cloud transition plan ensures you are ready to allocate resources and effort, and assign accountability for the next stages of the Cloud Adoption Lifecycle Model.

Cloud Modeling and Architecture Adoption Stage

The goal of this cloud adoption lifecycle stage is to perform the necessary cloud modeling and architecture steps in order to execute the cloud strategy. This adoption lifecycle stage leverages the Cloud Computing Reference Model (CC-RM) and its supporting modeling and architecture framework to develop a strategically-aligned cloud reference model, reference architecture, and cloud implementation that will support and enable the defined cloud strategy.

The cloud modeling and architecture adoption stage enables your organization to perform the appropriate cloud modeling and analysis, to develop a cloud architecture that will help you implement cloud either (1) internally as a private cloud, (2) externally leveraging a public cloud, or (3) in a hybrid model where you retain cloud capabilities internally while leveraging public cloud capabilities for aspects of your cloud strategy. The following activities are part of the cloud modeling and architecture adoption stage:

- Cloud modeling
- Cloud Computing Reference Model
- Cloud Deployment Model
- Cloud Governance and Operations Model (quality of service [QoS], security, and SLA planning)
- Cloud Reference Architecture

Each of these elements of cloud modeling and architecture phase is discussed in the sections following.

Cloud Modeling   The cloud modeling and architecture substage is a critical and emerging requirement for the transition to cloud computing. As organizations will learn early into their cloud planning, there are multiple patterns of clouds, as opposed to a one-size-fits-all cloud. In order to successfully leverage cloud for your enterprise, you must have a framework for analysis that enables you to map your business and technology requirements to the appropriate cloud patterns and the supporting cloud-enabling technology and cloud deployment model, and to viable cloud service and solution providers.

Cloud modeling and architecture is an important planning process because it will provide guidance on what cloud solutions fit your business and technical needs. Cloud modeling and architecture also provides guidance on your cloud deployment choices—internal private clouds versus leveraging external public clouds provided and operated by third-party cloud service providers. Cloud modeling and architecture will help you determine what business, technology, economic, and operational use cases are appropriate for deployment to the cloud. Whether you plan to implement cloud solutions internal to your organization, or to leverage public clouds provided by Amazon, Google, Salesforce, or others, you must still understand cloud patterns, architecture and technology patterns, and various deployment scenarios in order to best determine what cloud approaches are best for your business.

Cloud modeling and architecture begins with an understanding of cloud patterns. There are multiple cloud patterns available that address different business and operational requirements your organization may have. Next, we summarize the most common cloud patterns and the business, IT, and operational challenges that they satisfy.

Cloud Computing Reference Model (CC-RM)   Cloud modeling is the process of analyzing business, technical, and operational requirements against a set of established patterns or approaches, and then determining the optimal cloud pattern, architecture, deployment model, and appropriate cloud solutions to meet your target business needs. The output of a cloud modeling approach should be a complete cloud business solution, which has the following attributes:

- Is a *cloud strategy*, which articulates the business context and rationale for pursuing cloud for a defined class of business, technical, and operational requirements
- Is described and modeled using the appropriate *cloud patterns*, discovered through a *cloud modeling* exercise that meets targeted business, technical, economic, and operational needs
- Has a well-defined *cloud deployment model* that supports the requirements (internal/private, external/public, hybrid (integrated, federated)
- Includes a *cloud governance and operations model*, which describes the end-to-end governance of cloud as well as the necessary operations and management model
- Includes a *cloud provider plan*, which evaluates the universe of cloud-enablement technologies as well as cloud service providers in accordance with your cloud strategy
- Leads to a successful *cloud implementation*, or the cloud solution implemented based on the appropriate deployment model that meets the business and operational requirement
- Has a *cloud onboarding/offboarding plan*, which describes how you will move applications, data, business process, and business operations into a cloud deployment, whether internal/private, external/public, or hybrid
- Finally, includes a *cloud operations and support model*, which includes all cloud operations management, monitoring, and runtime support necessary for operational and support requirements of your enterprise

In order to define these Cloud requirements, we advocate the use of the Cloud Computing Reference Model (CC-RM), which we explain in great detail in Chapter 6, Cloud Architecture, Modeling, and Design. Recall Exhibit 5.2 for the illustration of the CC-RM.

The proposed Cloud Computing Reference Model (CC-RM) will establish a cloud modeling and architecture foundation from which an organization can realistically plan, model, architect, and deploy cloud computing in a pragmatic fashion to address real and pressing business and technical challenges. Cloud should not be treated as a solution looking for a problem, but as a collection of cloud patterns that can be configured to meet a wide array of business and technical requirements.

The Cloud Computing Reference Model is comprised of four supporting models or elements, as described below:

1. **Cloud Enablement Model.** The core of the Cloud Computing Reference Model is the Cloud Enablement Model. The Cloud Enablement Model describes the tiers of cloud computing foundation, enablement, and business capabilities provided by cloud platform and service providers to potential consumers of cloud-enabled technology and business capabilities. The Cloud Enablement Model is comprised of the full range of cloud technologies and enablement solutions such that all cloud patterns can be realized by providers and consumers.
2. **Cloud Deployment Model.** Describes the range of cloud deployment scenarios available to your enterprise—internal private cloud, external public cloud, hybrid cloud, and community cloud. These deployment scenarios may be mixed and matched to meet a variety of business use cases and requirements.
3. **Cloud Governance and Operations Model.** Describes the governance, security and privacy, operations and support, management and monitoring requirements for cloud computing to ensure you have considered all the potential operational risks of adopting cloud for your enterprise.
4. **Cloud Ecosystem Model.** The Cloud Ecosystem Model considers the requirements of developing and sustaining a cloud ecosystem comprised of cloud providers, cloud consumers, and cloud intermediaries, as well as the cloud network and "cloud dial tone" necessary to ensure the cloud is always there for you. The cloud ecosystem also includes the various cloud enablement technologies and cloud providers and consumers of those cloud enablement technologies to establish the cloud ecosystem.

The cloud modeling process should result in a fully described Cloud Computing Reference model, as well as the cloud patterns that implement the targeted cloud use case(s) you are contemplating.

Cloud patterns describe the specific combinations of cloud enablement technology, cloud-enabled resources and capabilities, and the various deployment models that make those cloud-enabled resources available to consumers. We use the following nomenclature to characterize what constitutes a cloud pattern:

- **Cloud Pattern.** A cloud pattern is a described combination of a cloud enablement pattern and a cloud deployment pattern that, taken together, satisfy the broad business, technical, economic, and operational requirements captured in a cloud use case and refined through application of the Cloud Computing Reference Model.
- **Cloud Enablement Pattern.** The cloud enablement pattern is a description, either written or symbolically, of the cloud-enabled resources or technical capabilities, and their relationships to one another, as they satisfy the technical and architectural requirements of a cloud use case and a defined Cloud Computing Reference Model.
- **Cloud Deployment Pattern.** The cloud deployment pattern describes the various cloud deployment models that satisfy the requirements of a cloud use case and a defined Cloud Computing Reference Model. The cloud deployment pattern describes the broad deployment options of private/internal, public/external, and hybrid, as well as more fine-grained variations of those and the architectural implications of those choices.

Based on these cloud patterns, the following steps represent a cloud modeling approach we will follow in this book:

1. Determine business drivers and business imperatives.
2. Obtain stakeholder alignment and agreement (business, IT, and operations).
3. Understand how business imperatives are addressed by cloud patterns.
4. Select appropriate cloud pattern(s) that support business, technology, and operational needs.
5. Evaluate and determine cloud deployment scenarios based on selected cloud pattern(s).
6. Determine cloud governance lifecycle requirements and establish cloud governance model.
7. Evaluate cloud solution providers and cloud service providers that meet requirements.

8. Select cloud business solution (cloud pattern, deployment model, and cloud provider).
9. Implement cloud governance model.
10. Implement cloud solution.
11. Begin cloud provisioning, resource management, billing, and accounting process.
12. Onboard business operation, process, application or data onto cloud solution.
13. Monitor, manage, and govern your cloud deployed solution.
14. Evaluate costs, performance, and business impact; adjust cloud strategy accordingly.

Based on the completion of the cloud modeling activities, you must then define the cloud deployment model that is defined during the cloud modeling process.

Cloud Deployment Model   The Cloud Deployment Model is a planning stage necessary to understand the various cloud deployment options you may pursue based on the specific cloud pattern that meets your business, technology, and operational requirements, as well as the cloud provisioning model that will enable your onboarding of business capabilities, applications, data, and business operations onto a cloud platform either hosted internally, provided by a third-party cloud service provider, or some hybrid deployment pattern.

The cloud deployment plan describes the range of cloud deployment options you may consider as you evaluate how best cloud applies to a given business, technical, or operational need. The broad cloud deployment choices are:

- Private
- Public
- Hybrid
- Community

Depending on your business, technical, and operational requirements, you may have a clear and obvious cloud deployment preference. In other cases, the cloud deployment scenarios may be ambiguous, such that you lean toward a private or hybrid scenario.

Cloud Governance and Operations Model Cloud governance is a critical dimension of cloud computing. It will span the following range of business, technical, and operational requirements:

- Onboarding and offboarding business operations, processes, applications or data to a cloud. The Cloud onboarding/offboarding process should consider the following dimensions:
  - Organizational readiness
  - Business readiness
  - Application and data readiness
  - Infrastructure readiness
  - Technical capability readiness
- Cloud architecture, pattern modeling, deployment planning, and implementation
- Cloud operations, monitoring, and management
- Cloud audit requirements, reporting, and compliance oversight
- Cloud provisioning processes
- Cloud lifecycle management
- Cloud governance lifecycle (from planning to operations, from cloud consumer to cloud provider, from cradle to grave)

As you develop your plans for cloud modeling and architecture, be very explicit with your cloud governance model. Do not overlook the multidimensional requirements of cloud governance from a complete, end-to-end perspective.

Cloud governance is a multifaceted discipline, and you should not limit it to the operational runtime dimensions of cloud. You should treat cloud governance as the end-to-end planning, architecture, deployment, and operation of cloud computing. In this vein, cloud governance takes on a much more significant footprint in the planning and execution of your cloud strategy. Also, understand that the cloud governance lifecycle is not well understood. That will be remedied by the industry soon.

Cloud Computing Reference Architecture (CC-RA) A Cloud Computing Reference Architecture (CC-RA) is necessary for all cloud deployment patterns–internal private clouds, external public clouds, and hybrid clouds that blend aspects of private and public clouds.

In all cases, you need to understand your cloud reference architecture in order to provision applications, data, or business operations to a cloud, and you need to understand cloud architecture to successfully deploy one internally and provision the cloud resources to your internal business customers.

The Cloud Computing Reference Architecture is an artifact that is derived from the Cloud Computing Reference Model. The CC-RM and CC-RA work together to help your enterprise follow a repeatable process that will lead to a successful cloud reference implementation. The CC-RM provides the cloud framework for modeling the critical dimensions of cloud computing. The CC-RA helps map categories of technology to the CC-RM, such that you can begin to select vendor products mapped to the cloud reference architecture, and such that you can evaluate and test cloud use cases and requirements against the cloud reference architecture in support of a future cloud implementation.

Based on the cloud pattern or patterns that fit business needs, the cloud architecture must be aligned to those business, technical, and operational needs. Cloud architecture is a critical dimension of cloud computing, especially given its newness, and in particular given the huge trust being placed on cloud as the future of the computing industry.

Cloud Implementation Planning

The goal of this cloud adoption lifecycle stage is to prepare for your cloud implementation. This stage focuses on selection of appropriate cloud technologies, cloud service providers, and cloud solutions to support your chosen cloud strategy. In addition, deployment models, and the necessary governance, operations and support, management and monitoring, and security challenges are addressed in this stage as well.

The cloud implementation planning stage of cloud adoption focuses on the following activities:

- Cloud provider analysis
- Cloud deployment and provisioning planning
- Cloud governance and lifecycle planning
- Cloud program go/no go

Cloud Provider Analysis and Selection   This stage of cloud adoption requires a thorough analysis of cloud providers based on the cloud strategy and planning process you are undertaking. Broadly speaking, you have three cloud deployment choices to consider:

1. **Internal Cloud Provider.** Does your organization have an internal cloud capability online and operational? Are machine images and virtual machines, and storage and network resources provisionable to you with a supporting chargeback model, at rates competitive with third-party cloud service providers? Does your internal cloud service provider (assuming you have a shared services construct or your IT organization has become a cloud service provider) offer the same level of cloud pattern and architecture support as external cloud providers?

2. **External Cloud Provider.** For external cloud service providers, you must evaluate their business viability, fundamentals, and security practices. Do they offer the range of cloud-enabled capabilities and resources to meet your organization's needs? How open or proprietary are their APIs? How will they integrate and interoperate with other 3rd party cloud service providers? With your future or current hybrid cloud deployment patterns?

3. **Hybrid Blend of Internal and External Clouds.** For hybrid cloud deployment scenarios, how will you intermix your internal cloud capabilities with public cloud resources provided by third party cloud service providers? What cloud service providers have experience supporting hybrid clouds? Will third party public clouds integrate and interoperate with your private cloud-enabled resources and capabilities?

In addition, you must consider the following dimensions in your analysis:

- **Cloud Technology Providers.** What cloud enabling technology solutions are available to meet your organization's cloud requirements? What cloud-enablement technology and tools match the cloud patterns and deployment models you feel best suit your needs?

- **Cloud Service Provider.** What cloud services are available from various third-party cloud service providers? Do they offer infrastructure virtualization, computing, storage, and networks? Are they strong on application (SaaS) or platform cloud services (PaaS)? What is their operational capability with respect to backups, redundancy, failover, and their overall ability to meet your SLAs and meet the terms of your cloud service contract?

These activities will help you determine who the providers are of the cloud enabling technologies, tools, as well as third party cloud-enabled resources provided by cloud service providers, that support your business and technology needs.

Cloud Deployment and Provisioning Planning   The cloud deployment and provisioning model is a critical planning tool to help your organization understand the various cloud deployment options you may pursue based on the specific cloud pattern that meets your business, technology, and operational requirements. The Cloud Deployment Model documents the range of cloud deployment options you may pursue to address your defined business requirements. A cloud-provisioning model is necessary as well, which will enable you to plan how to onboard business capabilities, applications, data, and business operations onto a cloud platform either hosted internally, provided by a third-party cloud service provider, or some hybrid deployment pattern. The following are key dimensions of the cloud deployment and provisioning planning stage:

- Cloud deployment plan describes the range of cloud deployment options you may consider as you evaluate how best cloud applies to a given business, technical, or operational need. The four broad cloud deployment choices are:
  1. Private
  2. Public
  3. Hybrid
  4. Community
- Cloud provisioning plan describes how you will provision cloud resources internally to your enterprise, or how you will onboard your data, applications, or business processes into a

third-party cloud provisioned to you. Cloud provisioning is essential in order to identify a consumer, profile their cloud requirements, obtain billing information, and then provision cloud resources to that consumer. For public clouds managed and provisioned by third-party cloud service providers, or for private clouds managed and provisioned by internal cloud service providers via chargeback models, the provisioning process will be similar.

Cloud Governance and Lifecycle Planning   Cloud governance is an emerging requirement of cloud computing, and encompasses a broad set of business and technical requirements, from the planning and architecture process through the design-time considerations of cloud computing, functional and nonfunctional requirements analysis, and the actual process of onboarding your enterprise onto a cloud (internal, public, or hybrid), and the critical monitoring and operational requirements of cloud once you have successfully deployed.

The end-to-end cloud lifecycle is not well understood, nor are the cloud governance requirements of that end-to-end cloud lifecycle.

Cloud onboarding and offboarding planning is a critical step to ensure a smooth transition into cloud computing, as well as a smooth transition back from cloud if your organizational no longer benefits from cloud, or if you are unsatisfied with your cloud service provider and need to switch to another.

Your organization will benefit from an appropriate planning process that documents your plan for onboarding a business operation, business process, an application, or your data onto a third-party cloud or into a private cloud you deploy internally.

Cloud onboarding planning should consider the following issues:

- Process for accessing the cloud resources applicable to your business needs
- How to migrate a business operation to a public cloud
- How to migrate applications to the cloud provider you have selected
- How to migrate data to the cloud provider you have selected (internal or external)
- How to migrate an application to a cloud while hosting your data in your data center

- How to back out of a cloud or switch cloud providers as needed
- How to monitor cloud operations and QoS
- How to track and obtain audit data for data integrity

Expect great progress in the definition, policy, and management of cloud computing from an end-to-end lifecycle perspective, as well as the enterprise governance requirements of the cloud lifecycle.

Cloud Program Go/No Go   The last step of the cloud implementation planning stage is a final go/no go decision. Based on all the effort you have poured into your cloud POC/pilots, developing a formal cloud strategy and roadmap, your cloud modeling and architecture, and your cloud implementation plan, you should have a final stakeholder review and decision as to whether to continue with your stated cloud strategy. This final go/no go decision is the final gate before you commit resources—both funding and personnel—to implementing cloud. If your implementation plans call for a public cloud deployment, you still have commitments to onboarding, moving your data and/or content to a public cloud provider, and monitoring the SLAs of that particular cloud implementation. While public clouds offer a relatively easy pathway to cloud implementation, you must still understand the total enterprise lifecycle commitments that it entails under a successful approach, as well as the rollback plans if you are not successful with your external public cloud implementation.

If you choose a private cloud implementation, you have other factors that play into the go/no go decision, such as potential license and maintenance fees, internal resource commitments, physical resource requirements, and more. Similarly, the hybrid cloud implementation will bring to the fore aspects of both. This go/no go decision gives your organizational stakeholders a final opportunity to weigh in prior to committing to the implementation of your Cloud strategy and roadmap.

Cloud Implementation Adoption Stage

This stage of the cloud adoption lifecycle focuses on the completion of your cloud reference implementation, the cumulative realization of the previous cloud adoption lifecycle stages. The cloud implementation stage signals organizational intent to begin its formal cloud program. At this stage you are fully committed to cloud and are executing the cloud strategy. The following activities are part of the cloud implementation stage:

- Cloud reference implementation
- Cloud governance and security plan
- Cloud management, monitoring, operations, and support
- Cloud feedback, metrics, strategy evaluation

Cloud Reference Implementation   During this substage, you are implementing cloud following the modeling, architecture, and deployment planning steps performed earlier as part of the cloud adoption model. As you transition from the cloud pilot into formal cloud implementation, you will leverage the artifacts, knowledge, and lessons learned from the previous steps to inform your formal implementation.

Your cloud reference implementation will leverage your Cloud Computing Reference Model and Cloud Computing Reference Architecture, as well as your cloud modeling and architecture artifacts, to lead to a successful cloud implementation:

- **Cloud Computing Reference Model.** A description of the appropriate cloud industry standards, the dimensions of the cloud problem space, and the decisions and choices that apply to your cloud computing framework for your organization.
- **Cloud Computing Reference Architecture.** A logical architecture artifact describing the layers of a cloud reference model, and categories of cloud enablement tools and technologies (without specifying any particular vendor tools), and mapped to and is derived from the Cloud Reference Model.
- **Cloud Reference Implementation.** The cloud reference implementation is precisely that—a specific cloud implementation that is based on the previous artifacts—the Cloud Reference Model, the Cloud Reference Architecture, and the Cloud Deployment Model. The cloud reference implementation implements real cloud tools and technologies that align to the Cloud Reference Architecture, and deploys them as described in the Cloud Deployment Model.

Following this approach will be a very helpful exercise to transition your organization into cloud based on a set of industry standards, which are very emergent at this time, based on a solid Cloud Reference Architecture and Cloud Deployment Model, and a Cloud Reference Implementation. The Cloud Reference Implementation should be applied to business challenges, and should be leveraged for iterative deployments of cloud to various business needs.

Cloud Governance and Security Plan   Cloud governance builds on the governance planning that was performed earlier in the Cloud Adoption Lifecycle Model. Cloud governance will be a critical enabler of your cloud strategy and provides the management and operational foundation to ensure cloud delivers on its promise for your enterprise. There are many dimensions of cloud governance to consider as you transition from the planning and pilot phase to production deployment of cloud, whether internally or leveraging third-party cloud service providers. The following represent the aspects of cloud governance and security that should be part of your Cloud implementation:

- **Quality of Service and Service Level Agreements.** For cloud to be successful for your organization, you must have assurances from your cloud providers that they can deliver reliable QoS to you, as expressed and documented in SLAs that become part of your service contract with the cloud provider. If you leverage third-party cloud service providers, you must establish a contract with appropriate SLAs with them. If you are obtaining cloud services from your internal cloud service provider, you must still document your required service levels, and obtain SLA commitments from your internal cloud providers. SLA and QoS are critical aspects of cloud computing models. You must be able to trust your cloud service providers and the level of service they provide to you.
- **Cloud Security.** Cloud governance must incorporate processes and tools to ensure security of cloud deployments. Many concerns are rightfully focused on securing access to data via access controls, encryption, and even aspects of physical security, including personnel-screening processes, background investigations, and security protocols relating to privileged user access. Security issues thread into areas of

data location and segregation, basically ensuring your data is not commingled with data from other firms or, worst case, your direct competitors, and also into regulatory and compliance, audit or related concerns. Can your cloud service provider give you assurances that your data and their security will meet the regulatory and compliance requirements you may be obligated to conform to?

However, beyond securing the data are security issues that span the end-user organization to the cloud provider, especially in SOA-enabled applications and data and the multifaceted security model that SOA requires.

- **Management and Monitoring.** Cloud management and monitoring are critical to ensure operational integrity of your cloud deployments. How will you instrument your cloud internally, or monitor your third-party cloud service provider, to ensure your business processes, applications, data and security are all within the terms of your contract and SLA? How will you troubleshoot failures, degradations, or outages of your cloud provider's infrastructure, network, or facilities?

- **Onboarding and Offboarding Process.** Cloud governance must explicitly develop the methodology and end-to-end process for onboarding into a cloud, offboarding from a cloud back to your own infrastructure if you change your mind, and switching from cloud to cloud if you are dissatisfied with your chosen cloud service provider. The last scenario should plan for switching from external to internal cloud and vice versa. With the hype associated with cloud, we advise thinking through all of these very realistic scenarios as you develop your plans for cloud, and consider how you will manage them all. Chances are you will be switching cloud providers, and chances are you may decide to go from private to public, or vice versa, so planning explicitly about how you will onboard, offboard, and switch will be critical to your success.

- **Cloud Enablement of Applications, Data, Operations.** Related to cloud onboarding and offboarding is performing the appropriate application design, analysis, and refactoring to determine which of your applications and data are cloud-ready, or can be cloud-enabled. How can you evaluate technically what applications will benefit from a cloud-based deployment? What do you need to do with your data to be able to onboard it into a third-party cloud provider's storage environment? How can you separate your data from your applications such that you can even cloud-enable them? These scenarios point to the very direct linkages that connect SOA adoption to cloud adoption. Organizations with some success with SOA will have well-defined logical and physical architectures, will have a data services layer that separates data from applications, and abstracts direct database access from data consumers via a data services layer. SOA-enabled enterprises will be able to cloud-enable portions of applications, chunks of data, and entire business processes in pursuit of a cloud strategy. As part of your cloud strategy, you should be very explicit on the areas of your business and IT operation where you feel cloud offers value, and focus on how to mitigate risk and drive those target areas toward a cloud deployment. The analysis as you mature your cloud strategy must involve appropriate decomposition and analysis of your business to be sure of what you can and cannot migrate to a cloud computing model.

Again, as stated above, the requirements of cloud governance are still very emergent, as are the security challenges of cloud competing. This is a partial list of major considerations, and you will need to fully consider the governance and security needs of your enterprise as described in the Cloud Computing Reference Model.

Cloud Management, Monitoring, Operations, and Support   Finally, the cloud operations and management processes must be implemented in support of your operational cloud deployments.

Cloud management and monitoring requirements must be clearly articulated and understood based on the Cloud Enablement Model and Cloud Deployment Model you have developed during your cloud planning and architecture process. You must consider the instrumentation and tooling necessary to monitor and manage your cloud, whether your deployment is an internal private cloud, or whether you are leveraging third-party external clouds from, e.g., Amazon or Salesforce. Either way, you must be able to integrate and automate the monitoring, performance management, alarming and alerting of cloud events, and performance metrics in order to respond to outages, performance degradations, and related operational concerns.

The absence of cloud monitoring and management tools must be addressed by the cloud vendor community to develop comprehensive management and monitoring solutions covering the range of cloud deployment models and integration scenarios. Currently, many SOA software firms are repositioning their tools for services hosted in the cloud, but those tools, while robust for pure SOA environments, may not be sufficient for the full breadth of cloud enablement and deployment patterns.

Cloud operations and support requirements are also essential to plan for in your cloud planning framework. Thus, they are also an explicit consideration of the cloud governance and operations submodel. As mentioned above, the entire Cloud governance lifecycle is poorly understood, particularly for cloud operations and support. While many of these processes can be adapted from current Information Technology Infrastructure Library (ITIL), Control Objectives for Information and related Technology (COBIT), and other IT management frameworks, you will also need to leverage your current data center and IT support, help desk, and operations processes, and adapt them based on your chosen cloud deployment model.

Operations and support for hybrid and public clouds will be a fast-moving area of emphasis, and you must spend appropriate time understanding the operations and support requirements based on the cloud deployment and on which cloud enablement tiers and cloud patterns you intend to exploit.

Cloud Feedback, Metrics, and Strategy Evaluation   Finally, as part of the cloud implementation stage, you must incorporate formal feedback, a cloud metrics framework, and strategy evaluation processes into your cloud adoption plans.

Cloud feedback processes and mechanisms should be defined and implemented for all communities of stakeholders, from the executive and finance stakeholders, to the business and process owners, to the IT operations, infrastructure, and data center communities. Feedback should be solicited periodically through surveys and formal review sessions, as well as through other ad hoc mechanisms.

Cloud metrics should also be defined and implemented to monitor your cloud implementation. Appropriate cloud metrics should include the following examples:

- Cloud business metrics (e.g., consumption, financial impact, business benefits, as defined in your cloud strategy and roadmap)
- Cloud operational metrics (e.g., SLAs, uptime, planned and unplanned outages, and overall cloud performance metrics)
- Cloud strategic metrics of overall business impact, strategic enablement, and so on

You must define the metrics necessary to help realize your Cloud strategy and roadmap. This sample list will be expanded and aligned to your Cloud goals and objectives.

Finally, cloud strategy evaluation must be an ongoing process of determining, at regular intervals, whether your cloud strategy is meeting its objectives or not. This decision must be objective, based on metrics and operationally defined aspects of your cloud strategy. It cannot be a hunch. Use regular cloud strategy review sessions with various categories of cloud stakeholders to gather data, assess cloud strategy effectiveness, and performance against defined cloud goals and objectives. Your cloud strategy evaluation process must be defined into your entire cloud adoption lifecycle and performed quarterly as well as annually.

Cloud Expansion Adoption Stage

This stage of cloud adoption is where an enterprise builds on its successful cloud reference implementation to expand its cloud capabilities. At this stage, cloud becomes a formal program within the enterprise, and is poised for expansion based on the initial success you have realized. Cloud expansion can involve progressing from private clouds to hybrid clouds, expanding private clouds via addition of new cloud patterns, or adding new cloud enablement capabilities onto existing cloud enablement patterns. This is a logical phase of cloud maturation and growth within the enterprise.

In the cloud expansion stage, cloud is a formal program in your enterprise. At this stage, your organization is executing cloud in a systematic, well-governed fashion. Your existing cloud implementations are performing well, and your organization continues to expand its cloud footprint and rollouts based on clear business, technology, and operational criteria.

The cloud expansion stage is as much of a milestone as it is a sustained model for your business and IT operations. As such, your organization is continually evaluating its current cloud deployments, and is evolving its internal, external, and hybrid clouds for opportunities to enhance its business model via cloud. Your organization is leveraging its persistent cloud program to continually evaluate new business, IT, and operational requirements and determines if and how cloud may be an appropriate model for satisfying these new requirements.

Your cloud program will also develop processes, technologies, and models to accommodate emerging cloud requirements such as cloud integration and interoperability, cloud collaboration and cross-cloud composition of highly distributed applications and capabilities via next generation composition, orchestration, and choreography tools. These emergent cloud requirements will be addressed in the next phases of cloud adoption.

Cloud Integration Adoption Stage

This stage of cloud adoption anticipates the need to integrate cloud capabilities and deployment approaches, as well as the need to ensure cloud interoperability as cloud computing matures.

At some point shortly after you deploy your initial formal cloud projects, you will naturally be faced with integration requirements or interoperability challenges. As with all previous generations of technology, cloud will usher its own challenges and shortfalls as it becomes widely embraced.

Cloud integration challenges will emerge in the following scenarios:

- Integrating internal private clouds with external public clouds
- Integrating internal SOA capabilities with your data hosted in an external cloud
- Integrating business processes and applications hosted internally with data that is hosed in a public cloud
- Security integration between your enterprise security infrastructure and your third-party cloud provider's security architecture

- Integrating hybrid clouds based on various cloud patterns, the combinations of which can be significant

In addition to the cloud integration requirements, we anticipate that given the absence of cloud industry standards there will be many instances of interoperability challenges between various cloud solutions providers and cloud service providers. While industry standards for SOA will help, cloud also represents the confluence of multiple other technology paradigms, for which industry standards are also in development but are far from adoption as de facto or de jure standards. Thus, interoperability challenges between cloud solutions for the same cloud pattern, such as virtualization, will occur as well as interoperability challenges between cloud solution providers that focus on different portions of the logical cloud layered architecture. For example, a platform cloud provider may have interoperability issues with lower-level virtualization cloud providers, or storage cloud providers. There are many scenarios where variations of cloud technologies may struggle for interoperability.

As cloud is in its infancy as a technology paradigm, we can only estimate the impact of integration and interoperability that will accompany the transition into cloud for most organizations. However, as with all emerging technologies, be hopeful for the best but anticipate the worst. Plan for integration and interoperability issues, and mitigate the risks accordingly.

Cloud Collaboration Adoption Stage

This stage of cloud adoption focuses on the emergent requirements of cross-cloud collaboration, composition of applications across clouds, and orchestration of distributed process across various cloud deployment patterns.

As cloud deployments expand beyond the initial pilots and small-scale initial programs, we should expect requirements to surface that demand tools and capabilities for cloud collaboration, cross-cloud application composition, orchestration, and choreography. In other words, how do we stitch clouds together to enable massively scalable, highly distributed applications that are composed across clouds, whether private, public, or hybrid? While the need for these types of tools is not yet an industry requirement, we expect this to become a clear requirement as cloud takes on more and more importance in the industry. The following challenges and requirements are anticipated in the cloud collaboration adoption stage:

- **Cloud Collaboration.** How will collaboration be performed over the cloud in support of chat, collaborative application development, information-sharing requirements, and other collaboration scenarios? While Internet tools available today support some of these anticipated use cases, there are some scenarios we have not yet explored given the nascent status of cloud as an industry strategy.
- **Application Composition.** How will highly distributed, massively scalable applications be composed, given that portions of them may be deployed to multiple public clouds, or to hybrids cloud deployment patterns? What next-generation tools will enable composite applications, mash-ups, and other application models to be leveraged to turn clouds into a platform that benefits end-user as much as back office operations people? As cloud matures, watch for a collection of tools that will explicitly address application composition across clouds.
- **Process Orchestration and Choreography.** How will business processes be designed, modeled, and orchestrated for execution across private, public, and hybrid clouds? What tools and industry standards will support intra-enterprise process orchestration for private clouds? What tools and industry standards will enable cross-enterprise process choreography leveraging hybrid clouds? While the requirements for cloud-enabled process orchestration and choreography are very emergent, there will be demand for these approaches as cloud adoption accelerates and matures.

Cloud Maturity Adoption Stage

The final stage of the Cloud Adoption Lifecycle is the cloud maturity stage. This is an idealized stage when cloud technology has matured and the next technology wave is underway. At this point in time, cloud is in a steady state, and major innovation has peaked, and industry adoption is mature.

The reality is that this is a very hypothetical stage, and the point when an organization realizes it is at this cloud adoption stage will not be obvious. Chances are, as with client-server and Internet technologies, they are at the maturity stage when they are so ingrained in our culture that they simply "are." Therefore, the cloud maturity stage is not a planning stage; it is an industry milestone that, when it is upon us, will matter very little because our attention will be focused on other emerging business and technology trends.

Cloud Adoption Lifecycle Summary

This chapter introduced two cloud planning tools to help accelerate Cloud adoption for your enterprise: The Cloud Adoption Lifecycle, and the Cloud Computing Reference Model. Both of these tools will provide valuable context and planning frameworks to accelerate your adoption of cloud to address business, technical, economic, and operational requirements.

The main focus of this chapter was the Cloud Adoption Lifecycle Model. This model will help your organization understand a set of idealized stages that characterize important dimensions of cloud computing.

The Cloud Adoption Lifecycle Model is not an industry standard. It is not a prescriptive framework for cloud planning and implementation. Rather, it provides a guide to assist your organization with its cloud planning and implementation based on logical stages that make sense for emerging technologies such as cloud computing. It is a hypothetical framework that we feel will provide guidance for organizations that are exploring or considering cloud computing.

The Cloud Adoption Lifecycle Model will help your organization ensure a set of repeatable, iterative planning processes to increase the chances of a successful cloud implementation. For startups, the cloud adoption lifecycle can be accelerated based on your need to get to market quickly with your new business model or technical innovation. For the mature enterprise, the cloud adoption lifecycle will help you document your current state and your industry pressures and drivers, and settle on an appropriate cloud strategy for your enterprise business requirements.

For any enterprise, we encourage the alignment to the broad steps and processes defined in the Cloud Adoption Lifecycle Model, and we also encourage you to tailor this framework as you see fit. Make it work for your organization. In the chapters that follow, we will develop the details of the Cloud Computing Reference Model, and then provide guidance for how to get started with cloud computing using both of these cloud planning tools.

Parting Thoughts

A Cloud Adoption Lifecycle and a Cloud Computing Reference Model are useful tools, however, their value is in how organizations utilize them for value. A few points to remember about these cloud planning tools:

- The Cloud Adoption Lifecycle is notional, idealized, and based on adoption of similar architecture breakthrough technologies, e.g. Service-oriented architecture (SOA). Therefore, use it to help make sense of cloud computing for your enterprise, and adapt it to meet your needs. This framework will continue to evolve based on market research and feedback.
- The many references to a Cloud Governance Lifecycle indicate the critical nature of governance in a cloud-enabled world. However, there is a lot of work left to define an end-to-end Cloud Governance Lifecycle that encompasses all the governance dimensions of cloud. Stay tuned.
- The Cloud Computing Reference Model, or CC-RM, is a useful planning tool we feel, to help you frame the critical requirements for Cloud in an integrative and holistic model. We have leveraged the industry convention of a Reference Model, Reference Architecture and Reference Implementation for cloud based on the OASIS SOA Reference Model.
- The concept of *cloud patterns* is similarly a new device we feel helps frame a more realistic and detailed perspective of Cloud adoption as applied to real business problems. There are no industry conventions for the modeling of various cloud patterns, but we hope to spur the discipline of cloud modeling on in the coming months and years.

One challenge with being first with some of these conceptual frameworks is that they will almost always need to evolve. We will learn and adapt these approaches as the industry matures.

6

Cloud Architecture, Modeling, and Design

The emergence of cloud represents the next evolution in distributed architectures. Much as service-oriented architecture (SOA) transformed information technology (IT) based on reusable standards-based services, cloud offers benefits unique to its place in the chief information officer's (CIO's) toolbox today.

This chapter explores cloud architectures, and how to architect for success with cloud for your enterprise. Whether you are a simple consumer of clouds provided by third-party cloud service providers or you are a large enterprise intermixing private, public, and hybrid cloud deployments, this chapter will bring benefit.

The fundamentals of architecting clouds matter. You simply must understand the variations and nuances of cloud. There is no "one-size-fits-all" model here. You must match cloud capabilities to your business and technology requirements, using a repeatable pattern-based framework we develop in this chapter, based on a cloud logical and physical architectural framework.

Cloud Adoption Lifecycle Model: Role of Cloud Modeling and Architecture

The Cloud Adoption Lifecycle Model described in Chapter 5, Cloud Adoption Lifecycle, offers an idealized set of stages that should ensure a thorough cloud planning, modeling, and deployment process for your enterprise. Key to success with cloud is the process of modeling and architecture. The cloud modeling and architecture process involves the following activities:

- **Cloud Modeling.** Determining, mapping, and alignment of business drivers and key requirements to the range of potential cloud technical and resource patterns available. Cloud modeling forces the explicit definition of business needs, and then establishing what cloud technical patterns and resource models best suit those business requirements. For example, a business need for a customer relationship management (CRM) application provided as a service (by Salesforce.com) is one cloud pattern that is distinct from a business requirement to achieve better internal server utilization through enterprise deployment of internal clouds focused on Infrastructure as a Service (Iaas).
- **Cloud Deployment Model.** Determining, based on the cloud modeling effort, what cloud deployment model(s) best fit your organization's business and technical needs. Is an internal/private cloud best for your current and pending needs, or are their third-party external cloud service providers that can satisfy your business requirements (e.g., Amazon S3, EC2, or Salesforce Force.com)? Your cloud modeling outputs will help determine what cloud deployment options are available to optimize your economic, architecture, and business choices.
- **Cloud Architecture.** Once the above choices have been made, the cloud architecture can be defined, which is important for all cloud deployment scenarios: internal/private, external/public, hybrid/integrated, and community/semi-private. Cloud architecture must be defined, documented, governed, and managed regardless of whether you are planning a purely internal private cloud or if you intend to leverage external public clouds. The decision to onboard your data or a business application onto a third-party public cloud does not eliminate the requirements to develop a robust cloud architecture, document it, and evaluate and test it—all prior to deploying that architecture.

In this chapter, we develop the Cloud Computing Reference Model as the master framework to support the cloud modeling and architecture processes described in the Cloud Adoption Lifecycle

Model. Before we get to the Cloud Computing Reference Model, we must first explore the volatile world of cloud computing industry standards.

Cloud Industry Standards

Cloud computing is an emergent technology paradigm. As such, it does not yet have wide-ranging industry standards to smooth the transition from a dream to a mainstream industry technology that can predictably be implemented in an enterprise to realize predictable outcomes, within an architectural framework described by a blend of industry standards—both de jure and de facto, to facilitate its adoption.

A number of cloud computing areas should be informed by the development of industry standards:

- *Cloud interoperability and integration standards,* covering cloud-to-cloud (C2C) integration, hybrid-to-private cloud integration, and interoperability of various cloud patterns with one another.
- *Cloud interface standards and application programmer interfaces (APIs)* to facilitate the consumption of cloud to support specific business requirements, standardize the access to and invocation of cloud computing, and more.
- *Cloud discovery, portability, onboarding and offboarding models, and cloud provider abstraction* to enable seamless switching of cloud providers without disrupting business operations.
- *Cloud performance benchmarks* to guide consumers on how cloud can increase asset utilization, resource optimization, and other performance guides, as well as pricing model standardization of various a la carte cloud models (e.g., comparing Amazon's web services to other cloud service and solution providers).
- *Cloud governance standards* for design-time planning, architecture, modeling, and deployment, as well as run-time standards for management, monitoring, operations and support, quality of service (QoS), and service level agreements (SLAs).
- *Cloud security and privacy concerns,* such as data integrity, physical and logical security, and all other related security requirements for services, applications, and interactions in a cloud ecosystem.

- *Cloud standards for various tiers of cloud enablement,* such as virtualization standards for physical resources, as well as virtualization of applications, application infrastructure and containers, and more. How the various types of cloud resources are accessed via APIs, and integrated into a cloud-enabled capability is a wide-open area of inquiry in the industry.

There are many gaps in the categorization of cloud standards, but most of the recent emphasis has been on the infrastructure and virtualization aspects of cloud (i.e., cloud foundation and enablement). Infrastructure and virtualization technologies are fairly well known, and as a result the efforts have tended to start at the lower layers. Note that this closely mirrors much of the commercial activity as well, in which technologies have generally tended to mature from the bottom of the stack towards the top[1]. While the industry has started with what is both essential and most well known, there is broad consensus that further development of standards farther up the stack promise to deliver even higher value, corresponding to the increase in value of the higher-level cloud tiers themselves.

A number of organizations are attempting to develop cloud industry standards, including the National Institute of Science and Technology (NIST), individual vendor frameworks forwarded to industry for consideration as de facto standards, and some newer standards bodies with particular agendas and points of emphasis. NIST is addressing cloud standards primarily for the federal government, which is an aggressive potential adopter of cloud computing, and thus can be counted on to drive frameworks and standards for broad industry cloud adoption. NIST is a trusted and respected entity, and we can count on its work being vendor-neutral and end-user-centric, rather than forwarding the objectives of individual cloud software or industry advocates.

In the absence of industry standards, individual vendors are submitting cloud reference models and related reference architectures to drive industry discourse around some de facto standards as well as preliminary consensus around approaches to industry standards. These are typically absorbed into vendor-neutral frameworks driven by standards organizations such as Organization for the Advancement of Structured Information Standards (OASIS), the Object Management Group (OMG), and others, typically for the overall betterment of the industry.

Development of cloud computing standards is certainly dynamic at this time-new efforts appear from time to time and gain momentum, while some existing efforts may lose momentum or even disappear altogether. Consequently any lists are simply guides, and most definitely subject to change. With that in mind, below are summaries of certain industry standards bodies and organizations working to develop cloud industry standards:

- **National Institute of Standards and Technology.** NIST's role in cloud computing is to promote the effective and secure use of the technology within government and industry by providing technical guidance and promoting standards. NIST is heavily focused on federal government cloud standards, including emphasis on cloud interfaces, cloud integration, and cloud APIs. NIST has a working definition of cloud computing, as well as a forthcoming special publication that will cover cloud architectures, security, and deployment strategies for the federal government.[2]
- **Open Cloud Consortium.** The Open Cloud Consortium (OCC) is a recent standards group comprised of a group of universities focused on improving performance of various cloud patterns—primarily computing and storage cloud patterns—across geographically distributed data centers. In addition, the OCC seeks open frameworks to enable cloud integration and interoperability across multiple vendors, benchmarks for cloud, open source reference implementations of cloud, as well as managing a testing sandbox for cloud computing, called the Open Cloud Testbed.
- **Cloud Computing Interoperability Forum.** The Cloud Computing Interoperability Forum (CCIF) is focused on establishing a global cloud community and ecosystem where organizations can work together to foster and enable wider adoption of cloud computing technology, solutions, and services. Its initial effort is on the Unified Cloud Interface (UCI), which is to act as a "singular programmatic point of contact that can encompass the entire infrastructure stack as well as emerging cloud-centric technologies all through a unified interface."[3] The CCIF's UCI will be an open and standardized interface to facilitate the unification of all cloud APIs to support cloud integration and interoperability. In addition, the CCIF is establishing a semantic cloud model, taxonomy, and ontology via

the Resource Description Framework (RDF), to enable cloud resources and APIs to be described using an industry standard resource model.

- **Distributed Management Task Force.** The Distributed Management Task Force (DMTF) is focused on developing standards for cloud management and operations across cloud and enterprise platforms. DMTF developed the Open Virtualization Format (OVF) 1.0, a preliminary standard focused on packaging of software intended to be deployed to virtual machines or run-time containers independent of the virtualization platform or the particular hypervisor or physical processor architecture. In addition, DMTF has a draft standard for System Virtualization, Partitioning, and Clustering. DMTF has also initiated the DMTF Open Cloud Standards Incubator to accelerate development of open cloud standards. ''DMTF's Open Cloud Standards Incubator will focus on addressing these issues by developing cloud resource management protocols, packaging formats, and security mechanisms to facilitate interoperability.''[4]

- **Cloud Computing Community and Cloud Standards Wikis.** The cloud computing community and cloud standards wikis have been excellent resources to see the state of the industry with respect to cloud standards, as well as concepts for developing a Cloud Computing Reference Model, cloud computing stack, and a cloud platform reference architecture. These industry grass roots efforts also have contributed two additional items of value to the cloud ecosystem: the Cloud Computing Manifesto for cloud providers, and the Cloud Computing Bill of Rights for end-users or consumers of cloud computing solutions.

  - ◆ **Cloud Computing Manifesto.** The Cloud Computing Manifesto (CCMF) is a set of principles and guidelines developed for the cloud providers' community as complementary guidance to the Cloud Computing Bill of Rights. The Cloud Computing Manifesto documents key cloud principles that should be supported and adhered to by cloud solution, technology, and service providers for the benefit of all cloud ecosystem stakeholders. Categories of information included in the manifesto are user-centric guidelines, philanthropic principles, openness, transparency, interoperability, representation, discrimination, evolution, balance, and security. Along with its companion, the Cloud Computing Bill of Rights, the Cloud Computing Manifesto proposes basic cloud computing principles and ideals to guide and support the cloud ecosystem as it rapidly evolves.

♦ **Cloud Computing Bill of Rights.** The Cloud Computing Bill of Rights (CC-BoR) is a set of rights developed in support of end-users of cloud computing solutions and services. The CC-BoR ensures that a base set of cloud requirements are supported to facilitate and protect end-user organizations as they consume cloud capabilities from cloud technology providers, cloud solution providers, and cloud service providers. The CC-BoR includes information supporting auditing, billing, backup practices, data, interfaces/APIs, legal, location, security, service, and standards.

• **Cloud Security Alliance.** Cloud security standards are sorely needed as well, which spurred the formation of a new standards group called the Cloud Security Alliance in April 2009. The Cloud Security Alliance is focused on promoting the development and use of best practices for cloud security, as well as providing education on how cloud-enabled security can benefit other computing models and architectures.

Exhibit 6.1 is one early cloud standards roadmap initially developed by members of cloudcommunity.org (and ad-hoc grouping), which intends to track the status of relevant multi-vendor standards efforts.

Exhibit 6.1 A Cloud Standards Roadmap

Layer	Description	Group	Project	Status	Due
Client	?	?	?	?	?
	Operating environment	W3C	HTML 5	Draft	2008
Software (SaaS)	Event-driven scripting language	ECMA	ECMAScript	Mature	1997
	Data-interchange format	IETF	JSON (RFC4627)	Mature	2006
Platform (PaaS)	Management API	?	?	?	?

(continued)

Exhibit 6.1   Continued

Layer	Description	Group	Project	Status	Due
	Management API	OGF	Open Cloud Computing Interface (OCCI)	Draft	2009
	System virtualization		System Virtualization		
Infrastructure (IaaS)	Container format for virtual machines	DMTF	Open Virtualisation Format (OVF)	Complete	2009
	Descriptive language for resources	DMTF	CIM	Mature	1999
Fabric	?	?	?	?	?

Source: Sam Johnston (CC-BY-SA 3.0)

Standards Monitoring Framework[5]

A cautionary statement about industry standards is appropriate here. As with any emerging technology with intense media hype, industry buzz, and venture capital speculation, cloud computing will suffer its setbacks and challenges, as much from the overhype as from lack of standards to smooth and accelerate appropriate adoption and application of cloud to key business and technology requirements. Industry standards fall into three broad categories, as illustrated in Exhibit 6.2.

We urge you to take appropriate care when evaluating cloud computing for your enterprise, so that you do not inadvertently leverage the wrong standards or immature standards, and thus expose your enterprise to unnecessary risk and cost. Determine what standards matter to your particular cloud requirements, and the subsequent cloud model, cloud deployment pattern, and cloud architecture. Be sure to map the relative maturity and industry acceptance of various key standards to your needs based on the three categories of enabling standards, evolving standards, and emerging standards. Deploy cloud accordingly, as Exhibit 6.2 suggests.

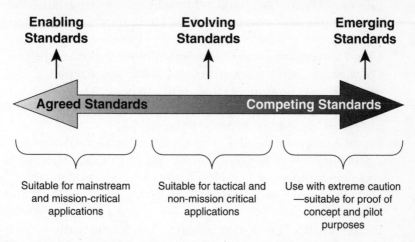

Which Standards Should I Use and When Should I Use Them?

Enabling
Standards

Evolving
Standards

Emerging
Standards

Agreed Standards   Competing Standards

Suitable for mainstream
and mission-critical
applications

Suitable for tactical and
non-mission critical
applications

Use with extreme caution
—suitable for proof of
concept and pilot
purposes

Exhibit 6.2   Spectrum of Enabling to Emerging Standards

Source: Eric A. Marks and Mark J. Werrell, *Executive's Guide to Web Services*, John Wiley & Sons, 2003. Used with permission.

A Cloud Computing Reference Model

In this section, we will develop a Cloud Computing Reference Model that will facilitate the process of cloud modeling, deployment planning, and architecture. As with SOA, until OASIS promoted the reference model, and reference architecture, and reference implementation constructs, there was not a sound standardized approach to realize a successful SOA implementation. The cloud computing reference model will hopefully establish a standardized process for modeling clouds. The Cloud Computing Reference Model we develop in this chapter is comprised of four supporting models:

1. **Cloud Enablement Model.** The core of the Cloud Computing Reference Model is the Cloud Enablement Model. The Cloud Enablement Model describes the fundamental technology tiers of cloud computing capabilities provided by cloud platform and cloud service providers to potential consumers of cloud-enabled technology and business capabilities.

2. **Cloud Deployment Model.** Describes the range of cloud deployment scenarios available to your enterprise: internal/private cloud, external/public cloud, hybrid/integrated cloud, and community or vertical cloud. These deployment scenarios may be mixed and matched.
3. **Cloud Governance and Operations Model.** Describes the governance, security operations, support, management, and monitoring requirements for cloud computing to ensure you have considered all the potential operational risks of adopting cloud for your enterprise.
4. **Cloud Ecosystem Model.** The Cloud Ecosystem Model considers the requirements of developing and sustaining a cloud ecosystem comprised of cloud providers, cloud consumers, and cloud intermediaries, as well as the cloud network and "cloud dial tone" necessary to ensure the cloud is always there for you. The cloud ecosystem also includes the various cloud enablement technologies, and cloud providers, and consumers of those cloud enablement technologies that comprise the cloud ecosystem.

The Cloud Computing Reference Model is depicted in Exhibit 6.3.

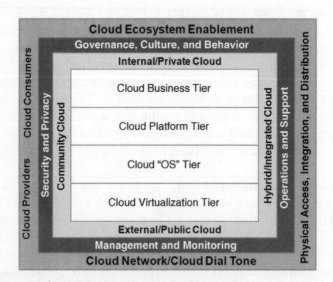

Exhibit 6.3   Cloud Computing Reference Model

The components of this Cloud Computing Reference Model are summarized below, and are explained in detail in the subsequent sections.

Cloud Enablement Model

- Cloud virtualization tier
- Cloud operating system tier
- Cloud platform tier
- Cloud business tier

Cloud Deployment Model

- Internal/private cloud
- External/public cloud
- Hybrid/integrated cloud
- Community/vertical/shared by community of interest stakeholders

Cloud Governance and Operations Model

- Governance, culture, and behavior
- Security and privacy
- Management and monitoring
- Operations and support

Cloud Ecosystem Model

- Cloud network/dial tone
- Cloud ecosystem enablement
- Cloud consumers and cloud providers
- Cloud physical access, integration, and distribution

Before we detail the specific submodels of the Cloud Computing Reference Model, we should establish the foundation for it. We need to establish the logical and technical foundation for our Cloud Computing Reference Model, and then we need to bring the logical foundation into life in the context of the cloud computing supporting models/submodels.

Exploring the Cloud Computing Logical Architecture

Developing the cloud computing logical architecture requires first a decomposition of the "layers" of a cloud architecture. In many respects, the cloud logical architecture represents the traditional layers of an enterprise architecture model, but with the ability to virtualize all the logical layers, as well as provide API access to cloud-enabled resources within each of the layers as cloud-enabled capabilities.

Cloud architectures have been variously illustrated using, naturally, pictures of clouds and other visual metaphors that allude to an amazing collection of technology packaged and available from a magic cloud in the sky. However, we all know there is much more nuance to cloud computing than the highly abstracted magic behind the cloud cartoon picture.

One widely-adopted cloud reference architecture is provided by NIST. The NIST cloud reference architecture is a high-level model comprised of three "tiers" of cloud capabilities "as a Service." In this NIST model, illustrated in Exhibit 6.4, there are three categories of cloud—Infrastructure, Platform, and Software—all "as a Service" architectures.

In this view, correctly, the respective layers build on one another. Platform as a Service (PaaS) layers and leverages the Infrastructure

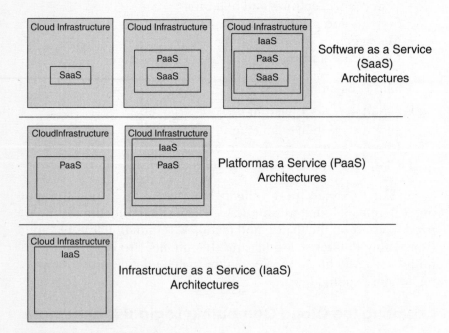

Exhibit 6.4   The NIST Cloud

Source: NIST

as a Service tier, and Software as a Service (SaaS) builds on the platform as a service architectural layer. However, this model does little to inform cloud architectures beyond these basic foundational insights. There is a lot more "magic" behind these tiers in the real world, and there are in reality more tiers of cloud capabilities as well.

For example, a cursory examination of the Infrastructure cloud tier will show how rich and complex the virtualization of Infrastructure, and the subsequent provisioning of Infrastructure as a "cloud service," truly are. For example, if we stipulate that the Infrastructure cloud tier must address network, computing, storage, and security capabilities, how do we architect these solutions so they can be virtualized and cloud-enabled as private internal cloud capabilities or as public external capabilities?

Virtualization technology is a robust and fairly mature capability these days. However, successfully virtualizing these related classes of computing infrastructure, and then layering over that the ability to provision these resources to multiple internal or external consumers, meter and bill their consumption by actual usage, flex the amount of capacity to address variable demand, all while elastically recovering capacity that is released back to the pool, is a different collection of technologies and solutions.

Virtualization of more than infrastructure (as a Service) is where cloud gets very interesting, and more complex, as more technology and business capabilities are cloud-enabled and available in a cloud ecosystem to the complete range of cloud consumers. Such a view requires a more detailed and extended view of a cloud computing logical model.

Exhibit 6.5 offers an extended cloud computing logical architecture that broadens the tiers and logical layers of cloud computing.

This logical cloud computing layered model consists of the layers of IT capabilities that must be virtualized in order to realize a cloud computing architecture. This model includes the following eight virtualized capabilities in support of attaining cloud computing:

1. Network virtualization (NaaS)
2. Infrastructure Virtualization (IaaS)
3. Application hosting virtualization (Container aaS)
4. Platform virtualization (PaaS)
5. Data virtualization (DaaS)

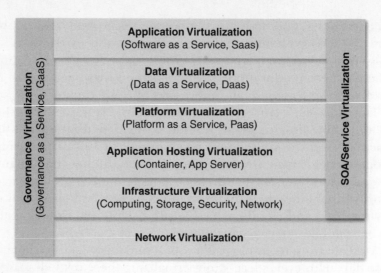

Exhibit 6.5 Logical Cloud Computing Model

6. Application virtualization (SaaS)
7. SOA/Services virtualization (SOAaaS)
8. Governance virtualization (GaaS)

Note that each of these tiers of virtualization build on one another, but are also accessible in and of themselves as cloud-enabled capabilities. A few comments on this cloud logical model are appropriate here.

First, this view emphasizes virtualization of every layer of a logical architecture, from basic infrastructure (computing, storage, network, security, etc.) to platform, applications, data, application hosting services, and more. We believe that the "as a Service" label can be applied to capabilities and technology services that have not heretofore been considered. For example, if we can provide Data as a Service (DaaS), what prevents extending on this to include Knowledge as a Service (KaaS)? Cloud enablement of capabilities and business solutions will extend to and touch many business requirements and capabilities. Our extended cloud logical model enables these other "as a Service" offerings to be incorporated into a cloud logical reference model explicitly.

Second, the SOA/services virtualization tier, which is illustrated as a vertical bar extending from the infrastructure virtualization tier all the way up to the application virtualization tier. SOA enablement and service enablement of capabilities is necessary to realize these higher layers of this cloud logical architecture model, hence the vertical orientation spanning many of the logical layers. SOA is both implicit and explicit in cloud computing, as we have maintained throughout this book.

Third, we depict in this view cloud governance virtualization, again, as a vertical tier that spans all the logical layers of this cloud logical model. Cloud governance is critical, perhaps more so for cloud than for SOA, and will require new approaches to the planning, design-time, quality assurance and test, and run-time management and operations of cloud, whether you are a cloud provider or cloud consumer.

Another view of a cloud logical stack is illustrated in Exhibit 6.6. Available from the Cloud Computing Community Wiki, this cloud stack is comprised of six layers or tiers as shown.

This cloud computing logical stack differs from that in Exhibit 6.5 in a few ways. Noteworthy, for example, is the treatment of cloud storage separate from cloud infrastructure, where the first model in Exhibit 6.5 considers storage, computing, network, and security virtualization as part of the infrastructure virtualization tier. In addition, the cloud stack of Exhibit 6.6 also includes the cloud clients tier. The cloud clients tier is essential in providing mechanisms to access and bind with the interfaces and/or APIs exposed by cloud

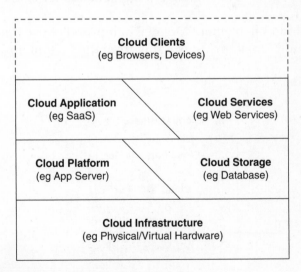

Exhibit 6.6   Logical Cloud Stack: Six Tiers

service providers in order to access cloud-enabled functionality for your organization's benefit.

Finally, Exhibit 6.6 explicitly identifies "cloud services," for example, web services, as one of its six layers or tiers. As stated previously, offering any computing capability "as a Service" means you are service-enabling that capability, whether it be infrastructure, computing, storage, application servers, or security. Thus, we applaud calling out the SOA/Services enablement dimensions of cloud computing in the cloud logical stack from the Cloud Computing Community Wiki site.

Developing a Holistic Cloud Computing Reference Model

With our review of come common cloud logical architecture frameworks completed, we can proceed to develop what we feel is a complete and holistic Cloud Computing Reference Model. Recall Exhibit 6.3, which illustrates the complete Cloud Computing Reference Model, and the four submodels that comprise it. The core of our Cloud Computing Reference Model is the Cloud Enablement Model.

The Cloud Enablement Model breaks cloud computing capabilities into four fundamental tiers of cloud enablement capabilities and technologies. The Cloud Enablement Model is illustrated in Exhibit 6.7.

The Cloud Enablement Model is comprised of five fundamental tiers of Cloud functionality, working from the bottom up, and listed below:

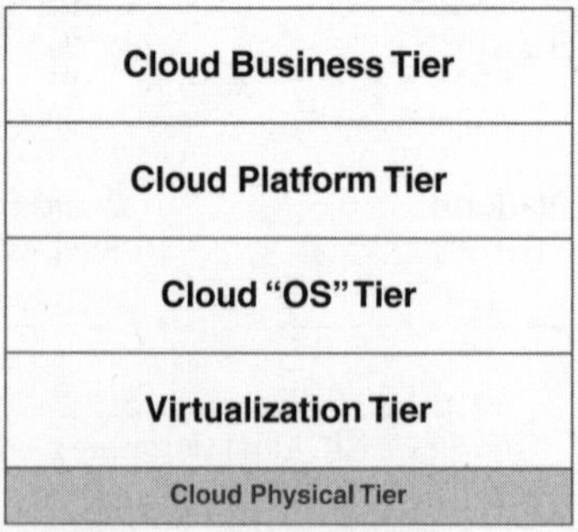

Cloud Business Tier
Cloud Platform Tier
Cloud "OS" Tier
Virtualization Tier
Cloud Physical Tier

Exhibit 6.7   Cloud Enablement Model Tiers

1. **Cloud Physical Tier.** Provides the physical computing, storage, network, and security resources that are virtualized and cloud enabled to support cloud requirements. The cloud physical tier has nothing to do with cloud, specifically. The physical tier provides the substrate on which cloud virtualization technologies and cloud operating systems platforms build to enable higher order cloud patterns to be realized. While we identify the Cloud Physical Tier in this discussion, we will not reference it further in the Cloud computing reference model.

2. **Cloud Virtualization Tier.** Provides core physical hardware virtualization and provides a potentially useful (in certain situations) foundation for cloud computing.

3. **Cloud Operating System Tier.** Provides the cloud computing "fabric," as well as application virtualization, core cloud provisioning, metering, billing, load balancing, workflow, and related functionality typical of cloud platforms. The Cloud OS tier is represented by a wide variety of new cloud platforms and cloud enablement technologies.

4. **Cloud Platform Tier.** Provides the technical solutions, application and messaging middleware, application servers, et cetera that comprise cloud- and/or application platforms, as well as pre-integrated cloud- and application platforms themselves, offered via PaaS delivery models.

5. **Cloud Business Tier.** Comprises the business or mission exploitation of cloud-enabled business applications, software, data, content, knowledge, and associated analysis frameworks, and other cloud consumption models that facilitate and enable end-user business value from cloud consumers' ability to access, bind, and consume cloud capabilities.

It is important to note that the Cloud Operating System and Cloud Platform Tiers in this more detailed model *together* form the Platform as a Service layer described in the higher level model defined by both NIST and in Chapter 2, Concepts, Terminology, and Standards.

Before we develop the detailed descriptions of the four primary tiers of the Cloud Enablement Model, there are a few principles and guidelines that must be explained first. The following rules are appropriate to make use of this Cloud Computing Reference Model.

- **Cloud Tiers Enable Higher-Level Tiers.** Each cloud tier, working from the bottom up in the Cloud Computing Reference Model, enables the cloud tier or tiers above it. The tiers build upon one another, but yet are independent and offer separately accessible cloud capabilities in and of themselves.
- **Cloud Tiers Are Individually "Atomic" and Individually Accessible.** Cloud consumers can access and consume cloud-enabled resources directly from any of these tiers, independent of the others, via cloud API and a portal or self-service user interface of some fashion. Exhibit 6.12 (shown later in the chapter) depicts the ability to access and consume resources from the four cloud tiers individually. The Cloud Enablement Tiers help organize various classes of cloud-enabled resources into the Cloud Computing Reference Model. In reality, cloud consumers do not access the "tiers" directly, but rather access cloud-enabled resources described by the tiers of the Cloud Enablement Model tiers.
- **All Cloud Tiers Need Ecosystem Enablement and Cloud Dial Tone.** Each cloud tier must have the necessary cloud network/dial tone and cloud ecosystem enablement capabilities in order to be discoverable, provisionable, and consumable as a service via the cloud. Furthermore, cloud providers and consumers must be able to find one another, communicate and negotiate, and then engage by establishing business and technical relationships via a service contract and appropriate technical interfaces to cloud capabilities, with clearly defined SLAs and QoS predefined and agreed to.
- **Cloud Consumer-Provider Continuum: Cloud Foundation, Cloud Enablement, and Cloud Exploitation.** Finally, implied in our Cloud Computing Reference Model is a continuum that describes the relationship of cloud providers to cloud consumers. We represent this continuum as three categories: Cloud Foundation, Cloud Enablement, and Cloud Exploitation. The Cloud Foundation is established by the tools and technologies that enable virtualization of network, computing, storage, and security resources, over a highly reliable network and computing infrastructure. The Cloud Enablement category refers to two of the tiers: the Cloud Operating System (OS) Tier and the Cloud Platform Tier. Both of these tiers are cloud enablement tiers that hit the core of cloud: The OS capabilities are

essential to create cloud-based capabilities, and the Cloud Platform Tier enables the broad range of platforms, applications, and business capabilities to be provided as a service via the cloud. However, we must be clear: Cloud enablement applies to all the Cloud Computing Reference Model tiers we have identified. The two middle tiers—OS and Platform—are especially critical to realizing the true potential of cloud. Finally, the cloud exploitation category refers to the consumption of cloud-based resources to address specific business, mission, information technology, infrastructure, and mission needs. The cloud exploitation category really can refer to the ability to exploit all cloud tiers and combinations of cloud patterns and deployment models to address business requirements. The cloud exploitation category is the consumer side of cloud.

With these general principles in place, we can now decompose the Cloud Computing Reference Model, beginning with the four tiers of the core: the Cloud Enablement Model.

Cloud Enablement Model Tiers: Overview

The Cloud Enablement Model is the framework that comprises the various cloud foundation and enablement technologies and solutions that enable the full breadth of cloud computing solutions to be realized. The four elements of the Cloud Enablement Model are explained in detail in the sections below.

Cloud Virtualization Tier (Infrastructure as a Service)   The cloud virtualization tier is a fairly mature class of technical solutions focused on the virtualization of physical IT infrastructure resources, primarily network, computing resources (server virtualization), storage resources (storage virtualization), and security resources. The cloud virtualization establishes the core resource model that enables shared, pooled physical resources that can be leveraged by cloud consumers in support of key business and technical needs. Typical physical resources included in the cloud virtualization tier include:

- Computing resources.
- Storage resources.
- Network resources.

- Security resources.
- Other physical infrastructure resources that may be virtualized and provided as foundational cloud infrastructure enablement capabilities.

Cloud Operating System Tier   The cloud operating system (OS) tier provides core cloud enablement capabilities that leverage the virtualization tier, and enable higher order cloud capabilities such as cloud-enabled platforms, applications, processes, and data. The cloud OS tier is typically provided by cloud technology platforms that provide core cloud functionality layered on top of the virtualization tier. Cloud OS provides application virtualization that builds on the cloud virtualization tier, which provides hardware resource virtualization.

The cloud OS tier provides many core functions of cloud solutions that enable clouds to be provisioned, managed, and reliably offered to consumers as a service. The cloud OS consists of a suite of capabilities and services that enable pooled cloud resources to be virtualized and offered to potential customers. In many respects, the cloud OS tier creates the fabric, resource, and operations management and provisioning capabilities to enable cloud platforms to deliver cloud enablement to cloud consumers.

The functionality of this layer includes the types of capabilities listed below:

- Virtualization technology
- SOA enablement technology
- Billing and metering
- Chargeback and financial integration
- Load balancing and performance assurance
- Monitoring, management, and SLA enforcement
- Resource provisioning and management
- Onboarding and offboarding automation
- Security and privacy tools/controls
- Cloud pattern enablement tools (see Exhibit 6.6)
- Cloud workflow, process management, and orchestration tools

Most cloud platform providers offer differing combinations of these features to enable various cloud patterns or deployments to be realized. In addition, while we show the cloud OS tier as a logical layer between virtualization tier and the cloud platform tier, in reality the cloud OS layer is ubiquitous to this model, and encompasses the entire logical cloud reference architecture model. Over time, we expect the cloud OS tier to absorb the cloud virtualization tier, as well as the technologies and middleware that comprise the cloud platform tier.

Cloud Platform Tier (Platform Enablement and Platforms Provided as a Service) The cloud platform tier provides the core platform functionality, virtualized and service-enabled, such that application platforms can be provided "as a Service" to organizations for application development, hosting and container support, web and application server, and messaging and mediation capabilities, all as a service. This is the application middleware tier that comprises an application platform, but is pre-integrated and provided as a service through cloud OS capabilities of provisioning, billing and metering, and related functionality.

The cloud platform tier is comprised of the enabling technologies and capabilities that help establish application platforms that are assembled, integrated, and provisioned as services to potential consumers. For example, Salesforce.com is a CRM application built on its Force.com platform as a service. Force.com is the application platform on which Salesforce.com and other business software applications are built, and within which its logic, data, and application infrastructure are hosted.

Figure 6.8 depicts the cloud platform tier as two sub-tiers: the Cloud Platform Middleware sub-tier, and the Cloud Platform sub-tier.

The **Cloud Platform Middleware** Sub-tier includes all the cloud and application middleware technologies and tools typically needed to build an application platform, e.g. SOA platform middleware, application servers, messaging and application middleware, web servers, runtime application containers, content servers, developer tools and integrated development environments (IDEs) typically associated with application servers, et al. The Cloud Platform Middleware Sub-tier is where SOA services would be hosted and deployed in a SOA framework.

The Cloud Platform/PaaS Sub-tier represented as the upper portion of the Cloud Platform Tier represents pre-integrated cloud and application platforms, which can be offered as a service (PaaS)

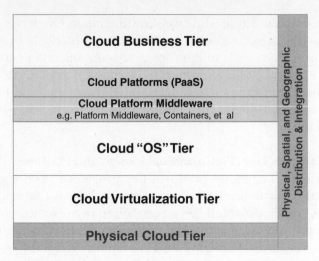

Exhibit 6.8   Cloud Enablement Model

as a standalone, virtualized application capability such as Force.com, Google App Engine, etc.

The fundamental difference between these sub-layers of the Cloud Platform Tier is that the Cloud Platform Middleware Sub-tier describes the technologies and tools that are leveraged to create application and cloud platforms, while the Cloud Platform/PaaS Sub-tier refers to the integrated, virtualized platforms available to consumers as a service.

The cloud platform is what enables Platform as a Service. The following capabilities are included in this cloud tier:

- PaaS as pre-assembled, integrated application platforms provided to others (e.g., Google App Engine, Salesforce's Force. com)
- SOA middleware, services and other related SOA enablement middleware and capabilities
- Application container services, application servers, and related application hosting and runtime services
- Web application and content servers, content hosting and delivery, and web server capabilities
- Messaging, mediation, integration, and related messaging services and middleware, provided as part of an application platform, as a service. This would also include event engines, complex event processing and related event middleware.

- Developer resources to support develop onboarding, application development, testing resources, sandbox functionality, and application provisioning, hosting, and the related application metering, billing, and support capabilities

The cloud platform tier is comprised of the technologies and tools that enable application platforms to be constructed, integrated, and provisioned to many unrelated application developers and application providers. The cloud platform tier provides a robust, feature-rich application development environment to incentive organizations to develop new applications on a given application platform, and it provides the application hosting and run-time services to operate and provision the finished application to new consumers via a cloud-enabled application delivery model.

Cloud Business Tier   This cloud tier consists of various business and application capabilities, provided via a cloud enabled platform, enabled by a cloud OS, and riding on the cloud virtualization tier, and of course, provided as a service. Included in this tier are Software as a Service (SaaS), and related cloud-enabled business capabilities such as Data as a Service (DaaS), business processes as a service (BPaaS), and knowledge as a service (KaaS). The cloud business tier represents the business consumer side of cloud, where business capabilities are consumed via the cloud logical architecture, as provided by other third-party cloud providers. While SaaS is well articulated from Salesforce.com, Google apps, and other related software applications, the other categories of business solutions are new constructs. DaaS is what Dun and Bradstreet provides, as well as Equifax, and other data providers. KaaS is what intelligence agencies provide to the Department of Defense, as well as other content providers who deliver knowledge or pre-analyzed content as a service. BPaaS is also included in the cloud business tier, since pre-assembled business processes will also be provided via cloud application platforms to consumers as well.

The cloud business tier is where business and mission capabilities are provided as services to business consumers via the other cloud enablement tiers. The cloud business tier includes the following business capabilities, provided as services, to end-user consumers:

- SaaS, including business applications, enterprise applications, desktop software, business utilities (e-mail, calendar, synchronization), portal, and so forth.
- DaaS/KaaS
- Business processes as a Service
- KaaS
- Anything aaS

The cloud business tier is a primary tier where the business and mission exploitation of cloud computing occurs for end-users who leverage cloud-enabled capabilities to perform their business and mission functions.

Cloud Deployment Model

We will now add the Cloud Deployment Model, or sub-model, to our Cloud Computing Reference Model. Cloud deployment models are critical aspects of the cloud computing paradigm. You must understand the basic cloud deployment models, and how you might mix and match various cloud patterns and deployment models to support a business need or operational use case that solves a business problem you may have. There are four basic cloud deployment scenarios to consider: internal/private cloud, external/public cloud, hybrid/integrated cloud, and community or vertical cloud. All cloud adoption scenarios will fall along this continuum.

The Cloud Computing Reference Model view with the various cloud deployment scenarios is illustrated in Exhibit 6.9.

The fundamental debate in the industry centers on the relative business value of public clouds, in which you effectively outsource a portion of your data centers and/or IT infrastructure completely to drive better use of capital and resources, or you implement cloud internally, as a private cloud, to support more effective utilization of computing resources while you ensure privacy and security of your data and information.

Many analysts suggest that implementing cloud internally defeats the purpose of cloud, in which you can obtain computing resources from a network of cloud service providers based on your particular needs, and dynamically add or subtract capacity as you go. Implementing internal clouds means you have internal capacity, even if its utilization is better than before, via virtualization technologies, but

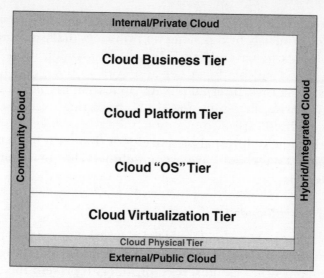

Exhibit 6.9   Cloud Deployment Model

you still have capacity that you have acquired, installed, and have to maintain, and you're stuck with it. In a public cloud, once you have no need for the computing capacity, you release it and stop paying for it completely. With private clouds, like internal data centers, you still have the amortized/depreciated costs associated with capital expenditures on hardware, software, and so on.

In fact, some would argue that an internal cloud is not a cloud at all, since you are tapping internal resources via a highly virtualized hardware and application platform model. Cloud computing, as defined, means a massively scalable set of IT resources provided to multiple consumers on a multi-tenancy basis. Internal clouds in a strict sense do not meet this definition.

Regardless of this debate, there are virtues and benefits of all the various cloud deployment models we will describe in this section.

We will review each of the primary deployment models in the sections below.

Internal/Private Clouds

An internal cloud, or private cloud, is an internal deployment where cloud computing capabilities are planned, architected, acquired, and implemented to support internal business requirements, while avoiding perceived risks around security, privacy, and the relative immaturity of the cloud industry and technology landscape. A private cloud primarily brings value via proven virtualization technologies, which can extend from the cloud virtualization tier up through the cloud platform tier and even to the cloud business tier. In this manner, internal private clouds can be highly valuable to an enterprise, bringing new capabilities that exceed the well established hardware virtualization model that we know today. Given this context, internal private clouds that push higher up the logical cloud stack can have a compelling value proposition for your enterprise.

External/Public Clouds

An external or public cloud is provided by an external independent entity, typically a cloud service provider. Amazon, Salesforce, Google, and many other cloud service providers represent the external public cloud deployment model. Key attributes of the public cloud deployment pattern are as follows:

- Provided by an independent third-party cloud service provider
- Accessed via the web and a self-service user interface
- Readily available user guides, onboarding APIs, and technical support
- SLAs and service contracts
- Multiple virtual machine instances available in varying configurations based on your specific requirements, including processor configuration and RAM, operating system, application server and development environments
- Multiple cloud resources types available; for example, Amazon provides the following cloud-enabled resources to potential consumers: Amazon Simple Storage Service (S3); Amazon Elastic Compute Cloud (EC2); Amazon Simple DB; Amazon CloudFront (Content delivery, similar to Akamai); Amazon Simple Queue Service (SQS); Amazon Elastic Map Reduce

Hybrid/Integrated Clouds

Hybrid clouds, or integrated clouds, are scenarios where an organization blends its internal private cloud with cloud capabilities provided through public clouds by third-party cloud service providers.

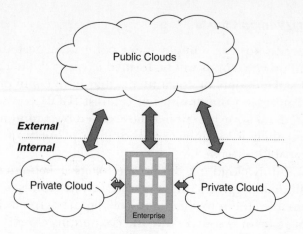

Exhibit 6.10   Hybrid Cloud Example

Hybrid clouds require cloud integration. Cloud integration and interoperability is an emerging challenge of the cloud industry, and is already spawning industry standards bodies to help address and standardize on frameworks for cloud interfaces and APIs, cloud integration and interoperability standards, and even tools that enable cross-cloud composition and orchestration of cloud resources in support of emerging business model needs.

Exhibit 6.10 illustrates a hybrid Cloud deployment model.

The following are attributes of hybrid, integrated clouds:

- Blend a combination of internal cloud and external cloud-enabled resources
- Take advantage of the cost economics of external third-party clouds, while mitigating some of the risks by maintaining an internal private cloud for critical processes and data
- Require integration of external and internally provided capabilities, which must overcome vendor-proprietary APIs and integrate them with your internal interfaces
- May segment the Cloud Enablement Model tiers into those you will cloud enable as private clouds (e.g., data and storage), while others may be pushed to third-party external clouds. Risk analysis and security assessments may help determine what cloud enablement tiers and resources within those tiers are best provided as private, public, or hybrid models.

Community/VerticalClouds

Community clouds are a deployment pattern suggested by NIST, where semi-private clouds will be formed to meet the needs of a set of related stakeholders or constituents that have common requirements or interests. Communities of Interest (COI) constructs typical of the federal government may be enabled by community clouds to augment their wiki-centric collaboration processes with cloud-enabled capabilities as well.

A community cloud may be private for its stakeholders, or may be a hybrid that integrates the respective private clouds of the members, yet enables them to share and collaborate across their clouds by exposing data or resources into the community cloud.

Cloud Integration and Interoperability

Clearly, as cloud deployments proliferate, and with the early interest in hybrid integrated clouds, the demand for cloud integration tools and the industry urgency behind standards for cloud interoperability will continue to be intense. Hybrid clouds are already pressuring the industry for open standards to enable integration of clouds with one another, regardless of the third-party cloud provider or the specific cloud technology provider's proprietary secret sauce. Watch for a new generation of cloud integration tools, followed by cloud development tools and suites, cloud collaboration tools, and cross-cloud composition and orchestration tools as well. The demand for cloud integration and interoperability is already high, and should be a ripe area for new solutions and tools to support these requirements.

A combination of vendor innovation supported by industry standards will greatly facilitate the realization of cloud integration and cloud interoperability.

Cloud Governance and Operations Model

The Cloud Governance and Operations Model establishes the governance, security, management and operations foundation to ensure you realize cloud with appropriate management controls, security and risk containment approaches in place. Exhibit 6.11 illustrates the Cloud Governance and Operations Model.

The Cloud Governance and Operations Model consists of the following elements:

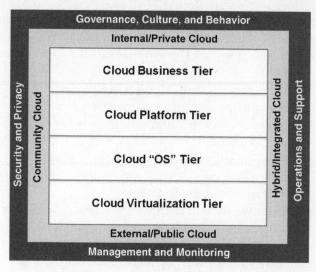

Exhibit 6.11   Cloud Governance and Operations Model

- Governance, culture, and behavior
- Security and privacy
- Management and monitoring
- Operations and support

Cloud Governance, Culture, and Behavior

Cloud governance is an emerging requirement of cloud computing, and encompasses a broad set of business and technical requirements, from the planning and architecture process through the design-time considerations of cloud computing, functional and nonfunctional requirements analysis, the actual process of onboarding your enterprise onto a cloud (internal, public, or hybrid), and the monitoring and operations requirements once you have successfully leveraged a cloud. There are significant gaps in the cloud governance domain, as highlighted:

- **Cloud Lifecycle Governance.** There is a lack of cloud governance process models for the complete cloud lifecycle, including cloud strategy, planning, modeling and architecture, onboarding and offboarding, cloud portability, cloud requirements analysis, and operations and sustainment.

- **Cloud Policy Models and Policy Enforcement Frameworks.** There is immaturity of cloud policies, policy enforcement models and frameworks to support runtime operations, policy enforcement for quality of service, SLAs, security, and more.
- **Cloud Management and Monitoring Tools.** The absence of cloud monitoring and management tools is being offset by SOA vendors and cloud technology providers offering their own management and monitoring solutions. However, more work is needed to develop comprehensive management and monitoring solutions covering the range of cloud deployment models and integration scenarios.
- **Cloud Operations and Support Models.** There is clear immaturity of cloud operations and support models for deployments that involve more than traditional data center operations and hardware virtualization concepts.
- **Cloud-based Application Lifecycle Governance.** There is a major industry gap in application lifecycle governance based on developing applications on cloud-centric platforms, such as Force.com, Google App Engine, and others, as well as architecting software applications specifically for cloud-based deployments models.
- **Legacy Application Migration to the Cloud.** There are few standards and application migration models to support migrating legacy applications into cloud deployments. Such application migration efforts are immature at best, and many cloud solutions today are oriented toward more contemporary design concepts and approaches (e.g., object orientation, service-enablement and SOA, and of course web 2.0 concepts of mash-ups, social computing frameworks, and collaboration). It will take a lot of work to close these application development, application migration, and application refactoring gaps.
- **Culture and Behavior.** A critical aspect of cloud computing is the behavior and cultural dimensions of cloud that will facilitate adoption within an enterprise, and enable the full potential of cloud to be realized by a given organization. We urge you to conduct an explicit examination of your cultural barriers and enablers, and understand the behavioral model necessary to move to cloud computing. This can be especially challenging when an organization is attempting to establish

its central IT organization and an internal cloud service provider. Cultural and behavioral factors will either create the environment for cloud success or will be the reasons for its failure. The technology will not be the reason for cloud failures.

- **Funding Models and Incentives.** Corresponding to the cultural and behavioral factors will be the funding models and incentive models necessary to support an enterprise cloud deployment. Funding models and incentives will support the desired behavioral transformation required for cloud success. Establishing the funding, budgeting, chargeback, and other financial mechanisms of your cloud strategy is a critical need. Creating incentives for cloud consumption from an internal cloud service provider will also be necessary. Together, funding, incentives, budgeting practices, behavior, and culture will establish the ecosystem and environment for cloud success.

We expect significant industry dialog focused on various dimensions of cloud governance, from design time and deployment to operations and runtime management. Furthermore, as is already occurring, many network management and web services management (WSM) vendors are repositioning their tools and products for the evolving cloud space. This will be a vibrant area in the coming years.

Security and Privacy

Cloud computing is certainly under scrutiny for its ability to securely manage data and information, without compromising data security requirements, privacy concerns, and data integrity challenges that accompany cloud deployments. Cloud security and privacy concerns will fuel more internal cloud deployments, initially, until the trust of cloud-based security can be established. Many business leaders, counter intuitively, feel their data is more secure in an external professionally-managed data center than in their own. This discovery demonstrates that perhaps the security and privacy concerns over cloud will be overcome more easily than those of SOA and web services.

A key element of the Cloud Governance and Operations Model, cloud security becomes an explicit dimension of our cloud architecture and planning process based on the business needs, as well as the cloud deployment scenarios you are considering. Understanding and planning for cloud security and privacy is critical to your success with cloud.

Management and Monitoring

As described previously, cloud management and monitoring requirements must be clearly articulated and understood based on the Cloud Enablement Model and Cloud Deployment Model you have developed during your cloud planning and architecture process. You must consider the instrumentation and tooling necessary to monitor and manage your cloud, whether your deployment is an internal private cloud, or whether you are leveraging third-party external clouds from Amazon or Salesforce. Either way, you must be able to integrate and automate the monitoring, performance management, alarming and alerting of cloud events, and performance metrics in order to respond to outages, performance degradations, and related operational concerns.

Again, the absence of cloud monitoring and management tools must be addressed by the cloud vendor community to develop comprehensive management and monitoring solutions covering the range of cloud deployment models and integration scenarios.

Operations and Support

Cloud operations and support requirements are also essential to plan for in your cloud planning framework. They are an explicit consideration of the Cloud Governance and Operations submodel. As mentioned previously, the entire Cloud Adoption Lifecycle Model is poorly understood, particularly for cloud operations and support. While many of these processes can be adapted from current Information Technology Infrastructure Library (ITIL), Control Objectives for Information and related Technology (COBIT) and other IT management frameworks, you will need to leverage your current data center and IT support, help desk, and operations processes and adapt them based on your chosen cloud deployment model.

Operations and support for hybrid and public clouds will be a fast-moving area of emphasis, and you must spend appropriate time understanding the operations and support requirements based on the cloud deployment, based on which cloud enablement tiers and cloud patterns you intend to exploit.

Cloud Governance and Governance as a Service?

The Cloud Governance and Operations Model points to gaps that are critical to the success of cloud computing. However, these gaps also point to new opportunities to deliver governance solutions as cloud-enabled capabilities as well. Can governance be provided as a service to enterprises based on incorporating policies, processes, and oversight mechanisms into a cloud delivery model?

And specific to cloud governance, how can the following governance requirements be addressed by cloud-enabled solutions, potentially provided as a service?

- Distributed governance and monitoring infrastructure
- Governance platform that spans private, public, and hybrid clouds to provide a single operational picture of operations
- Cloud onboarding, offboarding, and portability
- Cloud design-time and run-time considerations
- Cloud quality assurance and testing

Again, cloud solutions are nascent, and we have only begun to imagine the range of business and technology capabilities that can be cloud enabled and provided as a service. Governance as a Service and cloud governance solutions are wide open for new concepts and approaches to addressing these industry gaps.

Cloud Ecosystem Model (Supporting the Cloud Reference Model)

Next, we must extend the Cloud Computing Reference Model to incorporate critical environment dimensions of cloud computing. The Cloud Computing Reference Model must address the required environmental ingredients to enable cloud to be accessible to consumers that may be able to leverage cloud for the benefit of their enterprises. It must also address the essential elements that enable cloud platform and service providers to create business models based on providing cloud enablement and cloud-enabled business and technical capabilities.

The Cloud Ecosystem Model illustrated in Exhibit 6.12 surrounds the core tiers of the Cloud Enablement Model.

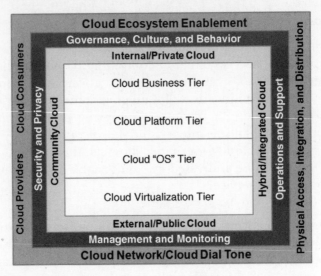

Exhibit 6.12   CC-RM Cloud Ecosystem Model

The following elements comprise the Cloud Ecosystem Model:

- Cloud ecosystem enablement
- Cloud consumers and cloud providers
- Cloud network/cloud dial tone
- Cloud Physical Access, Integration, and Distribution

Each of the Cloud Ecosystem Model elements is described below.

Cloud Ecosystem Enablement

Cloud ecosystem enablement is an environmental capability of the Cloud Computing Reference Model that builds on and extends the cloud OS tier to provide the core cloud enablement, provisioning, and management capabilities to all tiers of the Cloud Computing Reference Model. Essentially, cloud ecosystem enablement creates and enables the business and operational relationships between cloud consumers and cloud providers, as well as the technical and physical connections that enable business operations to be provided and performed over the cloud. The cloud ecosystem is the environment in which cloud providers, cloud consumers, and cloud solution and technology providers all operate to drive the economic and transactional foundation of cloud computing as a legitimate business and technology trend.

Do not mistake the cloud ecosystem as a purely technical capability or domain. The cloud ecosystem must also accommodate the behavioral, cultural, and trust dimensions of cloud, since in the end people determine whether and how to leverage cloud in support of their business, mission, and technology needs. As with other technology trends, the behavioral and cultural challenges to cloud computing must be understood and met head on.

Cloud Network/Cloud Dial Tone

Cloud network enablement describes the essential network and infrastructure capabilities that link cloud consumers, providers, and the related cloud enablement technology together into the "cloud," or the "net." This is the cloud dial tone. Cloud network enablement describes the ubiquitous and "always on" feature of the cloud that makes it attractive to potential cloud consumers—its reliability and the trust we place in it to be there when we want it, always. Cloud computing will succeed only if organizations trust that the network will always be there, and that their particular combination of cloud resources and deployment models will always be available based on the terms of the cloud service contract, SLA, and QoS. If cloud consumers lose trust in their cloud providers, then cloud will never be a viable industry. Much like electric utilities, if power is not on or available on a reliable basis, the trust would erode, and the utility system would cease to exist.

Cloud Consumers and Cloud Providers

The cloud ecosystem cannot be established without cloud consumers and cloud providers, connected via the cloud network/cloud dial tone, being able to establish an operational relationship to leverage cloud resources on behalf of the consuming entity or organization. The cloud consumer–provider relationship model is fundamentally the same as the SOA consumer–provider model.

In an SOA ecosystem, SOA services are developed by service providers, and then they are registered and published so they can be discovered by potential consumers. If service consumers find services of interest, they can try them out, or contact the service provider directly to negotiate a service contract, SLA, quality of service, and so on. Once the service contract is established, the service consumers can access the service provided by the service provider and leverage it to accomplish a specific business task. Cloud operates in much the same manner, and this should be no surprise. Cloud resources must be "service-enabled" via SOA platforms and tools in order to be discoverable and consumable by potential cloud consumers. The cloud ecosystem must provide the ability for cloud consumers and providers to find one another, and to technically "connect" via the cloud network/cloud dial tone to establish a business, operational, and technical relationship.

Cloud Enablement Continuum: Foundation, Enablement, and Exploitation

The cloud enablement continuum describes the range of cloud enablement and exploitation requirements necessary to establish a cloud ecosystem, comprised of cloud providers and cloud consumers. This continuum spans the cloud foundation of virtualization of physical infrastructure resources, to the more sophisticated cloud platforms and cloud enablement of platforms as a service, to the actual consumption of business applications and capabilities as a service. The cloud foundation is established by the tools and technologies that enable virtualization of network, computing, storage, and security resources, over a highly reliable network and computing infrastructure.

The cloud enablement category refers to two of the tiers—the Cloud OS Tier and the Cloud Platform Tier. Both of these tiers are cloud enablement tiers that hit the core of cloud: The OS capabilities are essential to create cloud-based capabilities, and the cloud platform tier enables the broad range of platforms, applications, and business capabilities to be provided as a service via the cloud. However, we must be clear: Cloud enablement applies to all the Cloud Computing Reference Model tiers we have identified. The two middle tiers— OS and Platform—are especially critical to realizing the true potential of cloud.

Finally, the cloud exploitation category refers to the consumption of cloud-based resources to address specific business, mission, information technology, infrastructure, and mission needs. The cloud exploitation category really can refer to the ability to exploit all cloud tiers and combinations of cloud patterns and deployment models to address business requirements. The cloud exploitation category is the consumer side of cloud, regardless of the type of consumer or the cloud-enabled resources consumed by them—the business end-user of Salesforce.com, the CIO consumer of virtualization, or the application developer consumer of a platform as a service, for example, Force.com.

Cloud Physical Access, Integration, and Distribution

A key part of the Cloud Ecosystem Model addresses the physical premises, including access controls, physical security, and related requirements,— all the ways cloud seamlessly supports physical integration of data centers, physical locations, and highly distributed users. Thus, the cloud ecosystem must address all the related aspects of the supporting physical environment. The physical integration and distribution of cloud-enabled resources and capabilities is why a cloud ecosystem must be established, via the Internet, via internal Internet technologies, and other technologies that connect highly distributed cloud consumers spatially, logically, and geographically.

Recall the Cloud Physical Tier described earlier in the context of the Cloud Enablement Model. Taken together, the Cloud Physical Access, Integration, and Distribution dimensions of the Cloud Ecosystem Model, along with the Cloud Physical Tier portion of the Cloud Enablement Model, represent the full range of physical resources that must be included explicitly in the discussion of Cloud computing. Regardless of all the ''virtualization'' of resources possible through cloud, the physical servers, storage devices, network routers and related infrastructure, and building, air conditioning and cooling equipment, and building automation capabilities all are part of the cloud equation, and someone must manage these resources very well to ensure cloud success.

If your cloud strategy calls for physical data center consolidation, then you must leverage the both dimensions of the Cloud computing Reference Model. If your strategy calls for server consolidation, you may not need to address the Cloud Physical Access, Integration, and Distribution dimensions of the Cloud Ecosystem Model, but you must address the impact of cloud on the Cloud Physical Tier.

Cloud computing is still dependent on physical implementations of computing, storage, network and supporting cooling, power management, and building automation tools. Always remember that someone ultimately has to host the physical gear, regardless of your Cloud strategy.

Consumption of Cloud-Enabled and Cloud Enablement Resources

It is essential to understand the consumption of cloud resources and capabilities, based on the Cloud Computing Reference Model tiers we have presented. Recall that a cloud consumer can access and consume cloud-enabled resources directly from any of the cloud tiers, independent of the others, via cloud API and a portal or self-service user interface of some fashion.

Exhibit 6.13 depicts the ability to access and consume resources from the four cloud tiers individually.

As depicted, each cloud resource, within a particular tier of cloud capabilities, is accessed via an interface, or API, such that application developers, solution architects, and the rest of the cloud consumer community can easily onboard their data or application, or their business, onto a cloud. While the illustration shows APIs at each of the tiers, the real world is more granular than that. Specific cloud-enabled resources are discovered and consumed, integrated

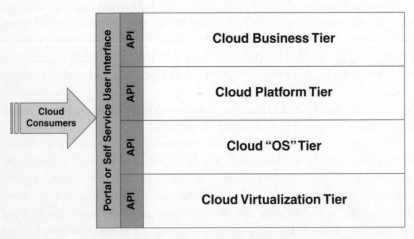

Exhibit 6.13   Cloud Consumers Accessing Various Cloud Tiers

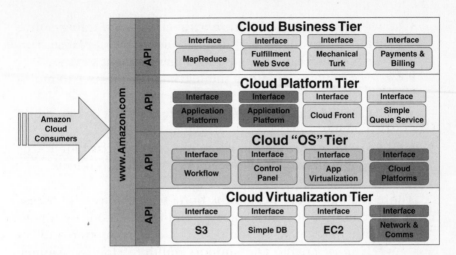

Exhibit 6.14   **Amazon Cloud Consumers Accessing Amazon Web Services**

together, and assembled into a complete cloud solution that addresses a specific organization's requirements.

Exhibit 6.14 illustrates how individual services from Amazon are accessible from www.Amazon.com as individual cloud services or in combinations of cloud capabilities based on various cloud patterns, by which you link or "integrate" multiple Amazon capabilities together into your cloud-enabled business solution.

As shown in the exhibit, an Amazon cloud consumer can access individual Amazon cloud capabilities, mapped to our Cloud Enablement Model tiers directly via APIs or cloud interfaces published by Amazon, to make it easy to access and consume their services, and to compose them into a cloud-enabled solution based on various cloud patterns.

Supporting the concepts around easy cloud consumption, there is a standards effort underway to address interface specifications for cloud-enabled infrastructure, or Infrastructure as a Service. This of course is mapped to the cloud virtualization tier of our Cloud Computing Reference Model. The Open Cloud Computing Interface (OCCI) standards body has developed a cloud computing Infrastructure as a Service interface specification, or API, for interfacing to Infrastructure as a Service. The new API covers the following scenarios:[6]

- *Cloud consumers* can interact with cloud computing infrastructure on an ad-hoc basis (e.g., deploy, start, stop, restart).
- *Cloud integrators* can offer advanced management services.
- *Cloud aggregators* can offer a single common interface to multiple providers.
- *Cloud providers* can offer a standard interface that is compatible with available tools.
- *Cloud service and solution providers* can offer standard interfaces for dynamically scalable service delivery in their products.

There is always more work to be done to enable ease of access and easier consumption of cloud capabilities based on the frameworks we have developed. In addition, cloud consumption and access models must enable and support multiple cloud consumer types to engage with and participate in the cloud ecosystem. Exhibit 6.15 illustrates how different communities or types of cloud consumers might access different Cloud Enablement Model tiers based on their specific business or technical requirements.

As Exhibit 6.14 suggests, data center technicians and architects are very much interested in the cloud virtualization tier as both internal and public external cloud deployments, based on the needs

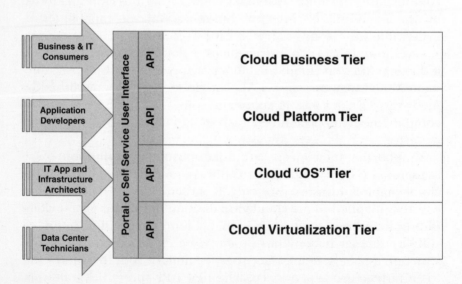

Exhibit 6.15   Consumers of Cloud Capabilities by Enablement Tier

of data center management (e.g., better asset utilization and optimized data center operations).

However, moving up the Cloud Enablement Model tiers, we show that application developers as cloud consumers accessing the Cloud Platform Tier capabilities do develop applications on third-party platforms provided "as a Service" by firms such as Google and Salesforce. Furthermore, we show business consumers accessing business resources and capabilities exposed via the cloud business tier. Again, this represents a completely different set of cloud consumers who may be accessing cloud computing models provided by internal or external cloud service providers. Cloud computing will succeed only insofar as various cloud consumers are engaged in and able to consume cloud resources based on their roles, interests, and business needs.

Cloud Computing Reference Model Summary

The CC-RM developed in this chapter provides a complete and holistic framework that supports the full cloud computing lifecycle, as well as the technical, deployment, governance and operations, and environmental or ecosystem needs of the cloud computing industry.

The CC-RM and its four supporting submodels—the Cloud Enablement Model, the Cloud Deployment Model, the Cloud Governance and Operations Model, and the Cloud Ecosystem model—together cover the full range of cloud requirements from a planning, architecture, and implementation and support perspective.

Furthermore, the Cloud Ecosystem Model and cloud consumption frameworks must address the needs and requirements of the complete range of potential cloud consumers, far beyond the technical IT audience we often typecast as the consumers of cloud computing models. In addition, the cloud ecosystem must provide the end-user tools to enable the composition and assembly of cloud resources and capabilities available to potential cloud consumers, based on preconfigured cloud patterns.

The CC-RM will facilitate the development of cloud modeling patterns. Development of preconfigured cloud pattern templates will be critical to help various organizations understand how various cloud-enabled resources can be linked and integrated into complete business and technology solutions to drive the value proposition of cloud.

The CC-RM submodel provides a clear framework for understanding cloud computing and all of its requirements from a strategy and planning perspective, from a modeling, deployment, and architecture definition perspective, and from a governance and operations perspective. Next, we briefly decompose the CC-RM into its Cloud Computing Technical Reference Model elements.

Cloud Computing Technical Reference Architecture

In this section, we will briefly explore some of the more technical aspects of cloud computing in the context of the CC-RM. Caveat: This chapter, and in fact the entire book, is not intended to be a technical implementation guide for architects and developers. While we decompose the CC-RM into its technical elements, we will go no deeper than that in this section, and what is covered will be only superficial. There are many other technical and developer reference guides available for the architect and developer communities.

The beginnings of a Cloud Computing Technical Reference Model are in place from our CC-RM, specifically in the four tiers described in the Cloud Enablement Model, described in detail in this chapter. We will revisit that model shortly. As we have commented, many cloud architecture diagrams begin with the oversimplified cloud cartoon, inside of which are various cloud capabilities provided by magic over the net. Exhibit 6.16 is an illustration of this.

As shown, we have the cloud cartoon, within which are depicted four cloud resources or capabilities available via the cloud:

1. Cloud platform
2. Cloud queuing service
3. Cloud storage
4. Cloud infrastructure

While this illustration can be quite easily mapped to our CC-RM, and specifically to the tiers of the Cloud Enablement Model, we will not spend more time on it other than to state that under the covers, there are a lot more technology components that underlie and enable this cloud cartoon illustration.

Exhibit 6.17 populates the tiers of the Cloud Enablement Model with many of the representative technologies, capabilities, and

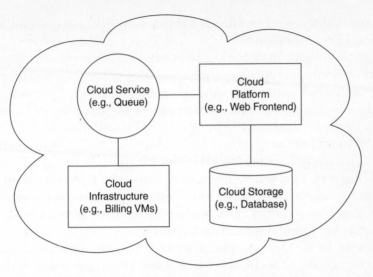

Exhibit 6.16   Cloud Computing Technical Architecture

Cloud Business Tier			
Data as a Service (DaaS); Knowledge as a Service (Kaas)	Software as a Service (SaaS)	Bus. Processes as a Service, BPM BPEL (BPaaS)	Web 2.0, Mash-ups, Composite Apps

Cloud Platform Tier

Content Mgt, Delivery and Web Servers	Semantics, Messaging, CEP/EDA Mediation, Integration (MWaaS)	SOA and Services Enablement (SOAaaS)	Platform as a Service (PaaS)	App Dev, QA/Test, Sandbox and Hosting (aaS)	App Hosting, Virtual Containers, App Servers

Cloud "OS" Tier

Resource Provisioning				Workflow
				Bus. Rules
Load Balancing	Capacity Mgt	Billing, Accounting, Chargeback	Resource Mgt	Onboarding and Offboarding Mgt.

Cloud Virtualization Tier

Storage	Computing
Network	Security

Exhibit 6.17   Cloud Enablement Model with Representative Technologies

resources that would be cloud-enabled, provided and consumed via a Cloud Ecosystem Model.

As illustrated, each of the four Cloud Enablement tiers is populated with various representative categories of technology and capabilities that are either provided via cloud in that tier, or contribute to the cloud enablement of capabilities provided by or accessed from that particular tier. The illustrated population of the Cloud Enablement tiers with various technology capabilities is not exhaustive or necessarily complete. It is not meant to be. Instead, we are building a representative framework that can be used to map and relate cloud-enabled and cloud-enablement resources into the tiers, and into patterns based on use cases, to simplify the concepts around cloud modeling and architecture.

As we show, for example, the cloud virtualization tier includes four categories of technology that must be virtualized in order to establish a cloud computing foundation or infrastructure, on which we can build the higher level tiers of the cloud enablement tier. Naturally, there are more technical details that help realize the cloud virtualization tier.

This architectural model was developed by Patrick Stingley, of the Department of Interior, to map cloud computing concepts into an existing Federal Enterprise Architecture Framework (FEAF). As you can see, it very nicely aligns with the NIST three-tiered model of cloud computing, which is illustrated in Exhibit 6.4 earlier in this chapter. Recall that NIST identifies three tiers of cloud delivery: Infrastructure as a Service (IaaS), Platform as a Service (PaaS), and Software as a Service (SaaS). However, as presented in this chapter, a more detailed and comprehensive Cloud Computing Reference Model clearly was needed to elaborate on the full breadth of cloud.

Stingley's SRM model expands on the technology categories and capabilities necessary to truly inform the Cloud Technical Reference Model, based on the initial mapping and alignment to the Cloud Computing Reference Model we have developed in this chapter. As you apply the Cloud Computing Reference Model to your enterprise requirements, by mapping to the very important cloud reference submodel models—the Cloud Enablement Model, the Cloud Deployment Model, the Cloud Governance and Operations Model, and the Cloud Ecosystem Model—you can then decompose these needs into the technology model that you will eventually implement in your enterprise.

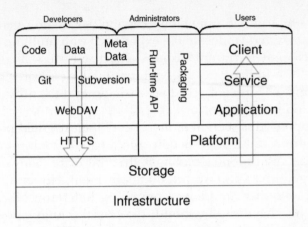

Exhibit 6.18   Cloud Computing Stack by Role

However, we urge you to first leverage the Cloud Computing Reference Model, before going to the fine-grained technical components listed in a lower level reference model. You must eventually get to this level of technical detail, to be sure, but only once you have performed a full cloud modeling and architecture exercise based on the Cloud Computing Reference Model.

For example, one such lower-level model is shown in Exhibit 6.18. This was an early model put forth at wiki.cloudcommunity.org, and serves to help illustrate this point.

As depicted, this cloud technical model relates to the cloud logical stack, with its six tiers identified, with three critical actors who interact with the cloud logical stack: developers, administrators, and cloud users. In addition, this exhibit denotes the additional technical standards used by cloud developers, as well as the technical interactions performed by cloud administrators. Again, once you have applied the Cloud Computing Reference Model to your enterprise, you can then go to the technical details to inform your choices derived through the application of the Cloud Computing Reference Model to your specific business and technology requirements.

In addition, this brings us back to the Cloud Ecosystem Model, where care must be taken to ensure all potential actors in the cloud ecosystem are engaged and able to interact according to the role or roles they play in enlivening the cloud industry. While this exhibit includes only developers, administrators and users, we have also illustrated how there are many types of cloud consumers available to interact with and consume cloud capabilities. As you mature your cloud strategy and gain valuable experience with multiple cloud deployments applied to your business objectives, you will continue to refine the Cloud Ecosystem Model that links cloud providers, consumers, and all forms of other actors in an end-to-end value chain of cloud computing.

Recapping, this section is *not* a developer-oriented part of this book. We only delve superficially into a Cloud Technology Reference Model discussion to highlight that there are many critical details that go into a successful cloud deployment. However, we firmly state that following the Cloud Computing Reference Model we develop in this chapter will establish the holistic cloud model and architecture foundation that will ensure successful cloud computing implementations aligned to key business and mission objectives. For the developers, application architects, and solution architecture community, there are other deeper technical resources at your disposal, aligned with our Cloud Computing Reference Model that will help you build operational cloud-enabled capabilities for your enterprises.

Parting Thoughts

In this chapter we explored cloud architectures, and learned how to create successful architectures for the cloud; we learned the basics of matching cloud capabilities to your business and technology requirements using a repeatable pattern-based framework. Finally, we developed the Cloud Computing Reference Model as the master framework to support the cloud modeling and architecture processes described in the Cloud Adoption Lifecycle Model.

In addition, we began to examine some interesting questions facing the industry as this transition progresses. In particular:

- How soon will Cloud Operating System and Cloud Platform tools replace the conventional application middleware typically required to host and operate an application?
- How soon will the Cloud OS Tier subsume the Cloud Virtualization Tier as well?
- Is it reasonable to envision that at some point for all application infrastructure and middleware needs, cloud OS tools and platforms will be the primary choice as opposed to buying

application servers, messaging middleware, runtime contain-ers, web servers, etc.?

These questions will be answered by the industry collectively—including all stakeholders—as this transition progresses.

Notes

1. A notable exception are the Software as a Service applications (Facebook, Salesforce, etc.) in which the standards discussions tend to be focused on in-ter-operability and data portability, and remain at this point generally early in development.
2. http://csrc.nist.gov/groups/SNS/cloud-computing/index.html.
3. www.cloudforum.org/
4. www.dmtf.org/newsroom/pr/view?
   item_key=aa9aec43563e9654b8d7eb4fe9c62bad25548aef.
5. Marks and Werrell, *Executive's Guide to Web Services*, John Wiley & Sons, 2002.
6. www.occi-wg.org/

7

Where to Begin with Cloud Computing

As with any emerging technology, organizations actively seek knowledge, insights, and best practices for how to begin their cloud computing initiatives. Organizations want to know how to prepare for their own cloud journey and how to avoid the risks and potholes associated with the early adopter stages of this emerging technology. This chapter offers insights and recommendations for the best path toward beginning your cloud computing journey. First, we must review the Cloud Adoption Lifecycle Model presented in Chapter 5. This is the first step to beginning with cloud.

Cloud Adoption Lifecycle

In order to know where and how to begin, you must first understand where you are in the generalized Cloud Adoption Lifecycle. Locating yourself in this lifecycle will point to your first steps in beginning the cloud transformation. In Exhibit 7.1, the Cloud Adoption Lifecycle Model is illustrated.

We believe you will be able to expand your cloud capabilities more quickly by following this adoption model, and by leveraging the recommendations that accompany each of these stages.

The idealized Cloud Adoption Computing Lifecycle follows nine core stages of cloud adoption:

1. **Cloud Proof of Concept/Pilot Project Stage.** The goal of this stage is knowledge and early learning about cloud technologies.

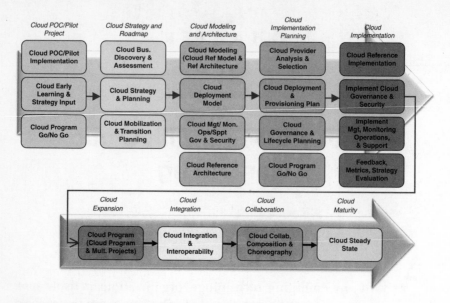

Exhibit 7.1   Cloud Adoption Lifecycle Model

This stage closes knowledge gaps, helps you understand what you do and do not know about cloud, and prepares your enterprise for a more formalized planning and implementation process going forward.

We strongly suggest that you begin your cloud initiative with one or more proof of concepts (POCs). These POCs or pilots should explore a range of business scenarios you are interested in (e.g., conduct a private cloud POC, followed by a public cloud POC, or vice versa). Either way, the intent of this stage is to learn, grow technical expertise, and develop an understanding of cloud sufficient to develop a robust cloud strategy.

2. **Cloud Strategy and Roadmap Adoption Lifecycle Stage.** The goal of this stage is to incorporate the lessons learned from your POC and pilots into a formal cloud strategy development process. The cloud strategy and roadmap stage establishes a formalized and actionable cloud strategy that will be executed to achieve stated business objectives.

It is essential to formalize your cloud strategy and roadmap through a strategy development effort that documents business drivers, imperatives, and goals, and develops a cloud strategy that will meet those stated business objectives. We urge formalization of your cloud strategy regardless of how long it takes—you may need a month, or three months. Take the time to formally plan and document a cloud strategy that is actionable, executable, and operationalized with dates, objectives, and metrics.

3. **Cloud Modeling and Architecture Adoption Lifecycle Stage.** The goal of this stage is to perform the necessary cloud modeling and architecture steps in order to execute the cloud strategy. This adoption lifecycle stage leverages the Cloud Computing Reference Model and the supporting modeling and architecture framework in order to develop a strategically aligned cloud reference model, reference architecture, and cloud implementation that will support and enable the defined cloud strategy.

   The Cloud Computing Reference Model (CC-RM) framework is one method you might consider to facilitate a cloud modeling and architecture effort. You should develop a Cloud Computing Reference Model, and from that you should develop a cloud reference architecture. These artifacts should be based on the goals and objectives of your cloud strategy.

4. **Cloud Implementation Planning Stage.** The goal of this stage is to prepare for your cloud implementation. The cloud implementation planning stage focuses on the selection of appropriate cloud technologies, cloud service providers, and cloud solutions to support your chosen cloud strategy. In addition, deployment models, and the necessary governance, operations and support, management and monitoring, and security challenges are addressed in this stage as well.

   It is critical to develop a cloud implementation plan that supports your formalized cloud strategy. The cloud implementation plan should include evaluation and selection of appropriate cloud technologies, cloud service providers, a cloud deployment and provisioning plan, and a cloud governance plan that supports the complete cloud lifecycle, including onboarding your data or applications onto a private cloud or public cloud. Monitoring, management, security and privacy, and operations and support requirements are also addressed in this stage.

5. **Cloud Implementation Stage.** This stage of the Cloud Adoption Lifecycle focuses on the completion of your cloud reference implementation, the cumulative realization of the previous stages.

   Following the idealized steps in this stage will accelerate your time to implementation, and mitigate the potential risks associated with cloud computing.

6. **Cloud Expansion Stage.** This stage of cloud adoption is where an enterprise builds on its successful cloud reference implementation to expand its cloud capabilities. Cloud expansion can involve progressing from private clouds to hybrid clouds, expanding private clouds via addition of new cloud patterns, or adding new cloud enablement capabilities onto existing cloud enablement patterns. This is a logical phase of cloud maturation and growth within the enterprise.

   By the time you are expanding your cloud implementations to add more capabilities, or moving more data or applications to the cloud, you will be well positioned to gain advantage from cloud.

7. **Cloud Integration and Interoperability Stage.** This stage anticipates the need to integrate cloud capabilities and deployment approaches, as well as the need to ensure cloud interoperability as cloud computing matures.

   While you may not be at this stage any time soon, you should plan in advance for the cloud interoperability and integration challenges you will face. As with all emerging technologies, the lack of industry standards will inhibit the industry adoption of cloud for many enterprises. Furthermore, there is already great concern with proprietary cloud lock-in based on the lack of industry standards for the various cloud application programmer interfaces (APIs), interoperability, and integration requirements. Many will avoid a technology if interoperability and integration standards are not well defined by industry standards bodies. So, reiterating, while you may not reach the cloud integration and interoperability stage soon, you should plan for it in your cloud strategy, cloud modeling and architecture, and cloud implementation stages.

8. **Cloud Collaboration Stage.** This stage of cloud adoption focuses on the emergent requirements of cross-cloud collaboration, the composition of applications across clouds, and

the orchestration of distributed process across cloud deployments.

This later stage of cloud will be important if your business requirements demand it. If you feel you have business requirements for this, plan for it in your cloud strategy. Otherwise, as an emerging cloud capability, you can wait until the industry moves in this direction.

9. **Cloud Steady State.** This is an idealized stage when cloud has matured and the next technology wave is underway.

At this point, you have deployed cloud within your enterprise, across all deployment variations—public, private, and hybrid—and like the industry, have moved onto the next technology trend. There are, of course, continuous improvement and ongoing optimization opportunities to tune your cloud strategies, refine your cloud operations models, and more. By and large, though, the cloud conversation will no longer be the water cooler discussion, and the dialog will focus on the next big thing.

The Cloud Adoption Lifecycle Model offers a baseline from which you can determine your entry point into cloud computing.

Where to Begin with Cloud: Using the Cloud Adoption Lifecycle

In order to make use of the Cloud Adoption Lifecycle, we suggest the following approach as detailed in the steps below. These are suggestions based on the Cloud Computing Adoption Lifecycle Model, which is of course based on real-world cloud adoption patterns from the industry.

- Review the Cloud Adoption Lifecycle to familiarize yourself with the stages, activities within each stage, and outputs of each stage.
- Determine which Cloud Adoption Lifecycle stage best fits where your organization currently is in relationship to cloud.
- If you have not started with cloud, you should begin at the first cloud adoption stage, or the cloud POC/pilot stage.
- Based on the stage your organization is in, determine if you have skipped over earlier stages recommended by the Cloud Adoption Lifecycle.

- Determine if and how best to close potential Cloud Adoption Lifecycle gaps. For example, if you have started developing a formal cloud strategy, but have not completed a POC or a cloud pilot, you may consider conducting one or more POCs to help validate and inform your cloud strategy.

While these recommended lifecycle steps are "generic" in nature, we will offer more specific cloud adoption strategies below based on deployment models, business use cases, and other relevant factors that can facilitate your organization's successful adoption of cloud computing.

Where to Begin with Cloud: Deployment Model Scenarios

In the early days of service-oriented architecture (SOA), there was great debate in the industry about where to begin with SOA and web services—internally within the four walls of your enterprise, or externally, with customer- and partner-facing web services. Central to the debate were the challenges around web services security. Cloud has surfaced the very same challenges, especially in the data security and privacy arena. Many of the cloud security challenges are those that have been by and large addressed through SOA and web services security standards and solutions, fundamentally because cloud is so heavily dependent on SOA and web services as the means of exposing prepackaged cloud-enabled resources and capabilities via interfaces that can be discovered, bound to, and leveraged via a service level agreement (SLA).

The question of where to begin with cloud revolves around the same internal versus external debate we had with SOA. In cloud vernacular, this relates to the various Cloud Deployment Models available—internal private clouds, external public clouds, and lastly, hybrid clouds that blend private and public cloud capabilities.

Public cloud deployments, in which an organization migrates an application, its data, or a business process onto a third-party cloud service provider's platform via the Internet, are excellent ways to begin exploring cloud computing in a cost-effective and agile rapid-time-to-market fashion. Leveraging various cloud offerings from Amazon, Google, Salesforce, and others is an excellent way to explore what cloud can offer to your enterprise.

Private cloud deployment scenarios, in which an organization implements cloud technologies on its internal network, or its Intranet, behind its security firewalls, enable the organization to explore cloud capabilities internally without the risk exposure of moving its data or applications outside of its own internal and corporate security controls.

Hybrid clouds leverage aspects of both public and private clouds to address a broader set of operational use cases and business scenarios. For example, an organization may use private cloud capabilities to federate two data centers and optimize utilization and availability of computer, storage, and network resources, and may also in parallel leverage public cloud capabilities from Amazon to offer a new application or service accessible via Amazon's e-commerce storefronts. This hybrid cloud mixes multiple cloud patterns to satisfy this requirement example.

There are a variety of advantages for starting with each of the three: public clouds, private clouds, and hybrid clouds.

Reasons for Starting with a Public Cloud

The following is a list of reasons an organization would choose to begin its cloud computing initiative with a public cloud service.

- **Low Cost.** Public clouds offer a very low cost of entry into cloud computing, which supports a POC or pilot project with limited research and development (R&D) funding.
- **Cloud Solution Variety.** There is a wide variety of cloud-enabled resources to assemble into complete cloud solutions, from virtualization and cloud operating system (OS) or platform technologies, to Platforms as a Service (PaaS) and Software as a Service (SaaS) offerings.
- **Low Risk.** An organization can quickly experiment with cloud computing solutions with minimal risk exposure.
- **Pay for What You Need/Use.** Public clouds are based on a completely variable, utility cost model, whereby once the initial project has completed, or if you no longer need the cloud services, you can stop paying the fees.
- **Rapid Accumulation of Knowledge, Skills, and Experience.** Public clouds offer a way to quickly gain experience, knowledge, and skills on the emerging technology trend of cloud

computing. Leveraging public clouds enables your organization to tap into the knowledge and experience of your third-party cloud service provider. This is a tremendous competitive advantage for any organization seeking first-mover advantage for its cloud computing strategy.

This list is not exhaustive, but it points to many reasons why you should give serious consideration to public clouds in the early learning, POC/pilot state of the Cloud Adoption Lifecycle model.

Reasons for Starting with a Private Cloud

The following is a list of reasons an organization would choose to begin its cloud computing initiative with a private Cloud Deployment Model:

- **Security and Privacy.** Mitigates privacy and security concerns by maintaining data behind your own firewalls.
- **Strategic Opacity.** Maintains strategic opacity, so your competitors cannot ascertain your intentions.
- **Focus on Internal Optimization First.** Internally optimize internal utilization of infrastructure assets.
- **Become an Internal Cloud Service Provider.** Beginning your cloud strategy with a private cloud focus will accelerate your ability to become an internal cloud service provider to the enterprise. This is a key benefit of beginning your cloud initiative internally with a private Cloud Deployment Model.

As with public clouds and hybrid clouds, there are solid reasons why an enterprise would begin its cloud initiative within its four walls and behind its security firewalls. While all of these reasons are valid, as are the reasons for starting with a public cloud, the specific decision will rest with the particular needs of a given organization.

Reasons for Starting with a Hybrid Cloud

The following is a list of reasons an organization would choose to begin its cloud computing initiative with a hybrid Cloud Deployment Model.

- **Begin with the End Game.** A hybrid cloud deployment as your cloud start point supports the ultimate end-state of cloud computing. Most industry analysts feel that in a short time, there will be only hybrid clouds, and the separation into public and private clouds is an artificial distinction given the infancy of the cloud industry.

- **Cloud Solution Range.** Hybrid clouds offer a great magnitude of solution variations that address business models and solutions that we can barely imagine now. Why not begin with hybrid clouds early to better understand what the true potential of cloud is in the bigger picture? There is no reason why you should constrain your learning process out of the gate. Hybrid clouds offer that to you.

- **Explore Cloud-Based Business Models.** Hybrid clouds allow you to explore and create new business models that exploit the combination of private and public cloud use cases. In this manner, you can actually explore business model innovation through new channels to market, and new distribution models of internal processes across your extended value chain. Hybrid clouds offer this unique experience to your organization.

- **Extra-Enterprise Thinking.** Hybrid clouds encourage extra-enterprise thinking with respect to business processes, cloud solutions, and capabilities. If you begin your cloud initiative with an extended enterprise frame of reference, you will be in a better position to innovate your business model, operations model, and business processes by leveraging cloud solutions.

- **End-State Knowledge Acceleration.** Beginning with hybrid clouds allows your organization to practice the cloud end state sooner by learning, gaining expertise, and accelerating the knowledge accumulation your team will benefit from in the short and long term. The more you understand about how cloud will evolve and the sooner you develop that understanding, the sooner you can exploit first mover advantage.

The respective reasons for beginning your cloud initiative with private, public, or hybrid Cloud Deployment Models will vary by industry and business need. Every organization must justify its decision based on tolerance for risk, stance toward emerging technology adoption, and other factors.

In addition, every pro for one particular cloud deployment decision is a con for a different cloud deployment scenario. As with anything, you must objectively balance risk, time to market, and value to your enterprise as you make these decisions. Regardless, you must begin your cloud early learning process as soon as possible, regardless of which deployment model you ultimately settle on.

Cloud Business Adoption Patterns

Another thought process for considering how to begin with cloud computing is based on the business requirement you are addressing. Depending on the requirements, you may vary your cloud adoption sequencing, or vary the durations of the various planning and implementation tasks.

We characterize cloud business adoption scenarios into four broad approaches:

1. **Agile Cloud Adoption Pattern.** Ideal for both simple public clouds and simple private clouds.
2. **Accelerated Cloud Adoption Pattern.** Suited for moderate complexity clouds, both public and private, in which time to market and cost outweigh risks.
3. **Nominal Cloud Adoption Pattern.** Appropriate for moderate to complex cloud deployments, including hybrid clouds, moderate to complex public clouds, and moderate to complex private clouds.
4. **Conservative Cloud Adoption Pattern.** Targeted for complex private, complex public, and moderate to complex hybrid clouds, where significant risk is introduced either through the cloud-enablement technologies, the chosen deployment model, or the targeted business use case for cloud enablement.

The approaches and rationale for each of these business adoption patterns will vary, but the key decision criterion is the type of business requirement you are applying cloud technologies to. Some business requirements will allow your organization to take an agile, iterative approach toward solving that requirement, while others are higher-risk and will necessitate a more conservative or measured pattern of cloud adoption.

Agile Cloud Adoption Pattern

The agile cloud adoption scenario is based on leveraging quick cloud sprints that accomplish the fundamental requirements of the Cloud Adoption Lifecycle Model, but in a rapid, iterative fashion using 30-day (or whatever time boxes make sense) increments. The agile cloud adoption pattern will quickly initiate POC and pilot projects, then perform the business discovery and assessment tasks, rapidly devise a formal cloud strategy, and as soon as possible move into the cloud implementation process in parallel with the formalized planning process. Each of the activities represented in the Cloud Computing Adoption Lifecycle will be performed in individual cloud sprints, in parallel or sequentially, or they will collectively be structured as a single cloud sprint with aggressive time boxes around each of the collective adoption stages.

From a cloud business adoption perspective, the following business "patterns" or demographics are expected to leverage some form of Agile Cloud adoption:

- Start-up company:
  - Needs rapid access to core IT infrastructure capabilities
  - Will deploy in rapid iterative sprint-like projects
  - Will aggressively adopt public cloud capabilities
- Innovation project within mature enterprise:
  - Needs access to cloud-enabled capabilities quickly and cost effectively
  - Time to market and competitive dynamics force rapid, sprint-like planning and implementations
  - Will aggressively adopt public and hybrid cloud deployments that meet business needs
  - Will leverage the agile approach to cloud to compress time to market
- Skunk works project:
  - Requires access to necessary cloud-enabled capabilities in support of a research and development project
  - Low-profile nature of the skunk works means accessing capabilities outside of the enterprise IT infrastructure to maintain secrecy of the project
  - Agile cloud adoption pattern will emphasize low cost and rapid time to market benefits of cloud

◆ Obtaining cloud resources external to the enterprise will support both the cost and secrecy demands of a skunk works project

Accelerated Cloud Adoption Scenario

An accelerated cloud adoption approach is ideal for certain business requirements or use cases, where speed is essential, yet certain cloud planning and adoptions steps must be performed in some detail. The accelerated cloud adoption pattern emphasizes speed for some aspects of the Cloud Adoption Lifecycle, while practicing a more cautious and pragmatic approach for other aspects of the Cloud Adoption Lifecycle.

For example, an accelerated cloud adoption pattern might leverage an agile approach by sprinting through a POC and sprinting through a cloud business discovery assessment, then performing a more thorough cloud strategy effort to formally document the cloud strategy, roadmap, business model, funding needs, and return on investment (ROI). There are multiple variations of an accelerated pattern where cloud sprints are blended with more traditional adoption approaches for emerging technologies. Appropriate projects for the accelerated cloud adoption pattern include moderately complex private clouds, moderately complex hybrid clouds, and public clouds leveraging many cloud capabilities from one provider or one or more cloud capabilities from multiple providers.

The following business use cases are good candidates for an accelerated cloud adoption pattern:

- Skunk works project (discussed in the previous subsection)
- R&D Project:
  - ◆ Accelerated cloud adoption pattern for speed
  - ◆ Depending on the R&D focus, may take on more risk through an accelerated cloud approach, while mitigating risk in some aspects of adoption
- New business application with uncertain demand and scaling requirements:
  - ◆ Must achieve rapid time-to-market
  - ◆ Exploring infrastructure virtualization and rudimentary private cloud approaches to address this need
  - ◆ Must blend rapid learning and experimentation with speed of application development, hosted platform as a service,

and utility model for scaling infrastructure requirements as the application demand increases

- Need a business capability quickly and cheaply delivered via SaaS:
  - Speed to market to address a business capability or application need
  - Offers easy-to-access cloud capabilities with little to no risk
  - With proper documentation of business requirements and analysis of cloud solution provider offerings, can blend risk management, requirements alignment, and time to market with an accelerated cloud adoption pattern
- Developing a new business application via a PaaS model:
  - Speed to market is a major concern
  - Rapid application development and deployment is essential
  - Cost is a major factor for this need
  - Will be conservative in documenting requirements and selecting PaaS alternatives, but will leverage agile development concepts to build the application on the PaaS

Nominal Adoption Scenario

A nominal cloud adoption approach is a more conservative cloud adoption pattern that is ideal for business requirements where speed is essential, yet certain cloud planning and adoptions steps must be performed in some detail. The nominal cloud adoption pattern emphasizes a more cautious and pragmatic approach for the Cloud Adoption Lifecycle. A nominal approach can blend parallel execution of portions of the Cloud Adoption Lifecycle with sequential development of your cloud strategy, implementation planning, and the implementation. The nominal approach to cloud will be focused on a crisp but conservative execution of the Cloud Adoption Lifecycle. Emphasis for the nominal cloud adoption pattern is risk mitigation but it also emphasizes time criticality and time-to-market, but only insofar as corporate risk can be managed.

For example, a nominal cloud adoption pattern might focus on a rapid, serial execution of the Cloud Adoption Lifecycle stages, while emphasizing risk mitigation throughout. Thus, risk factors always outweigh speed and time to market in the nominal approach, as opposed to the agile and accelerated cloud adoption patterns, where speed, agility, and time-to-market always trump security and privacy concerns. There are multiple scenarios where a nominal cloud adoption pattern makes perfect sense, such as complex private clouds, complex public clouds that involve multiple cloud enablement patterns from one or more cloud service providers. A few of these are explored below:

- New business unit of established enterprise:
  - Concern for risk outweighs all other factors
  - Need to maintain corporate intellectual property protection and strategic opacity
  - Will apply cloud as it makes sense to realize the business objectives, but will not be on the bleeding edge
  - Nominal approach to cloud adoption mitigates risk within a well-defined framework for cloud planning and execution
- R&D project:
  - May take on a nominal cloud adoption profile depending on the overall risk of the R&D effort
  - If the R&D focus is an emergent technology, perhaps more risky than cloud, a nominal cloud adoption profile may be appropriate, where cloud is leveraged in a more conservative and pragmatic approach, while supporting the needs of a R&D effort
- Lab consolidation:
  - Due to impact on operational development and testing facilities, may opt for a nominal cloud approach due to risk
  - Since cloud affects multiple sites or locations, will not be able to leverage an agile or accelerated cloud adoption profile; nominal is fast enough while ensuring risks are mitigated
- Data center consolidation:
  - Due to potential impact on operational systems and customer-facing or revenue systems, may opt for a nominal cloud approach due to risks of customer impact
  - Focus on internal optimization demands careful planning, while consolidation activity merits an aggressive approach to realize the benefits of consolidation
  - Emphasis will be on preventing customer and operational outages or disruptions, thus the nominal cloud adoption approach is appropriate

- Moderately complex hybrid cloud:
  - ◆ May involve new applications or business capabilities developed on a PaaS or obtained via SaaS from a third-party cloud provider
  - ◆ Complexity of the business use case demands caution and risk mitigation, despite the cutting edge aspects of a hybrid cloud approach

Conservative Adoption Scenario

For certain requirements, a more cautious approach might be considered for cloud adoption. This approach is what we label the conservative cloud adoption pattern. The conservative cloud adoption pattern applies to cloud opportunities where the risk is high, and risk trumps all the benefits of time-to-market, cost variabilization, and related benefits of public cloud scenarios. Initiatives that merit a more conservative cloud adoption approach might include major data center transformations, large private cloud implementations, or transitioning your internal central information technology (IT) organization into a cloud service provider for the enterprise.

As such, the conservative cloud adoption pattern emphasizes a steady, serial, and risk-averse approach to the Cloud Adoption Lifecycle. The following scenarios may merit the conservative cloud adoption pattern:

- Datacenter transformation/green datacenter project
- Enterprise-wide testing and quality assurance (QA) environment
- Storage consolidation and cost reduction
- Enterprise data center migration to private cloud
- Complex hybrid cloud that blends data center federation with PaaS/SaaS capabilities in a public cloud

Where to Begin with Cloud: Consumers and Internal Cloud Providers

Finally, the question of "where to begin with cloud" must be based on being an end-consumer of cloud capabilities as well as being a provider of cloud capabilities. We will focus on two scenarios most common today in the early adoption of cloud: cloud consumers, and the transition of an internal central IT organization into a cloud service provider.

Cloud Consumers: How to Begin?

From a cloud consumer perspective, your entry point into cloud should still follow the Cloud Adoption Lifecycle Model. In addition, however, you can accelerate your cloud initiative by mapping your requirements into the Cloud Computing Reference Model (CC-RM), using the Cloud Enablement Model.

Your cloud adoption pattern as a cloud consumer will map into the layers of the cloud enablement model as defined in the CC-RM.

As shown in Exhibit 7.2, your entry into the cloud paradigm will be primarily driven by the cloud capabilities you need to access or deploy to meet targeted business, economic, and technology drivers. Those business, technology, and economic driver inputs will in many respects dictate the cloud enablement requirements of your organization.

As a cloud consumer, you must first understand what your requirements are, as defined by an appropriate cloud use case, vignette, or cloud scenario. From this, you should understand what

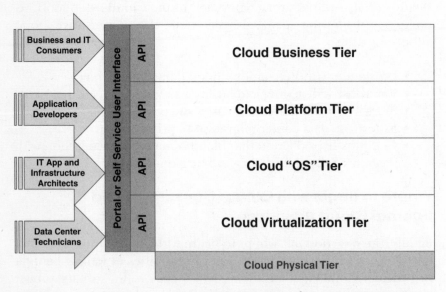

Exhibit 7.2   Consumers of Cloud Capabilities by Enablement Tier

your cloud enablement requirements are, and the deployment models that support your requirements.

The approach we advocate is as follows:

- Perform a Cloud Adoption Lifecycle assessment to determine where your organization is with cloud.
- Based on your position in the Cloud Adoption Lifecycle, determine the relative complexity of your cloud requirements.
- Based on your cloud adoption pattern complexity, determine how you will apply the steps of the Cloud Adoption Lifecycle to your requirements (e.g., agile, accelerated, nominal, or conservative).
- Conduct POC/pilots as needed.
- Develop a formal cloud strategy for your business requirements.
- Develop a Cloud Reference Model and reference architecture; begin cloud implementation planning, including selection of vendors, technologies, and cloud service providers that meet your requirements.
- Begin cloud mobilization steps, including education and awareness, evaluation of alternatives, funding requirements analysis, and transition to cloud implementation.
- Begin your cloud implementation, depending on the deployment model you have selected that satisfied the Cloud Enablement Model requirements.
- Learn, iterate, and expand as needed.

This approach is a simplistic summarization of the steps required to plan and successfully implement cloud as a cloud consumer. The detailed steps are included in the Cloud Adoption Lifecycle and in the Cloud Reference Model that is detailed in Chapter 6, Cloud Architecture, Modeling, and Design. Refer to that chapter for the details of those cloud-planning tools.

Cloud Adoption Use Case Development

In order to facilitate your adoption of cloud computing, we have developed the following framework to accelerate the development of cloud use cases that document your requirements in support of a formal cloud strategy and implementation process. These seven steps build on and map into the cloud planning models we develop in this book.

1. **Develop cloud scenarios, vignettes, or user stories**. Develop the cloud scenarios, vignettes, and user stories supported by the specific business use cases that help flesh out the cloud scenario you envision.
   - *Develop the business "concept of operations,"* or the detailed business operational threads that represent the range of business requirements to be accommodated by the particular cloud scenario.
   - *Develop cloud business scenarios*, which represent how the consumers of the cloud capabilities will operate, as well as the IT operations scenarios, or how the IT organization will support or enable the business to leverage cloud.
2. **Identify the cloud consumer(s) and potential cloud provider (s) of the cloud scenario**, regardless of whether the cloud is a private or a public cloud. Next, develop the cloud consumer/provider scenarios, which describe the end-to-end interaction model of cloud computing for your target business scenarios. This step helps explicitly develop a sense of the end-to-end cloud interactions and relationships that will ensure success with cloud computing.
3. **Develop the CC-RM cloud enablement model** as it supports the requirements of our cloud computing business scenarios (see Chapter 6 for the details).
4. **Define the CC-RM cloud deployment model** (see Chapter 6 for the details).
5. **Define the CC-RM cloud governance and operations model** (see Chapter 6 for the details).
6. **Develop the CC-RM cloud ecosystem model** (see Chapter 6 for the details).
7. **Complete the detailed cloud use case** that includes all the functional and nonfunctional requirements of cloud, as well as the detailed analysis based on the CC-RM.

Upon completion of the documented cloud use cases, you can use these to plan your cloud POCs and pilot projects. In addition, they are a core requirement to develop a formal cloud strategy and roadmap for your enterprise.

Develop as many cloud use cases as you need to document the complete range of cloud enablement patterns and deployment scenarios that you anticipate including in your cloud strategy and roadmap. Below, we provide some sample cloud scenarios that apply aspects of the cloud use case format we developed above. Of course, for your operational planning and formal strategy development needs, you must develop the details of these cloud use cases to support your needs.

Cloud Patterns Mapped to Common Cloud Use Cases

In the paragraphs below, we explore some common cloud use cases where different Cloud patterns can be used to support specific business and operational scenarios. In these use cases, we will explore them in the context of the CC-RM described in detail in Chapter 6, Cloud Architecture, Modeling, and Design.

We hope that this section will stoke the imagination of our readers to explore and push the envelope of cloud into all of its potential, again, by leveraging the Cloud Reference Model to ensure you have examined all the potential pros and cons of the complete range of cloud use cases and scenarios you may explore.

We Need a Hosted CRM Capability to Support Our Expanded Sales and Marketing Efforts

Scenario Synopsis: An enterprise seeks a customer relationship management (CRM) application capability, and currently does not have a system installed. The organization is growing at a rapid pace, and needs a CRM solution to manage its customer and marketing requirements, as well as accelerate its growth with a more professional sales and marketing process and the necessary supporting tools. The firm is exploring hosted CRM solutions, and settles on Salesforce.com's hosted CRM. This use case is illustrated in Exhibit 7.3.

Cloud Consumer: Sales management, sales IT support, sales reps

Cloud Provider: Hosted CRM providers via the cloud business tier

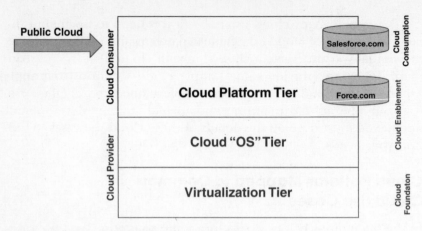

Exhibit 7.3 Hosted CRM Cloud Use Case

Cloud Enablement Model Patterns: This use case leverages the cloud business tier, specifically by consuming Salesforce. com CRM from Salesforce. Salesforce-hosted CRM is built on the Force.com platform, also provided by Salesforce. While the use case primarily leverages the cloud business tier, via Software (SaaS), it also accesses the cloud platform tier indirectly by leveraging the capabilities of Force.com in the background.

Cloud Deployment Model Pattern: The CRM use case leverages a public Cloud Deployment Model, where Salesforce.com hosts the CRM solution in a multitenant environment, and the firm's customer data are maintained by Salesforce.com in its cloud.

Cloud Governance and Operations Model: This use case requires little internal governance and operations support, since the cloud pattern is a hosted CRM SaaS available as a public cloud via the cloud business tier. No additional cloud governance and operations requirements are necessary from the end-user enterprise.

Cloud Ecosystem Model: Requires a range of users of the Salesforce-hosted CRM application, from a sales administrator, an IT support technician, and the range of sales end-users, from sales management to individual sales representatives. No special requirements from the end-user organization are necessary to ensure the cloud ecosystem is in place.

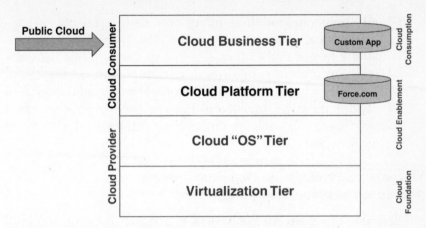

Exhibit 7.4   Platform as a Service Cloud Use Case

I Need a Hosted Application Platform to Build New Custom Business Application—PaaS

Scenario Synopsis: A small business enterprise is developing a new business application and prefers to build it on a hosted Platform as a Service to minimize investment in application infrastructure, as well as optimize time to market, while controlling fixed costs. This use case is illustrated in Exhibit 7.4.

Cloud Consumer: Application developers, IT management, IT administrators

Cloud Provider: Platform as a Service providers (e.g., Amazon, Google App Engine, Salesforce's Force.com platform, etc.)

Cloud Enablement Model: The firm will provide its new application via the cloud business tier, but this use case primarily involves access to the cloud platform tier to leverage a cloud-enabled application development platform for application development and application hosting of the finished application.

Cloud Deployment Model: Public cloud, hosted Platform as a Service.

Cloud Governance and Operations Model: Need application lifecycle governance and architecture oversight, but other cloud governance and operations requirements are provided by cloud service provider

Cloud Ecosystem Model: Requires application developers, application architects to be in the cloud ecosystem, as well as the target end-user customers of the application once it is completed, provisioned, and deployed via the cloud providers Platform as a Service. The Cloud Ecosystem Model must be broad enough to incorporate internal developers as well as customer end-users of the to-be application.

We are Having Problems Scaling a Custom-built Application for Global Use by the Business

Scenario Synopsis: An established enterprise has a mission-critical internal application that is experiencing degraded performance, and will not scale to meet the needs of a planned global expansion. This scenario is illustrated in Exhibit 7.5.

Cloud Consumer: Enterprise architects, application administrators, application business owners

Cloud Provider: Internal IT data center and operations team

Cloud Enablement Model: This use case leverages the cloud virtualization and cloud operating system tiers of the cloud enablement model.

Cloud Deployment Model: Private, internal cloud focused on hardware and application virtualization.

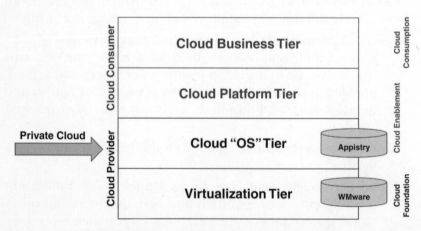

Exhibit 7.5   Application Scalability via Cloud Use Case

Cloud Governance and Operations Model: Emphasis on onboarding the existing application and data into the private cloud; potential application refactoring to provision it to the cloud; may require attention to the operations and support model based on the new cloud enablement patterns.

Cloud Ecosystem Model: Internal ecosystem consists of the same business end-users, business management users, and technical and help desk support personnel as before. No fundamental changes.

We Want Better Utilization of Datacenter Resources and Server Consolidation

Scenario Synopsis: An established Fortune 1000 firm seeks efficiencies and cost saving by optimizing its datacenter operations, achieving better utilization of hardware and personnel resources as well as cost reductions from a server consolidation initiative. This scenario is illustrated in Exhibit 7.6.

Cloud Consumer: Datacenter management, datacenter operators, and infrastructure engineers

Cloud Provider: Internal IT datacenter and operations team

Cloud Enablement Model: This use case leverages the cloud virtualization and cloud operating system tiers of the cloud enablement model.

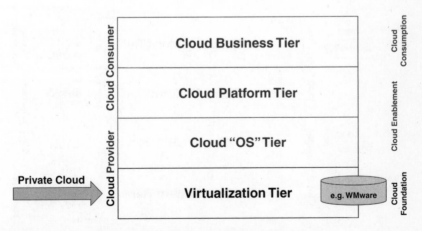

Exhibit 7.6   Datacenter Optimization Cloud Use Case

Cloud Deployment Model: Private, internal cloud focused on hardware virtualization and, potentially, followed by application virtualization.

Cloud Governance and Operations Model: Emphasis on simplifying and consolidating server and storage infrastructure through virtualization technologies. Governance and operations processes will be largely the same, with staff reductions based on a reduced number of servers and associated maintenance and support for them.

Cloud Ecosystem Model: Internal ecosystem consists of the same business end-users, business management users, and technical and help desk support personnel as before. No fundamental changes.

We Want a Distributed Data Model for a Real-time, Event-driven Architecture Business Model

Scenario Synopsis: An established Fortune 500 firm is focused on implementing a more real-time business model supported by event-driven architecture (EDA), and enabled by a robust data services layer supported by cloud enablement capabilities. This scenario is illustrated in Exhibit 7.7.

Cloud Consumer: Business leadership, business operations and management, IT management, business architects, and business analysts

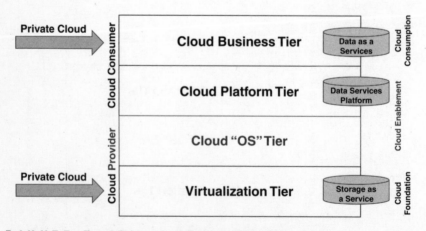

Exhibit 7.7   Event-Driven Architecture Cloud Use Case

Cloud Provider: Internal data architects, database architects, process analysts, business application owners, business architects

Cloud Enablement Model: This use case primarily leverages three cloud enablement model tiers: the cloud virtualization tier, the cloud platform tier, and the cloud business tier as shown in Exhibit 7.7.

Cloud Deployment Model: Private, internal cloud focused on storage virtualization, and data as a service, and data enablement middleware, and a data services layer enabled via SOA

Cloud Governance and Operations Model: Emphasis is on data governance, and application lifecycle management based on leveraging and deploying data services and a new data architecture in support of an EDA and associated business processes that leverage both of these. Operations model will demand data support as event-driven and data service–enabled business capabilities are rolled out and established in the operating model of the firm.

Cloud Ecosystem Model: Internal cloud ecosystem consists of business end-users, business management users, as well as business architects, business analysis, data architects, and business process analysis.

We are a New Internet Startup, and Need Basic IT Infrastructure to Operate Our New Business Model

Scenario Synopsis: This is a new startup, an Internet firm that needs basic IT infrastructure—storage, computing, and network—to get its new business model off the ground. The infrastructure must scale as the company gains traction with new customers. This scenario is illustrated in Exhibit 7.8.

Cloud Consumer: Business technical leadership and application developers

Cloud Provider: Any standard cloud service provider with robust computing, storage, network capabilities as a service.

Cloud Enablement Model: Primarily leverages the cloud virtualization tier of the cloud enablement model.

Cloud Deployment Model: Public Cloud Deployment Model.

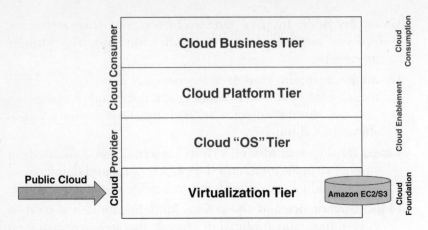

Exhibit 7.8   Cloud for a Start-Up Company Use Case

Cloud Governance and Operations Model: N/A, will establish its customer support processes and operations processes as adjuncts to what the cloud service provider offers.

Cloud Ecosystem Model: Will require a cloud ecosystem for internal personnel as well as customers of the new startup. Ecosystem must accommodate all processes involved in attracting customers to the startup as well as internal personnel who are accessing cloud resources from the provider.

We Need to Integrate Our Internal Private Cloud With amazon EC2

Scenario Synopsis: This is an established firm that has already deployed an internal private cloud, but also seeks to access business capabilities via Amazon web services as a public cloud. This is a hybrid cloud scenario, and is illustrated in Exhibit 7.9.

Cloud Consumer: Business leadership, IT leadership, IT architects and developers, data center operations personnel

Cloud Provider: Internal cloud provider for internal resources, and public cloud resources from Amazon

Cloud Enablement Model: This use case illustrated an internal cloud based on cloud virtualization and cloud operating system tier functionality, as well as external cloud resources that span all four cloud enablement tiers.

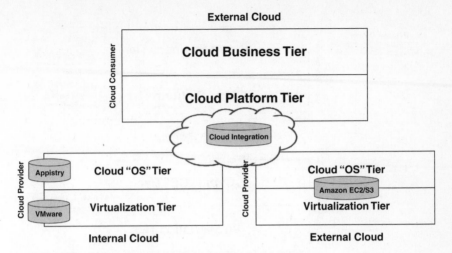

Exhibit 7.9   Cloud-Based Integration Use Case

Cloud Deployment Model: Hybrid; internal private and public provided by Amazon

Cloud Governance and Operations Model: Must clearly understand the end-to-end governance requirements of this hybrid cloud, which will require integrating internal cloud lifecycle governance processes with those of the external cloud service provider, Amazon in this case. The operations model must incorporate instrumentation and management processes and tools provided by Amazon into the operations and management processes and systems deployed internally. Significant effort is expected in the Cloud Governance and Operations Model.

Cloud Ecosystem Model: Will involve internal IT resources involved with datacenter operations, integration personnel, as well as processes that link external and internal customers into the cloud patterns that involve the cloud business tier and cloud platform tiers.

We Need a Private Data Cloud Supported by a Public Cloud "OS" and Infrastructure as a Service

Scenario Synopsis: This is an established firm that desires to leverage a data cloud pattern, as an internal private cloud, while pushing IT infrastructure and cloud OS capabilities

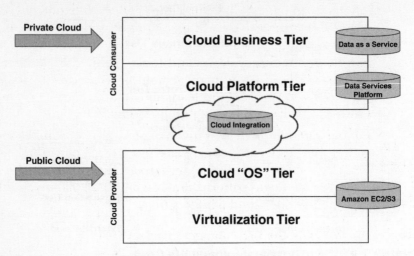

Exhibit 7.10 Hybrid Cloud Use Case

out to a public cloud deployment. This model keeps company data private, while leveraging economics of outsourced cloud-enabled infrastructure. This is a hybrid cloud scenario, and is illustrated in Exhibit 7.10.

Cloud Consumer: Business management and operations, customers, IT leadership, IT architects and developers, data center operations personnel

Cloud Provider: Internal cloud provider for the data cloud, with the public cloud resources provided by a third-party cloud provider (e.g., Amazon).

Cloud Enablement Model: This use case illustrates an internal private cloud based on the cloud platform tier and the cloud business tiers, which are key to establishing a data cloud pattern, while leveraging public cloud capabilities that concentrate on the cloud virtualization and cloud OS tiers.

Cloud Deployment Model: Hybrid; internal private data cloud, and public virtualization and cloud OS provided by Amazon.

Cloud Governance and Operations Model: Must clearly understand the end-to-end governance requirements of this hybrid cloud, which will require integrating internal cloud lifecycle governance processes with those of the external cloud service provider, Amazon in this case. In addition, the emphasis on an internal data cloud pattern integrated with public infrastructure cloud capabilities must be understood. The operations model must incorporate instrumentation and management processes and tools provided by Amazon into the operations and management processes and systems deployed internally. Significant effort is expected in the Cloud Governance and Operations Model.

Cloud Ecosystem Model: Will involve internal IT resources involved with datacenter operations, integration personnel, as well as processes that link external and internal customers into the cloud data patterns that are delivered via the cloud business tier and cloud platform tiers.

We Need to Integrate Our Two Primary Business Offices to Enable Sharing and Collaboration

Scenario Synopsis: This is an established small business on the Inc 500 list. While minimizing overhead and IT costs, it still must integrate two physical locations and remote employees, while creating collaboration and content sharing across the distributed organization. This firm has a headquarters in Massachusetts and another headquarters office in Virginia. This is an integrated public cloud scenario, and is illustrated in Exhibit 7.11.

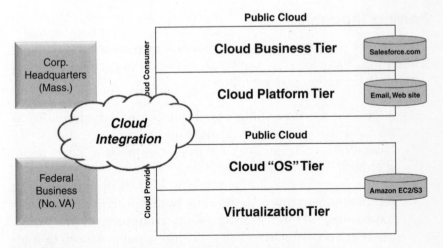

Exhibit 7.11   Enterprise Integration and Collaboration Cloud Use Case

Cloud Consumer: Business management, business professionals, and delivery personnel, as well as select customers who are allowed access to the content in a secure fashion

Cloud Provider: External public cloud resources provided by a third-party cloud provider (e.g., Amazon, Saleforce.com, Replicon, or web hosting)

Cloud Enablement Model: This use case illustrates an integrated public cloud that spans all four tiers of the cloud enablement model, although they are provided by multiple different cloud providers.

Cloud Deployment Model: Integrated public cloud

Cloud Governance and Operations Model: Must understand the governance requirements of cloud integration across multiple functional requirements of the business, as well as the support and management processes required to manage this integrated public cloud deployment.

Cloud Ecosystem Model: Will involve business leadership, management and staff consultants, as well as internal IT support and multiple cloud provider support teams, and the engagement with external customer who may be allowed access into the integrated public cloud for specific project requirements.

Parting Thoughts

This chapter presented some ideas on how to get started with cloud computing. Some ideas to ponder as you begin your cloud planning and implementation process follow:

- A process for describing cloud computing requirements as business use cases or scenarios is missing in the industry. We have offered a framework for this in hopes it will accelerate standardization of cloud use case development.
- Reiterating some earlier comments, we feel that the concept of *cloud patterns* offers great value to the process of planning, modeling and architecting cloud computing frameworks, whether your intent is a private cloud, a public cloud, or a hybrid cloud. Stay tuned for more developments from the industry in general and this author in particular.

- We firmly support the concept of exploring cloud with combinations of public and private cloud pilots or POCs. However, if you cannot afford both deployment scenarios, begin with a hybrid or public cloud to gain experience as soon as possible.
- Agile development concepts applied to cloud is an interesting approach, and the question is, how soon will this take hold? If cloud offers a ready-to-use platform or IT infrastructure (as a Service), shouldn't your organization leverage agile development of applications to capitalize on the fundamental agility imbued through cloud computing strategies?
- The variety of cloud use cases illustrated using the Cloud Computing Reference Model are examples of how to perform cloud modeling and architecture. Again, a cloud modeling and pattern framework is yet to be defined by the industry, but hopefully you can see the value of documenting your enterprise cloud requirements using the CC-RM to get started.

Of course, having taken all of this carefully into account, the most important step is in fact to simply set a course and get started. We are confident that when looking back on the decision from some point in the future, it will have been a step well worth taking.

All Things Data

Now it is time to take a few steps back and look at some of the developments that are not only enabling the practical adoption of cloud computing, but in turn will be themselves driven by that same adoption.

Much of the thinking about cloud revolves around operational models, reliability, security, the adoption of commodity infrastructure, or, some would argue, simply the location of the computing resources "out there in the cloud." In many ways, though, these may not even be the most crucial changes that cloud is bringing to conventional computing.

In fact, the changes underway in "all things data"—how data is organized and accessed, where it is located, even what sort of infrastructure on which it is stored—these are the changes that are, in the long run, perhaps the most crucial.

Surprising? Probably. Very likely? Absolutely.

These changes are being driven by the relentless drive for scale which is so emblematic of this age, and which impacts everything involved with data.

What does this drive for "big data" mean? How will it change how we store and consume data?

Over the next 5 to 10 to 15 years, some changes are more or less inevitable. In particular, we will see at least these three:

1. The decline and fall of the near-monopoly of the relational database—it will no longer dominate and simply be assumed; rather it will be relegated to relatively modest to mid-sized and legacy use cases.

2. The nature of archiving, disaster recovery, and geographic distribution will fundamentally change—archiving and disaster recovery will be accomplished by multiple, optionally live, geographically dispersed copies of the same data; this will be true for the most crucial, mission- critical, high-volume data.

3. Computing and storage infrastructures will merge—first for the highest volume applications, then eventually for most applications.

The reasons for these three developments are very fundamental, simply endemic to cloud computing.

To understand these changes more clearly and what they mean to the enterprise, let us dive a bit deeper. We will start by looking at the present state of affairs in the storage and management of data, with an initial focus on the enterprise.

The Status Quo

As we finish the first decade of the new millennium, the "best computing practice" for data has been fairly well established for perhaps 20 years—for most enterprises, most operational data is:

- Stored in a relational database
- Running on a cluster of large servers or mainframes
- Accessing data stored in a storage area network (SAN), network attached storage (NAS),[1] or a combination of both
- Archiving statically onto physical or off-line media (tapes, DVDs, etc.)

Enterprises that have implemented a data warehouse for studying long-term trends and generally analyzing operational data (without impacting operational systems) will store their operational data in the same manner, though in the last step they will also feed the operational data to the data warehouse.

Relational Database

In the early days of data storage (1960s and 1970s) most applications stored their data either in groups of files or in a simpler, non–relational database system. However, the need for consistency of data, transactional integrity (the ability to know that the data has been updated safely), manageability, and the flexibility to use the same data for many different purposes ("views") became fertile ground for adoption of relational database systems.

In turn, this enabled organizations to separate the development of applications from the design, acquisition, and maintenance of data of all kinds. While it is true that those lines are always slightly blurry—the needs of the application and reporting of data always interacts, and properly so, with the design and operation of data repositories—the general distinction has been quite healthy for most organizations.

An entire ecosystem of design, development, and operational tools has developed around the relational database sector, and are both sophisticated and well entrenched. Some would say that might be a kind way of saying slightly musty, stale, and "long in the tooth," but that is a discussion for a bit later.

Physical Storage Infrastructure

Up until the early 1980s most storage arrays, or "disk farms," were attached to servers and mainframes, and accessed directly by applications running on those same computers.

As a logical evolution in this situation, SANs emerged, in which the storage hardware (both the "controllers" and the disk drives themselves) were separated from the servers and mainframes, and then connected via dedicated, relatively high-performance network connections. This allowed multiple servers to access the same storage pools, which made it simpler to administer the storage, change out faulty server hardware, and so forth.

NAS devices provided similar benefits, but were generally targeted at lower-performance applications, since they generally ran on the lower-speed networks that were shared across datacenters, operated on entire files at one time, and generally made use of more-commodity-oriented hardware.

Computing and Storage Infrastructure Separate

With the advent of SANs that were capable of serving the largest, most powerful servers and mainframes along with NAS that could provide similar benefits for lower-performance applications (at a much lower cost), it became possible to separate physical infrastructure for computing from the physical infrastructure focused on storage. Similar to the separation of data from the software applications that operated on them, the separation of the physical infrastructure enabled a much cleaner operational focus on each area, and generally resulted in lower costs and greater flexibility.

Still, in the very act of gaining these benefits the built-in limitations of these approaches became apparent. As the last millennium drew to a close, there were many clear signs that new ideas were needed.

Cracks in the Monolith

For as long as there have been computers, there has been the universal, perpetual quest to do more—in this case to handle larger and larger stores of data—in terms of total amounts of data stored and in the amount of data that factored into given operations.

Over time various breaks from the typical model—a relational database, running on servers, storing data on a SAN or NAS—were developed to push beyond the boundaries of what was typically possible from the norm.

Each of these was, in a certain fashion, evidence that the typical model itself was in increasing need of fundamental improvement, of something—or several somethings—completely new.

Caching, In-Memory Databases

Since accessing data from memory is normally several orders of magnitude faster than accessing that same data off of disk, over time a range of products were developed that, in one fashion or another, converted as many data access operations from disk as possible into data access operations from memory.

Some of these were purely about speeding up individual operations, but even these had an incidental effect of increasing the overall capacity to process data. Depending on the application, moving key data to an in-memory database or a cache could also increase the total size of the database that could be reasonably maintained.

Data Warehousing

In the last 10 to 15 years a class of tools focused on analyzing large amounts of operational data has emerged, under the general banner of data warehousing (i.e., on-line analytical processing

[OLAP]). Along with these tools most organizations have developed an architectural style in which two separate types of data repositories are kept:

1. Current operational data stored in an relational database
2. A long-term "warehouse" of data, stored in a manner optimized for analytics (which may or may not be a relational database, or perhaps a particular store friendlier to analytics)

These have been generally positive developments, though these tools, while already useful, are in relatively early stages of their evolution.

Development Languages "Go Object"

Over the past 10 to 15 years most software development became "object-oriented," which is not conceptually very friendly with the ideas that underlie relational databases. Around 2000, many thought that databases that were natively able to store objects would replace relational databases—these at least had a sort of "conceptual resonance."

However, that did not happen for a number of reasons—instead, tools were developed that mapped the ideas of objects into the ideas from relational databases.[2] While those work fairly well for many applications, at the same time much simpler tools were developed that mapped those same objects into simple strings of text—which could then be passed along to a web site, stored in a file, and so forth.

In any case, this tension between the conceptual frameworks of the development languages and the conceptual frameworks of the databases can be thought of as an indication that a cleaner fit is possible.

Unstructured Data/Enterprise Search

Data stored in a relational database is generally "structured data," that is, it is organized in a particular form, with particular relationships that may be thought of between itself and other sets of structured data. However, as more and more of the economy has gone onto a digital footing, there has been an explosive growth of data that does not fit this model—data such as e-mails, notes, text documents, phone calls, images, web sites, video streams, and so forth—all of this may be incidentally available as a result of some business interaction. This data is generally large, voluminous, and rather messy (i.e., it is unstructured), and comprises the majority—more than 95%—of data stored, as well as the fastest-growing type of data.[3]

Searching through all of this data looking for certain patterns, perhaps particular occurrences—all references to a particular client, for example—has become increasingly useful. Perhaps spurred on by the capabilities of general web search, many enterprises have implemented, to one degree or another, enterprise search capabilities—that is, the ability to search these mountains of unstructured data.

Approaches to implementing this have generally resembled shrunken-down versions of web search—none of which can utilize relational database technology, as it is simply not suitable.

Content-Addressable Storage

For certain archival situations (such as storing compliance documents required for securities compliance regulations for a public company) the dynamic, structured nature of the mainstream case—relational database, on a server, storing data in a SAN or NAS—is not very suitable, since it is harder to ensure that data may not be altered, and much of the data is likely to be unstructured.

In those situations a specialized type of storage mechanism—a Content Addressable Store (CAS)—may be quite helpful. While good at what they do, these types of stores are not very good at much else. This is not to diminish their value—rather, it is an excellent illustration of just how the "store everything in a relational database" monolithic empire is, of necessity, breaking down.

Cloud Scale

There are many ways to think of scale, but as discussed in Chapter 1, The Sound of Inevitability, the cloud is taking scale to another dimension entirely. As the progeny of the Internet, cloud has, by definition, inherited many of its progenitor's characteristics—including the insatiable need to scale. Scale here, scale there, scale everywhere . . . scale, scale, scale . . . and then scale some more.

Increase in websites per year (in millions)

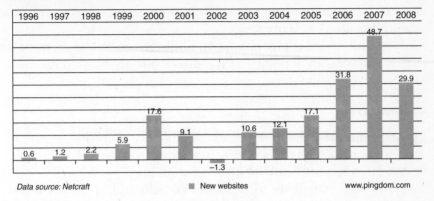

Data source: Netcraft ■ New websites www.pingdom.com

Exhibit 8.1 Increase in Web Sites per Year

Source: Pingdom.com

Lest this sounds implausible, here is a vignette to illustrate. First examine Exhibit 8.1 (from Pingdom[4]) showing the number of new web sites each year since 1996.

Erick Schonfeld of TechCrunch noted that this exhibit shows that the growth of web sites (since the beginning of the Internet) has been in two five-year cycles, roughly corresponding to the global economy.[5] This is a rough estimate, because the number of new web sites in 2009 had already exceeded the down year of 2008 *less than halfway through the year.*

In other words, despite the continuing economic travails, web site growth has already resumed, apparently without even going close to a decrease (as in 2002, after the bursting of the Internet Bubble).

So when Larry Page and Sergei Brin were conducting their research at Stanford in automatically indexing all the content of the web, there were about 4 million web sites. Halfway through 2009, just over ten years later, there were more than 216 million web sites . . . and the web sites themselves, as you well know, have generally each become much larger.

Even if the web sites had not grown in how much data each contained (and they most definitely have), this amount of growth is difficult to comprehend.

While thinking through the technology that led to the creation of Google, Page and Brin may not have been able to anticipate the growth rates that we have actually experienced, yet they at least understood that they needed to address the possibility of nearly incomprehensible levels of growth.

While all of these were crucial, in hindsight one more factor was clearly essential in forcing the need to think through some new ideas with regards to data.

Commodity

In particular, the general desire to use large numbers of commodity computers to support this new search infrastructure turned out to be crucial in forcing fundamental new thinking.

While that may seem to be rather paradoxical, in reality it was crucial. Embracing an infrastructure built out of cheap, failure-prone, relatively low-capability computers a priori precluded the use of conventional database and storage technologies. As a result, the architects never had the luxury of leaving the "scale problem" to the storage layer.

Database Will Always Be the Limitation

An early prospect for Appistry[6] (in the 2003 timeframe) initially became very excited about the prospects of using commodity infrastructure to reliably support their web-based commerce operations. Yet upon further investigation it became clear that their real problem was in their database. As is all-too-typical in enterprise applications (web-enabled or otherwise), this company had kept all the "problems of state" (i.e., the hard stuff) out of any portion of the application outside of the data tier.

This turns out to be very, very common. Most people familiar with building out applications to any sense of web scale will directly state that at some point, some place, somewhere, and somehow, the database *will* be the bottleneck—it is really only a matter of time.

The Core Issues

At the beginning of this chapter, we mentioned that the reasons that data storage would need to change fundamentally to cope with web scale were fundamental—and they are. While a detailed discussion of these issues is certainly outside the scope of this discussion, for many readers it may be helpful at least to understand why changes are necessary.

False Dependencies (Co-Dependencies Are Bad)

Imagine that we are looking at a database containing credit card transactions. While it is reasonable to see that multiple transactions from a single cardholder have some relationship to each other (e.g., they are subject to the same credit limit, and therefore have some level of interdependence), it should also be reasonably clear that transactions from two different people (for most cases) have no natural interdependence.

Unfortunately, by placing all of these transactions into the same relational database we have, in effect, created *false dependencies* between transactions that are not naturally interdependent. All of these false dependencies are essentially like the plaque that forms in coronary heart disease—they should not be there, they inhibit performance, and when pushed hard enough they will bring the whole show to a grinding halt.

Another example is a practice that was encouraged during much of the past 20+ years—the idea of putting small portions of an application (generally to do some basic calculations on data, or to ensure a consistent presentation) into the database itself. These bits of software—generally known as *stored procedures*—execute on the servers that are running the database systems themselves, and can heavily tax computers that are often already the most heavily utilized. Furthermore, since most relational databases run on a relatively small number of servers, these are generally the least efficient place to execute additional software.

There are many other forms of false dependencies, but in general most result from unnecessarily being placed into a common database.

Bandwidth

Bandwidth is a measure of how much data can be moved from one spot to another in a given amount of time. Whether one is examining data movement within a server (between processors and memory), between servers and storage within a datacenter, between datacenters, or between a datacenter and an end-user (mobile or fixed), the amount of bandwidth available for transferring data is very likely to be the most limited resource. In fact, Exhibit 8.2 shows the relative throughput of basic computing building blocks (in millions of bytes per second).[7]

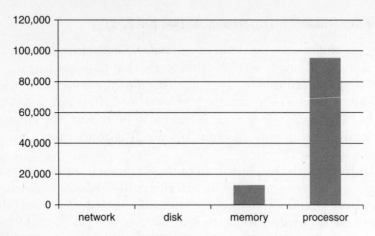

Exhibit 8.2   Relative Bandwidth of Basic Components

There is a very large increase in bandwidth capability at each step up in this exhibit—in fact, the relative speeds of a network and disk connection are so small they do not even show up on this chart. So even at a first-order look one can intuit that bandwidth limitations have everything to do with encouraging new data architectures.

Yet even though this is already a pervasive problem, technology trends for the foreseeable future suggest that it will become worse—far worse, and quickly. The reason for this is simple: Examine storage, processor, and network capacities and it is clear that storage and processor capacities are increasing far more rapidly than bandwidth capacities.[8]

In other words, not only is bandwidth a problem at every level of a computing architecture today, as each year goes by it will become far more of a limitation.

In any case, this problem is significant enough that in data-intense sectors (e.g., processing satellite imagery) it is commonplace to transport large datasets by sending physical commodity disk drives by overnight package delivery. Not surprisingly even leading public cloud providers accept data in the same manner—by the modern equivalent of pony express.

Consider another example. Recently there was an interesting set of tweets in which an engineer at Google, desiring to use the cloud in his own personal work (in this case high quality photography and videography, both generating relatively large volumes of data), initially tried backing up his data from home over the network to a cloud-based storage facility. After a few days of waiting for the first backup to complete he realized the impracticality of this approach, so then the engineer decided to create backups on commodity disk drives and take them with him to work each day. Being an engineer he had to calculate the "bandwidth" of carrying the data with him. It turned out that even including traffic and walking through parking lots, he was able to transport data in his car more than an order of magnitude faster than over a network connection!

Network Distance (Latency)

The network distance that data has to move, both in terms of physical distance covered and the number of network steps (known as *hops*) determines the responsiveness of a remote storage facility. This is also known as latency, and is another important constraint that will drive the evolution of cloud-friendly data stores.

Of the three central issues discussed here, this is perhaps the most directly driven by "the way things are." That is, the amount of time that it takes to transport a small amount of data (such as a response to a request for a single customer's basic information) over larger distances is mostly determined by the speed of light.

Across large geographic distances this reality is dealt with by creating local copies of data (where possible)—this is the service that content-delivery/distribution companies[9] provide; across smaller distances—such as within a datacenter or a server—local copies are provided by caching software.

Lessons Learned

While these realities have been a source of consternation to some (primarily those who prefer things to remain the same), for others these very same realities have been the fertile ground for significant progress.

Here are some of the lessons that have already been learned, and are evidenced in one form or another in many of the cloud-friendly storage technologies. In particular:

- **Maintain Independence.** As discussed previously, data often has a high degree of independence in a given problem. Unfortunately much of that independence is lost by choices that are made when storing and processing the data. One of the most crucial lessons learned to facilitate cloud-friendly scalability is to respect and maintain the inherent independence of data in any given problem. Highly effective, but it can be culturally challenging to learn.

- **Simpler Is Often Okay.** Many of the newer cloud-friendly storage technologies are actually simpler in the way they describe, store, and operate on data. Unlike the complexities of a full-featured relational database, some cloud-friendly offerings do no more than store an object and allow you to retrieve that same object; others provide more capability. While clearly less powerful, the reality is that these simpler systems are sufficient for many applications.

- **Relax (Transactional Rules** *Sometimes*). One of the tenets for many years of building applications that utilize traditional database systems is that all changes made to a closely related set of data must be made at the same time—that is, all or nothing. Upon further investigation we now understand that many applications are actually fine if sets of data are allowed to be slightly inconsistent, if only for a short time—the storage facility will eventually catch up and make everything consistent again. Allowing "eventual consistency" (where acceptable) can lead to significant scaling improvements.

- **Closer Is Better.** As discussed earlier, moving data is the scarcest resource in web-scale computing and storage. Consequently, where that data can be positioned closer to where it will be consumed (whether it is a particular server within a datacenter, or a customer in another datacenter, or across the Internet) then both performance and scalability improve.

- **Replication Wins.** In order to position data closer to where it's needed it is often necessary to create multiple copies of that data. While that is not suitable for every application in every situation, it is an important principle that is exploited early and often in cloud-friendly storage technologies.

- **One Size Does Not Fit All.** Unlike much of the past 20 years, in which it was nearly always presumed that all data of any significance would be first placed in a relational database, then operated on, it is now clear that different storage approaches are suitable for different situations. While a simple, highly replicated file system might be suitable supporting one class of applications, it is unlikely to work for another (which may retain the need for a traditional relational database), or yet another which would work best with a data store that is entirely in memory.

These lessons are being incorporated into a wide variety of new, often extraordinarily scalable cloud-friendly storage approaches. Let us now examine a few of these, along with some example use cases.

Solutions and Technologies: A Few Examples

This is by no means a comprehensive list of newer, cloud-friendly approaches to storing and processing data in a more scalable manner, but in these examples, we will illustrate some of the notable developments.

As noted earlier none of these will ever be as universal as the relational database in its heyday, yet each is better at what it does than a generalized relational database could ever possibly be.

Bucket and Big-Object Storage

At a very foundational level are scalable, self-organizing file systems. Unlike traditional file systems that are designed to organize files within a single server, these are designed to expand to thousands, tens and hundreds of thousands, perhaps even millions of servers; all of which may be breakable, modest-capability, commodity equipment.

This almost embarrassing simplicity is the source of much of their utility. While they do not do much more than store bucket- or file-sized sets of data,[10] look up and retrieve that data, and perhaps perform a few simple searches, what they do they do well, and do it at extraordinary volumes. Examples include the Google File System (GFS), the Hadoop File System (HDFS), S3, Appistry CloudIQ Storage,[11] and other specialized offerings.

Deconstructed Databases

One step up the food chain are databases that provide more services than the bucket/file stores, yet remain far simpler than a full-fledged relational database. These remain very simple to understand and use, and as with the previous case much of their scalability is a direct result of their simplicity. Examples include offerings such as SimpleDB (Amazon), CouchDB, BigTable/HDDB, and others.

Map-Reduce

Map-reduce refers to a group of programming techniques in which data is processed in sets.[12] Inspired by techniques developed in artificial intelligence research 30+ years ago, Google pioneered the adaptation of these techniques to web-scale sets of data. While these were initially applied to problems such as creating the indices that support Google's search functions, it soon became apparent that these techniques (and many others like them) have applicability across a much broader set of problems.

A very common use case would be the batch processing of sets of any type of transactions. For example, suppose that a credit card processor needs to process all of their customers' transactions each day. At the highest level this will involve receiving the day's transactions; separating those into groups (such as for each merchant); going through each merchant's transactions to look for fraud, assign a fee, and so forth; then delivering the results to each merchant.

This is a perfect problem to be done in the map-reduce style, with no database of any kind (relational or otherwise) involved whatsoever. In fact, it is such an excellent fit that a new credit card processor (Clearent[13]) was able to match the processing capabilities of a current mainframe/relational database combination with less than a dozen commodity computers. Tens of millions of dollars of capital versus $10,000, much cheaper operations, and the map-reduce implementation actually had a far better ability to scale to much higher volumes—all because this approach maintained the independence inherent in the data for that problem.

This is the type of technical advantage from which fundamental competitive advantages are built, from which a competitor gains the upper hand.

This same type of problem can be applied across any industry that has customer data that is processed in groups, such as weekly insurance transactions, stock settlement data for a brokerage, and so forth.

Hadoop and Its Ecosystem

Hadoop is an open source implementation of the map-reduce approach which is gaining some popularity. It has a number of components (many loosely modeled after Google's internal toolkits), some better than others. Due to its popularity, an ecosystem of tools, companies, and technical communities are forming that know what works well and what does not, and more importantly are providing more scalable solutions to particular portions (such as HDFS, the file system).

Enterprise Search

Lucene is a relatively modest open-source search engine which is also gaining a significant community—in this case for its flexibility, simplicity, and ability to customize. In addition, since it also maintains a hands-off approach to respecting the independence of data, it has the potential to scale significantly. As with Hadoop, a community of companies, people, and technology are forming around Lucene that provide various approaches to significant scaling.

Live Archive

Sometime in the past two years two thresholds were passed. First, storing data on commodity disk drives became cheaper than storing that same amount of data on enterprise-grade archival tapes. Then just a bit later it became cheaper to store the same amount of data on commodity drives than to burn a whole stack of blank DVDs.

Note that these comparisons do not include the robotic tape systems, servers, or any other such costs for either side: These simply look at the media costs, which are the dominant costs at volume.

Those costs are likely to continue to diverge for some time, with the cost advantage for storing data on a commodity disk drive increasing over time.

What this opens up are some very profound possibilities—where archiving data can be a byproduct of operating in geographically dispersed areas, where archival data is always live and available for analysis, and so forth.

These types of live archive facilities are just now beginning to appear, and tend to be done on a case-by-case basis. Still, they hold many interesting possibilities over the near to midterm.

A Look Below: Need for Combined Computation/ Storage

Most of these new approaches have primarily impacted either the storage mechanism, the processing software, or both. None of these approaches, however, change the most fundamental property of the physical infrastructure—namely that pools of computing power (servers) are separate from storage pools. This has generally been the case since the rise of specialized storage infrastructure in the 1990s, and in fact remains the case for a surprisingly large percentage of deployed clouds.

Recall that the scarcest resource today remains network bandwidth and that network distance (latency) significantly impacts performance. The question is: What can be done to fundamentally change this?

The answer is surprisingly simple, actually enabled by the commodity infrastructures of most clouds: Merge the compute and storage pools.

In other words, change the atomic building blocks out of which we construct most clouds—instead of compute-oriented servers for compute pools where the applications will run, and storage pools that are separated by some sort of network, simply place a small amount of processing power right next to a small amount of disk.

This new building block—one commodity processor, a modest amount of commodity storage, and a commodity network connection[14]—will become the basic building block for construction of the cloud infrastructure (for example, in mid 2010 that might be a 2.5 Ghz two core processor, one or two 2-terabyte drives, and a gigE network connection), as shown in Exhibit 8.3.

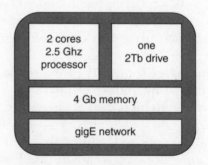

Exhibit 8.3   The New Basic Building Block

In this way data does not generally have to be moved for work to be done; rather, the work to be done is moved to the data. That is a much simpler and quicker operation (much less data is moved), which will in turn result in much higher scalability.

The merging of the compute and storage pools will not be suitable for all applications, but it will be well suited for many—and for the appropriate applications, it will open entirely new levels of capability.

Parting Thoughts

When cloud computing is discussed, much of the attention, understandably, is on the applications themselves. Yet for reasons necessitated by web-scale, what we are already beginning to see is that even more fundamental changes are in progress in all things data—how data is stored, where it is stored, how it is processed, and so forth.

While it may have been surprising at first glance, for very fundamental reasons—shaped by such things as the speed of light and other basic realities—over the next five to ten years, for many applications, we are going to see:

- The decline and fall of the relational database near-monopoly
- The nature of archiving, disaster recovery, and geographic distribution will fundamentally change computing
- The merging of storage infrastructures

While much of this may seem surprising from the perspective of mainstream computing practice in 2010, a very eloquent case can be made for this evolution from a key inventor of much of that very mainstream, Dr. E. F. Codd (inventor of both the relational database and OLAP)[15]:

> Attempting to force one technology or tool to satisfy a particular need for which another tool is more effective and efficient is like attempting to drive a screw into a wall with a hammer when a screwdriver is at hand: the screw may eventually enter the wall but at what cost?

Notes

1. While there are significant architectural differences between the two, for the purposes of this discussion they are equivalent.
2. These are generally known as Object Relational Mappers; the most popular at this time is probably an open-source project called Hibernate.

3. Gantz and Reinzel, "As the Economy Contracts, the Digital Universe Expands," IDC (sponsored by EMC), May 2009.

4. Web Growth Peaked in 2007 but Might be Back with a Vengeance in 2009, pingdom.com, Royal Pingdom, May 7, 2009 http://royal.pingdom.com/2009/05/07/Web-growth-peaked-in-2007-but-might-be-back-with-a-vengence-in-2009/; as cited in the following note.

5. Schonfeld, "Is the Growth of the Web Slowing Down or Just Taking A Breather?", Techcrunch, May 8, 2009, www.techcrunch.com/2009/05/08/is-the-growth-of-the-web-slowing-down-or-just-taking-a-breather/

6. Appistry was then known as Tsunami Research.

7. The network is a gigE at a typical 30% utilization, the disk is a Western Digital 2Tb SATAII drive at its sustainable throughput, the memory is a typical Intel Core2 processor with DDR2 memory, and the processor is an estimate for the internal transfer speeds of an Intel I7 Nehelam processor, 3 Ghz, 4 cores, separate data and instruction fetches, 4 instructions per core.

8. In the aggregate. While it is true, for example, that chip companies are struggling to increase the speed of individual processing cores much beyond their speeds of the past five+ years, they have made tremendous strides in packaging many cores into a single processor. This also influences software architectures, but that is outside the scope of this discussion.

9. Of which the most notable at this time is probably Akamai (AKAM).

10. A bucket would generally correspond to an amount of space similar to a single disk drive, or perhaps several disk drives, while a file would be much smaller (such as a single image, video, or document).

11. CloudIQ Storage is an internal working name for a technology that has been developed, though has not yet been released at the time of this writing. The actual product name(s) may be different.

12. Broadly speaking, map-reduce occurs in two steps: a *map* step in which incoming data is grouped with like data, and the *reduce* step in which each of these groups of similar data are processed. The results of all of the reduce operations are then collected together into the results.

13. Clearent (www.clearent.com) is a credit card processor that was created with a clean-sheet approach, at least in part to gain full advantage from a cloud computing technical infrastructure.

14. Other combinations are certainly possible, and technical considerations (as well as the particular types of applications) will dictate the right balance of processor, memory, storage, and network capacity for the basic building block. But the main idea is to keep small bits of each together in a unit, keep them in balance, and build the aggregated cloud infrastructure out of these basic building blocks.

15. Codd, "Providing OLAP (On-line Analytical Processing) to User-Analysts: An IT Mandate," E.F. Codd and Associates, 1993. This white paper defined OLAP, and presents business cases for its need and usefulness. Dr. Codd wrote seminal whitepapers defining both the relational database and OLAP.

CHAPTER 9

Why Inevitability Is . . . Inevitable

In the summer of 2001, amidst the financial rubble of the collapse of the Internet Bubble, there were many who proclaimed that the Internet was over—that those predictions of universal connectivity, a life on the web wherever one went, and businesses completely integrated with partners and customers at all times were all no more than over-hyped, vacuous pipe dreams and that it was time to look elsewhere for vision and fundamental innovation. While a full analysis of the "irrational exuberance"[1] of that period ought to be left for others, given the benefit of hindsight at least one fact is very clear.

The technology infrastructure at the turn of the year 2000 was, and would forever remain inadequate to handle what we now know as web-scale.

In other words, the big-server-centricity of most circa-2000 computing architectures placed an intrinsic cap on our ability to grow, though for macro economic reasons most did not fully realize these limits. Still, survivors such as Amazon, eBay, and others realized—to one degree or another—that their technological foundations needed to change, and change fundamentally.

Yet in research labs and startups—some focused on applications (such as search), others focused on enabling applications—work continued on building applications that could scale. At the same time there was a useful confluence between the newfound interest in reducing the cost of computing and the emerging computing techniques.

In a sense it did not really matter whether it was even possible to achieve a certain level of scale, or if having achieved that scale whether it was economically viable to build a business around that technical foundation—either way, both problems needed to be solved, and the answer to both problems lay (at least in part) in utilizing commodity.

During this time other teams focused on enabling a wide range of applications to run on a commodity foundation, and to do so with enterprise characteristics (e.g., reliability and security) that met or exceeded those of the conventional big-server architectures. For example, the founding team of Appistry envisioned a general purpose platform capable of running any enterprise application on breakable, commodity computers. By anticipating failure the group of computers could sustain many failures without losing any data; by teaching these computers how to organize themselves so that they acted like a single big server—deciding how to apportion work as it arrived, and how to reorganize as computers came and left the group—the cost of operating this group of computers was significantly reduced as well.

By the summer of 2002 an early version of this new platform was running and being shown to prospective customers. It was eye-opening to "pull the plug" on computers without the running applications even missing a beat. While it was true that this sort of capability had been possible for years in high-end fault-tolerant servers,[2] this was being done on commodity computers costing only a few hundred dollars apiece.

In fact the reality of what was now possible in this new world was, in a certain sense, difficult to comprehend—the relative numbers were simply staggering. One demonstration really made the point eloquently. With a group of about 100 commodity computers running this new platform software, the team was able to handle more transactions—more than 15,000 per second—than the central datacenters for a major credit card association at their peak that year, with one key difference: Instead of several hundred million dollars, this facility had cost less than $100,000. It was at least as reliable, simpler to manage, easier to scale.

At that moment we "knew that we knew that we knew"—this was the new reality of computing. It was simply a matter of time.

Driving Scale

The drive for scale is certainly a major factor any discussion of cloud computing—it must be, really, since scale that is extraordinary by historical standards is now a daily fact of life.

There are three key factors driving the need for scale:

1. **Ubiquitous Access.** While mobile devices have had some form of Internet capability for nearly ten years, the devices themselves have been either limited in functionality, fairly uncommon, costly, or all of the above. That has obviously changed with the advent of mobile computers (which happen to be able to make phone calls): the iPhone, Android, Blackberry, and all the rest. What separates these from the past is that they present a serious, useful web experience—as borne out by their instant dominance of mobile web traffic—and are becoming cheap enough[3] to be truly ubiquitous—and they will only become more so.

   Equally if not more important is the pervasive generation of data via sensors, embedded computers, and the like—in a sense, the other "side" of the network. Retail, autos, satellite, even our running shoes: sensors and data everywhere, available for processing and consumption.

2. **Nearly Pervasive Connectivity.** At every level of the Internet—industrial strength backbone networks, high-speed fiber to homes and office, as well as wireless networks for mobile access—sufficient network connectivity is available most places, most of the time. Of course, this too will only get better. In practice this means that it becomes practical to assume that services built on a cloud computing foundation—public, private, or any combination—may be utilized from just about anywhere.

3. **Cheap Storage and Computing Power.** This could also be called "because we can"—as a result of continued technological progress (generally following Moore's Law) our raw ability to store and process data is beginning to surpass practical limits. Utilizing this raw ability, of course, is another matter—thus the need for the advancements at the platform (Platform as a Service [PaaS]) and application (Software as a

Service [SaaS]) layers that enable clouds to fully utilize these raw building blocks.

In other words, we now have the ability to collect, transport, process, store, and access data nearly anywhere in nearly arbitrary volume—and that continues to expand and grow at a rapid pace. The limiting factors are the software architectures at every layer—hence the need for adoption of native, cloud-friendly software architectures that we have discussed throughout the book.

Objections and Concerns

As with any other transition there are a number of concerns and objections that may reasonably be raised when considering cloud computing. A full exploration of this section could easily fill a book of its own. A detailed discussion is most definitely outside the scope of this section, but we will provide brief summaries of each potential concern.

Losing Control

A common objection is a concern over losing control—losing control of the infrastructure, applications, everything. This is a valid concern: Some cloud offerings do not provide sufficient controls for operational control over quality of service, location of data, and so forth. But, others do provide those controls.

In another sense it may be more psychological—after all, there can be a certain comfort to walking into a room and seeing a well-run, well-designed enterprise datacenter. If this is sufficiently important then the best choice might be a private cloud (which of course might be the best choice for any of a number of other reasons as well).

In still another sense "losing control" may be completely necessary. After all, does any organization really want to decide what each and every server is doing at all times, when there might be 100,000 of them? What made sense with a handful of mainframes, or maybe a few dozen large servers will be completely intractable with large numbers of commodity boxes.

The best cloud implementations provide control over the high-level behavior, while allowing (but not requiring) lower-level observation and control, when desired.

Security

Security may be the ultimate weapon for sowing Fear, Uncertainty, and Doubt (the proverbial FUD). After all, by alleging a security concern one can put others in an indefensible position—having to disprove a negative.

But there are legitimate security concerns when evaluating specific cloud computing offerings, as there are with any computing infrastructure. With that in mind, here are a few observations.

A private cloud can be protected in the same manner as a traditional big-server architecture: by a combination of perimeter access, internal controls and procedures, and so forth. This is true whether that private cloud is located within a premise controlled by the consuming enterprise, or elsewhere in a facility controlled by an enterprise-oriented private cloud provider.

The greater scale of most public clouds provides the opportunity for a higher level of expertise and security protection than might generally be provided in a private datacenter. This certainly has some real promise, but must not be assumed—each public cloud offering needs to be evaluated on its own merits.

Of course, there will always be situations where nothing less than the full segregation, physical isolation of a private cloud will do—obvious examples include secure clouds for national intelligence agencies, deployed military forces, and so forth. While it is true that a special form of public cloud may well make sense for these situations within mutual-trust communities that form appropriately. Those specialized public clouds will, at some level, continue to rely on physical boundaries (along with all the other appropriate measures).

In other words, security within cloud computing offerings can be evaluated in much the same manner as conventional computing architectures—the same rules generally apply.[4]

Cost

In early 2009 there was a brief firestorm of discussion[5] over a McKinsey study[6] which seemed to show that the "emperor had no clothes"—that cloud computing was, in fact, more expensive than a traditional big-server datacenter. Upon slightly closer examination it becomes clear that the study had an intrinsically limited scope: It really was comparing retail pricing of certain public cloud offerings to some basic conventional scenarios. In the ensuing discussion it became clear that this study, while valid in a certain narrow sense, was much more of a reflection of a limited view of cloud computing—public clouds or nothing, no meaningful sense of a platform (Paas)—than of cloud computing as a whole.

Also, the study was done at a time when there were relatively few offerings from which to choose, and hence relatively modest competition.

The simple reality is that by incorporating a strong platform (PaaS) an enterprise can ensure real choice in cloud providers for their own applications, and with choice always comes the ability to drive down costs; by building on self-operating commodity building blocks the aggregate infrastructure costs will inevitably be reduced significantly (both acquisition and operational costs); and with that same strong platform comes the ability to more tightly control energy costs.

While cost of a cloud, as with any other criteria, must always be examined closely, in truth this is already a very strong advantage of the transition to cloud computing, and that advantage will increase as the industry matures.

Change and Disruption

That cloud computing presents the opportunity for change is undeniable. Whether that is good or bad, and furthermore whether that change is disruptive or not depends entirely on the approach and the receptivity and perspective of particular organizations and individuals.

In Chapter 5, Cloud Adoption Lifecycle, and Chapter 7, Where to Begin with Cloud Computing, there are discussions about various approaches to adoption. As you can see in these chapters, there are very clean methodologies and approaches that enable an organization to gain the necessary expertise to fully utilize cloud computing.

As for receptivity and perspective, the rapid adoption of cloud computing as an explicit (and implicit) part of each individual's personal computing lives (e.g., Google, Facebook, Youtube, Twitter, and many more) is going a long way to laying helpful groundwork in this area. In a similar vein, the high profile of SaaS offerings in the enterprise (such as Salesforce.com) are also quite helpful. Time is on the side of cloud computing on this one—adoption of cloud computing is increasing, and will continue to increase for the fore-seeable future.

The bottom line is that the adoption of cloud computing in-volves change that must be managed well. Furthermore, lingering fear over any type of change in general, and adoption of cloud com-puting in particular—and fear can be a barrier to adoption—is going down rapidly as social reality continues to plow this ground ahead of enterprise adoption.

Nothing New to See Here

"Cloud computing is just marketing hype around everything we al-ready have." Interestingly enough, this objection is most often raised by those involved in the computing business, usually in tradi-tional computing architectures and operations.

Unfortunately it is simply not true, as we have discussed in many different dimensions throughout the book. Yes there are many cases of "putting lipstick on a pig"—taking existing offer-ings and slapping a "cloud" label on them—but those may be easily seen and taken for whatever they are worth, outside of their "cloud claims."

Of course, novelty itself is not sufficient to recommend a course of action—as with anything else, simply evaluate cloud computing on its merits . . . and that is very favorable for cloud computing.

Lock-In

Lock-in is a serious, multifaceted concern that demands careful con-sideration. Here are some general observations.

Lock-in is less of a problem at the infrastructure layer, more of a problem at the application layer, and somewhere in between at the platform layer.

If one uses a strong platform capable of operating on a wide variety of infrastructures, or if one has written an application to as-sume nothing more than basic building blocks out of the infra-structure layer, then there is very little lock-in. In other words, an enterprise can shop around for the lowest cost providers of VMs and terabytes, and go from there. This is true flexibility.

At the platform layer, some platforms are designed to work very closely with only particular infrastructures, or perhaps with only cer-tain programming languages. In those cases lock-in becomes more significant, because of the tendency to constrain one to that particular infrastructure or programming language.

For example, a fairly high-profile example is Google App-Engine, which supports two languages (Python and Java), and one native data store (BigTable). The close integration with BigTable is a significant contributor to lock-in, as other platforms have not yet provided a storage facility that is both API- and capability-equivalent.

Consider a platform like Engine Yard, which provides a very targeted platform for Ruby on Rails applications. The trade-off with this is that it provides a type of lock-in—you are definitely committed to Ruby on Rails. This is a lesser type of lock-in, since there are few other, perhaps less-well integrated options for deploying Ruby on Rails applications.

In most cases, though, it is better to reduce lock-in by utilizing the more generalized platforms mentioned earlier, though of course they do involve some level of commitment to that platform. Still, the best platforms understand this and ensure that applications can easily be moved to another platform, should the customer ever desire.

The highest degree of lock-in is potentially at the application (SaaS) layer. For example, if an enterprise utilizes a particular set of manufacturing applications, then their ability to switch to another provider is modest. This is largely no different than for conventional applications, yet it can be a difficult reality should major problems develop with a particular provider. Having said that, the best applications provide strong capabilities to migrate data out of that application, if the customer ever wants to.

Lock-in needs to be well-understood for each situation. With that business-specific information, each enterprise can decide what level of lock-in they are willing to tolerate for that situation.

Summing Up Objections and Concerns

These concerns are best thought of as evaluation criteria. That is, various cloud computing offerings will differ in the amount of control offered, the type and level of security, the amount of lock-in, and so forth. Therefore, understanding these concerns can provide useful guidance when selecting a cloud offering for a particular situation at a particular organization.

Overwhelming Rationality

As discussed throughout this book, there is an underlying resonance to cloud-computing, a fundamental coherence, a raison d'être driven by the pervasive drive for scale that is characteristic of the Internet.

This coherent drive for scale is enabled by the ubiquitous access, near-pervasive connectivity, and commodity storage and computing discussed at the beginning of this chapter, but it also has several properties which are structural, which will in and of themselves help ensure that the adoption of cloud computing is an absolutely inevitable transition for nearly every organization.

Inexorable Commoditization

Commoditization has just begun, but what has already been accomplished is meaningful.

In particular, adopting commodity infrastructure forced software architects to deal with breaking past a single machine, and to do so straightforwardly. Historically many of the forms of distributed computing—the broad technical category for utilizing many computers to accomplish a coherent set of work—are thorny to utilize well, and consequently tended to drive architects either to adopt greatly simplified distributed architectures,[7] or to assume, simply, that key components of an application could execute within the bounds of a single server (one factor in the tendency of traditional architectures to gravitate towards fewer, larger servers).

This has led to tremendous innovations in software architectures, tooling, data storage, and platforms that greatly simplify the process of creating a coherent, distributed application.

In addition the adoption of commodity really drove the next step to fully decouple software from servers—a very aggressive form of virtualization in which applications are not tied to particular servers, network, and so forth. Those applications may well execute on a very large number of machines, a little bit at a time. This will in turn allow aggressive optimization of the commodity infrastructure (see the next section). In any case, once this decoupling has occurred and enabled this whole new round of infrastructure commoditization, there is no turning back to the old, less flexible, more costly big server architectures.

Finally, the most significant aspect of commoditization as found in cloud computing is actually not about the infrastructure directly. Instead, it is the commoditization of operations. Self-organizing, self-operating infrastructures, platforms, and applications are, to one degree or another, key elements of a true cloud infrastructure. All contribute to a reduction in operational costs (primarily labor), and consequently make significant contributions to the benefits gained by cloud adoption.

Efficiency: Energy, Financial, and More

Imagine that you are trying to ship a laptop somewhere, so you dutifully pack it in the original inner box and head down to the local FedEx office. Expecting to find a reasonable, laptop-sized shipping container in which to enclose your laptop, you are surprised to find a new policy has been put into place–you have only two choices in shipping containers: (1) letter-sized, or (2) a 10-meter × 10-meter × 10-meter steel contraption suitable for moving a delivery truck.

Having no real choice, you select the 10-meter mega-cube, pay the now-extraordinary shipping fee (after all, you *did* pick the 10-meter monstrosity), and warn the recipient that they might want to reserve a forklift to receive the laptop.

Absurd? Of course—while the 10-meter mega-cube makes sense if you were shipping a thousand laptops, it certainly is not a very good fit for a single laptop. In other words, it is not very efficient.

This situation is analogous to most pre-cloud, big-server computing architectures—rather tricky to match up the need with the capacity, particularly since that capacity was acquired in big steps.[8]

In contrast, capacity in a cloud can be acquired in much smaller increments—bite-sized commodity chunks, so to speak—and those increments can be acquired for only the period of time in which they are needed. This is true for all real clouds—public, private, or hybrid.

Two other aspects of cloud efficiency deserve at least a brief mention.

Since applications assume that they are on a varying number of small servers, the operators of a cloud can examine the utilization of the cloud as a whole, turning off as many servers as may be turned off without compromising service levels. Of course just what is desirable may be set on a case-by-case basis by each organization. In any case, this enables the operators of each cloud to ensure the highest utilization levels possible, constantly fine-tuning capacity to precisely match the requirements at that moment.

Again for the same reason, the physical infrastructure may be selected for optimal energy efficiency, space efficiency, cost efficiency, or whatever mix of those priorities are appropriate for each organization. For example, rather than using "server grade" commodity equipment, some future organization may decide that mobile device processors (which are highly optimized for maximum computing power per energy consumed) would be better for a particular cloud. That organization would be free to optimize their energy efficiency in that manner, with the cloud infrastructure and platform layers insulating the applications from the change.

In short, a cloud can always be operated more efficiently – in many cases far more efficiently, in many dimensions than can a traditional technology infrastructure.

Cost

As discussed earlier in the chapter, over time cost reduction will be the second most cogent reason the transition to cloud computing is inevitable. The necessary initial expenditures, the ongoing operating expenses (energy, labor, etc.), the ability to vary expenses to precisely match varying needs, and the ability to entirely avoid initial expenditures when desired—all this adds up to a compelling proposition in favor of the transition to cloud.

Exascale

The top reason that the transition to cloud computing is inevitable is the drive for scale—over time this will simply overwhelm conventional architectures. While traditional applications can certainly continue to run on traditional architectures for quite some time, eventually many of those will need to scale beyond their intrinsic ability.

So what does "exascale" mean? The cold mathematical definition (for storage) is

1 exabyte = 1,000 petabytes

1 petabyte = 1,000 terabytes

1 terabyte = 1,000 gigabytes

1 gigabyte = 1,000 megabytes

So in a formal manner we could define exascale to be a class of computing that can routinely process a billion gigabytes of data.

Consider that an average digital photograph might be about 5 mb, then this would be about 200 billion photographs, which is more than 30 photographs of every man, woman, and child alive today. Even an average one hour high-definition video is about 2 gb, so one exabyte would contain about 500 million videos, all available all the time.

No matter how we think about it, an exabyte is a substantial amount of data. Substantial, yet we are most definitely driving towards these amounts in many areas.

It is interesting to note that limits of scale are being pushed first in two very divergent areas. The first are in the basic plumbing of the Internet—search engines, social networks, and so forth—and the second are in the areas of national intelligence and defense. In both cases, as we examined in Chapter 8, All Things Data, this inexorable drive for scale is forcing radical changes in how data is stored, retrieved, and processed.

For example, a typical commercial satellite (circa 2009) generates more than five terabytes of raw data each and every day. That means nearly two petabytes of raw information each year—and that information must still be processed, which is where the real value is discovered . . . and stored. And that is only one satellite, one sensor.

Now let us look at a seemingly innocuous example—the growth of Facebook through 2009 (see Exhibit 9.1).

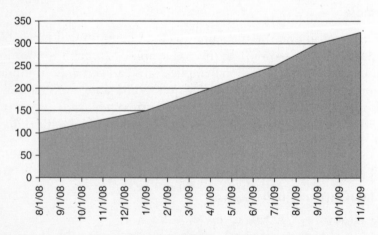

Exhibit 9.1   Recent Facebook Subscriber Growth, in Millions

This means that Facebook is adding *500,000 new customers each and every day!*[9] Each of these people can load videos, photographs, send messages to friends, run applications, and so forth. It does not even really matter how long this can be sustained—it is happening now (as of this writing), and if Facebook wants to succeed they must deal with this seemingly insatiable growth in demand.

This is exascale, the type of scale that is now the "price of success," and the only meaningful chance for handling this types of success is to adopt cloud computing.

A Natural Evolution

Cloud computing is certainly real today, and practical for startups, commercial enterprises, and government organizations. Yet when thinking about what is possible, we are much closer to the starting line, both for cloud computing in particular and the Internet in general. Here are a few areas of innovation in and around cloud computing likely over the next five to ten years, though some of these are obviously in progress even now:

- **Business Models.** In many ways the innovations in business models are at least as crucial as, if not more crucial than the technical innovations driving cloud computing. For example, the post-bubble advertising-based revenue models that enable monetization of communities based on activity have become crucial over the past decade. Key to this model is their foundation on micro-events—customer relationships each as small as the viewing of a single page, or the clicking of a single ad—combined with a social-based community to provide longevity.

    These micro-events correlate very well with the fine-grained variability of cloud computing, and enable new flexibility in constructing business models.

    Recent "freemium" business models, in which basic, ad-supported free services are combined with one or more premium services offered for a fee are likely to become the norm.
- **Interoperability.** As discussed previously, concern over lock-in can be a deterrent to cloud computing adoption. Consequently there will be much effort to ameliorate this concern—some voluntary, some not so voluntary—among cloud computing vendors. Voluntary effort will include various standards, both

formal and de facto, covering application programmer interfaces (APIs) at every level (both inside the cloud computing stack and outside), data migration, and so forth. Where voluntary interoperability either does not occur or is slow in coming, involuntary interoperability may occur—typically with the creation of a software layer, usually encouraged by customer behavior.

- **Software Development, Part II.** In a rather surprising trend to many, most organizations are now back into software development—even those who still claim that they do not do any software development. In particular, due to the very nature of cloud-based applications many organizations are combining applications in ways that are most useful to themselves with relatively modest bits of software that glue disparate applications together.

  Quite similar to the composite applications in a service-oriented architecture, these mash-ups often operate at a higher level than the individual applications themselves. They are also quite similar to the common scripting traditionally done to combine various programs.

  Even though they might not be considered "software development," the reality is that these composite applications have become crucial. For example, we are familiar with organizations in which anywhere from 30 to 50% of the software that they write is of this nature—and that percentage is likely to go up for most organizations over time. This newer type of software development is crucial to meshing cloud-based applications with the business processes in each organization.

- **Commodity Will Become Radically More So.** The endgame of commoditization will be quite different than what is considered "commodity" today. Once software has been freed from both individual as well as the number of computers on which it operates, and operations have been freed from the burden previously imposed by managing large numbers of servers, and everyone is freed from the fear of infrastructure failures, then the vendors of infrastructure are free to innovate far more aggressively with commodity. Over time this is likely to take several forms, including very large numbers of very efficient (typically mobile-oriented) processors, as well as new combination building blocks in which combination disk drives are combined with one or more of these same very efficient processors (into a package essentially no bigger than the drive itself).

Many other, currently unforeseen innovations are likely, and all of these will be enabled by the widespread adoption of cloud-friendly software architectures, both current and future.

- **Semantic Web.** There are many efforts, some in research organizations, some in large enterprises, some at startups, others collaboratively across the web, that may be loosely grouped as moving toward a "semantic web"[10]—that is, an Internet in which the information is understood at higher levels than just raw data, in which many of these interactions can be done entirely by software "agents" automatically on the behalf of people.

  Long a dream and goal of many in computing, the one thing that is common across all of these efforts is an insatiable appetite for computing resources.[11] In other words, the very development of cloud computing is a necessary precursor to the practical development and deployment of most, if not all, of the envisioned semantic-web services.

This is only a partial list, only a small fraction of the innovations to come in all things cloud . . . some in progress, some on the horizon, and others not yet even a fleeting thought in anyone's imagination. A very bright future indeed, yet grounded in the solid foundation of a useful, practical, and valuable present reality.

Parting Thoughts

What then, is next?

In the near term we will see—indeed are already beginning to see—the emergence of the fully connected, truly responsive organization: the "real-time enterprise"—an enterprise in which the flow of data and decisions is both more rapid and contemporaneous with the actual events that trigger them. These same events—when aggregated into meaningful trends—will cause meta-adaptations in the enterprise that, as a result, will then truly enmesh with their customers at a very high number of touch points.

When done well, this new type of enterprise will be both simultaneously open—quite transparent to customers—and sticky—keeping customers for much longer than average.

This level of responsiveness, this level of transparency, this level of close interaction with customers—this will be directly enabled by the broad adoption of cloud computing. Organizations that understand, embrace, and take advantage of this new reality will prosper. Those that do not will struggle, and face extinction.

When thinking about these new realities it is very easy to get excited, very easy to let the mind run. Mostly this is a very good thing, opening the mind to think of all that may be vastly improved and how that may be accomplished.

Yet there are some who have, unfortunately, taken this excitement and dabbled in ponderous, overwrought metaphysical speculation; these excursions are ultimately pointless and misguided, at best. We suggest they calm down a bit—they simply miss the point, and as a result run the risk of missing out on the truly remarkable opportunities before us.

Cloud computing is a fantastic new reality for those who plan, run, and ultimately set the visions for what is possible in their organization. A reality in which the organization can be largely freed from the traditional constraints that computing has placed on all for so long—constraints based on the cost, availability, capabilities, and the difficulties of using computing-enabled stuff.

Cloud is a new reality to be embraced, understood, and acted upon.

Imagine the possibilities.

Notes

1. "Irrational exuberance," a memorable phrase coined by Alan Greenspan (Director of the U.S. Federal Reserve), came to signify much that was overwrought about the business, cultural, and technological climate of the late 1990s, particularly as seen in the speculations surrounding the initial growth spurt of the Internet.
2. Such as specialized, fault-tolerant servers from Tandem and Stratus, both of which were staples in financial services.
3. For example, in July 2009 Apple reduced the price of the entry-level iPhone to US$99 (in the United States, subsidized with a service contract with the carrier).
4. It is interesting to note that the larger number of commodity servers can actually provide significant opportunities to better survive direct attacks, rather than being more vulnerable to those attacks (as might be a first reaction). In essence this is because a compromised server can be treated just like a broken one—the cloud cuts out the broken server and continues on, without much loss in capability.

5. For example, see "McKinsey Cloud Computing Report Conclusions Don't Add Up," Golden, Virtualization and Cloud Advisor blog, *CIO* Magazine, April 27, 2009.
6. "Clearing the Air on Cloud Computing," McKinsey & Company, March 2009.
7. In general these tended to simplify most of the application in exchange for placing even more pressure on the database (and other data storage components). While suitable up to a point, this brings the scale-drive "day of reckoning" about sooner.
8. In this analogy server consolidation would become the same thing as bringing together every laptop shipment into the same 10-meter container, in the hope of filling it up as much as possible—and with that this analogy is probably exhausted.
9. Subscriber (user) counts provided by Facebook, except 11/6 estimated by All Facebook. All counts cited in Parr, WOW: "Facebook Adding Half a Million New Users Every Day," Mashable, November 10, 2009.
10. The term "semantic web" was coined by Tim Berners-Lee in the book *Weaving the Web*, HarperOne, 1999.
11. For example, the founding team of Appistry had been thinking through this type of technology in 2001 when the need for such a platform (now known as PaaS) became clear, leading to the founding of the company.

A P P E N D I X

The Cloud Computing
Vendor Landscape

At the beginning of the new millennium there was not yet such a thing as a cloud computing vendor, though (as we have seen) teams were already hard at work on several significant efforts . . . and several of these eventually blossomed into key cloud computing vendors.

In fact, only a few years after a modest beginning for the nascent industry, there is a vibrant vendor ecosystem, with everything from relatively established players to the latest, most hopeful startups, and much in between. Hardly a month passes without numerous, significant product announcements, nor a quarter without new vendors and open source projects.

Cloud computing is clearly an area of rapid evolution. As a result, in order to ensure the most useful (current) information this brief appendix contains information that is least likely to change rapidly—overview information for the major categories, including examples of some of the vendors in each category. Comprehensive, current listings of companies and products, including industry trends and recent developments are available on the web site for this book.[1]

The major categories include three that correspond to the major layers of the cloud technology stack, and two for those providing expertise in one form or another. Each category includes vendors focused on public, private, and hybrid cloud offerings; those focused on commercial as well as government markets; startups and the established; open source, open distribution, and traditional distribution models; and in many cases, all of the above.

Of course certain vendors have offerings in more than one category; a handful intend to cover each category, though that will likely be difficult to achieve and maintain.

In any case, here are the major categories, along with a few notes about the history that shaped each category.

Infrastructure as a Service (IaaS)

Vendors in the Infrastructure as a Service (IaaS) category primarily fall into two broad groups: those that provide an existing IaaS and those that provide technology to enable IaaS. Vendors that provide an existing IaaS generally come from cloud technology providers (e.g., Amazon), managed services or hosting providers (e.g., Rackspace, Savvis, etc.), and integrated vendors such as HP, IBM, and Dell.

The technology providers include those who provide software stacks to manage physical or virtualized infrastructure (such as VMWare) as well as those who provide hardware (of varying degrees of commodity) that is intended for easy stacking, replacement, and so forth (all of the major hardware providers, several startups, and certain fresh entrants from nontraditional vendors, such as Cisco).

This is a category that is likely to see significant innovation–in particular, as the trend towards commoditization of the infrastructure matures, then very-high volume providers of commodity infrastructure are likely to dominate, both amongst the ready to consume IaaS and the technology providers.

Platforms as a Service (PaaS)

As discussed in Chapter 2, Concepts, Terminology, and Standards, and Chapter 4, Strategic Implications of Cloud Computing, there are two major subcategories here—offerings that focus on providing management, operations, billing, provisioning, and related functions for cloud-based applications, and offerings that focus on providing application frameworks and fundamental capabilities (such as cloud-friendly data storage). Of course, too, there are offerings that bundle all of the above.

Examples of those that provide management, application frameworks, and fundamental capabilities include Amazon, Appistry, and

Google. Examples of those that provide only management are 3Tera, Rightscale, Enomaly, and Eucalyptus. Examples of those that provide primarily application frameworks or fundamental capabilities include Cloudera, Gigaspaces, Terracotta, and VMWare/Springsource.

Vendors in this category have generally come from one of two perspectives: either from the "top of the stack" and therefore they had an initial application focus, or from the "bottom of the stack" and therefore they were extending the infrastructure (typical for most management vendors).

Software as a Service (SaaS)

In many ways this category is both the most familiar and the most extensive, in that a significant portion of early cloud deployments were in this category. Whether it was search and e-mail by Google; e-mail and instant messaging by Yahoo, Google, and Microsoft; social networks such as LinkedIn, Facebook, and Twitter; customer management by Salesforce, and others; commerce from Amazon; content delivery from YouTube or any of dozens or hundreds of other examples—any reader of this book, and for that matter a very high percentage of the general population has personal experience with vendors in this space.

The reason for this is simple—making an application available over the Internet implies a commitment to providing web-scale, which in turn is an implicit commitment to cloud.

It is that desire for—or fear of—scale that drove many of these vendors to initially develop and embrace cloud computing principles throughout the stack. This category generally includes those who best understand these principles, and as a consequence best exhibit cloud characteristics such as scale, elasticity, and so forth.

Systems Integrators

Most large-scale systems integrators are in various stages of developing cloud computing capabilities, some more aggressively than others. Due to the broad nature of the adoption cycle, over time this will tend to affect most areas of each integrator. While only certain practice areas will be focused on cloud-specific topics (such as all aspects of how to transition a virtualized datacenter to a true private cloud), most practice areas will need to broaden and adapt to include cloud-enabled capabilities (such as developing enterprise capabilities for handling "big data" problems that exceed the capabilities of traditional approaches).

Analysts and Service Providers

More or less the same comments apply to the smaller service providers. However, both the analyst community and certain specialized boutique service providers have been more aggressive in developing deep cloud expertise, which befits their expected role of guiding and evangelizing planning, experimentation, evaluation, and adoption of significant new technologies.

Parting Thoughts

In many ways the cloud computing vendor community reflects the history of cloud computing itself: a convergence of firms coming from many different backgrounds, each bringing unique perspective and capabilities to the rapid innovation and extremely dynamic nature of this relatively new market.

At the same time, there are many encouraging aspects of the vendor community: Amongst this energy and innovation there are many with a deep understanding of enterprise expectations, of precisely what it means to deliver capability upon which an enterprise—commercial or government, casual or classified—can depend.

Note

1. The site for this book is www.execsguidetocloud.com. A link to the vendor guide is featured on this home page. Note that this site is (naturally) resident on a cloud.

About the Authors

Eric A. Marks (Newburyport, MA) is president and CEO of AgilePath Corporation, a leading management and technology consulting firm. Eric Marks is a recognized technology strategist and visionary with six business and technology books to his credit. He continues to explore the impact of emerging technologies on business strategy, how organizations absorb and internalize technology, and the enterprise governance implications of new technology acquisition and absorption . . . Mr. Marks is an information technology veteran with 22 years of experience with firms including PricewaterhouseCoopers, Cambridge Technology Partners, Novell, Electronic Data Systems, StreamServe, Ontos, and Square D Company/Schneider Electric.

Mr. Marks is the author of six business and technology strategy books including, *SOA Governance for the Services-Driven Enterprise* (2008), *Service-Oriented Architecture (SOA): Planning and Implementation Guide for Business and Technology*, (2006), *Executive's Guide to Web Services* (2003). He also wrote *Business Darwinism – Evolve or Dissolve*, (2002), and he also edited and contributed to *Manufacturing Leadership through the Extended Enterprise* (2000). He also contributed to *Coherency Management: Architecting the Enterprise for Alignment, Agility, and Assurance* (forthcoming).

Mr. Marks graduated from Syracuse University in 1983 and the University of Wisconsin-Milwaukee in 1986, and serves on the Advisory Board for Syracuse University's top-ranked School of Information Studies, as well as being an Adjunct Professor. He also serves on the National Board of Advisors for the Kauffman Campuses Initiative (Enitiative), is on the Advisory Board for Northeastern University's School of Information Services, and is a Visiting Scientist at Carnegie Mellon's Software Engineering Institute (SEI).

Roberto (Bob) Lozano (St. Louis, MO) is chief strategist and founder of Appistry, a leading provider of cloud application platforms (i.e., software for building, deploying, and managing a wide variety of applications and services for all types of clouds – public, private, community, and hybrid). He previously served as the company's president and CEO.

He is an experienced entrepreneur with a history of building successful companies. Prior to Appistry Lozano founded and led PaylinX, a leader in the payment solutions market, from its inception through significant growth. He has also held management and technology positions with Southwestern Bell (now AT&T, he was a founding member of the Advanced Computing Laboratory at the nascent Technology Resources R&D organization), Monsanto, and Sandia National Laboratories, and he founded Intelligent Computer Systems. Mr. Lozano served as an adjunct faculty member at the Washington University in St. Louis for several years, lecturing on artificial intelligence, and has frequently helped to foster successful entrepreneurs wherever they find themselves.

Mr. Lozano received his BS in Electrical Engineering from the University of Missouri in 1979 and his MS in Electrical Engineering (Computer Engineering Program from Stanford University in 1980.

He blogs at www.thought soncomputing.com, micro-blogs as @boblozano on twitter (among other places), and speaks frequently at industry events, conferences, and other forums.

Index

A

access, ubiquitous 30
acquisition processes 62, 80
adoption 4, 7, 29, 31, 41, 74, 77, 82,
    87, 107, 110, 114–15, 120,
    130–1, 138, 140–5, 149, 151,
    176, 195, 198, 204, 206, 209,
    211, 227, 229, 248, 250–1,
    253–4, 259
  accelerated pattern 204, 206–7
  agile pattern 204–5
  cloud business patterns 204–5,
    207
  cloud collaboration 142–3
  conservative pattern 204, 207, 209
  discover steps 120
  lifecycle xii, 35, 48, 63, 111–12,
    114–45, 148, 195, 197–9, 202,
    206–7, 209, 211, 250
  lifecycle model *see* model, Cloud
    Adoption Lifecycle
  logical stages 111–13, 115, 118,
    123, 130–1, 135, 140–2, 144,
    198–9, 207
  nominal pattern 204, 206–8
  obstacles 107
  pattern 94, 210
age of computing
  first 7–8, 11
  second 8–9, 15
  third 10, 13–15
ages of computing 6–7, 9, 11, 13
agile development 53

AgilePath xiii, 96, 98–9, 110, 267
agility 69, 78, 86–8, 92, 95, 207, 267
  enterprise 92, 95, 109
Agility Double Play 92–3, 95–6, 98,
    101, 103, 107, 109–10
Amazon 14–15, 22, 27, 30, 34, 37, 47,
    50–1, 67, 83, 90, 108, 124, 138,
    172, 178, 185, 200–1, 215, 220–
    4, 240, 245, 264–5
  EC2/S3 220–3
  Simple Storage Service (S3) 172
API 17, 20, 41, 51–2, 61, 108, 131,
    149–52, 161, 164, 173, 184–6,
    198, 210, 258
Appistry xiii, 12, 26, 43, 67, 83, 216,
    221, 234, 244, 264, 268
application 11–12, 14, 16–18, 26–7,
    29–37, 41, 43–4, 46–8, 50–1,
    53–4, 56–9, 61–5, 67–8, 77, 82,
    95–6, 106, 127–9, 132–3, 137–8,
    148–50, 160–1, 165–6, 168–9,
    191–2, 229–31, 234–5, 238–9,
    242–8, 250–5, 257–8
  architect 186, 192, 210, 216
  architecture 7, 10, 17, 52, 99–101
  capabilities 94, 168–9, 213
  cloud-computing 67
  cloud computing pattern 106
  cloud-optimized architectures 20
  composite 51, 143, 258
  composition of 94–5, 99–100,
    142–3, 198
  conventional 36, 252

application (*continued*)
  cost reduction 77
  definite 48
  developers 29, 47, 53, 184, 186–7,
    210, 215–16, 219
  development 82, 101, 167, 176,
    206–7, 215, 229
  distributed 141–2, 253
  frameworks 264–5
  hosting 98, 159–60, 169, 215
  infrastructure 79, 150, 167, 215
  maintenance 99, 102–3
  mobile 30, 70
  native 36, 50, 56
  newer 59
  portfolios 103
  scalability 106, 216
  servers 10, 53–4, 67, 162–3, 167–8,
    172, 193
  typical 17
  virtualization 62, 150, 160, 163,
    166, 216, 218
applications 31, 36, 169, 230
  cloud enablement 137
approaches 121, 124
  hybrid 38, 209
  nominal 208
  robust enterprise 38
architects, business 218–19
architecture
  adoption stage 123
  Cloud Computing Reference
    129–30, 135
  Cloud Computing Technical
    Reference 188–9, 191
  enterprise 103
  master reference 100
  platform reference 152
  processes 133, 138, 148, 175, 178,
    192
  style 67, 231
architectures 10, 17, 244, 248, 253,
  259

archiving 228, 243
asset 73–4, 79
  better utilization 78–9, 99, 187
asymmetric competitor 86–7, 91
  cloud–based 86

B

benefits 46, 63, 69, 74, 76–82, 84, 88,
    91–2, 101–3, 110, 117, 133, 137,
    140, 147, 152–3, 171, 179, 203,
    208–9, 229–30, 245, 254
Berners-Lee, Tim 2, 261
The Big Switch 68
Bill of Rights, Cloud Computing
    (CC-BoR) 152–3
BPaaS (Business processes as a
    Service) 169–70, 189
broad enablers 15, 17, 19
business
  drivers 99, 112–13, 127, 148
  emerging 111, 144
  goals 98, 101, 110, 112–14
  impact 128, 140
  leadership 78, 218, 220, 224
  small to medium 65
business model 5, 28, 42, 52, 80, 83,
    86, 88–91, 97, 141, 179, 203,
    206, 257
  cloud-based 74, 82, 84, 87–92,
    203
  innovation 72, 75, 81, 203
  new concepts 75
  web-based 90–1
Business Processes as a Service
    (BPaaS) 169–70, 189
business scenarios, cloud
    computing 212

C

capabilities xii, 16, 20, 30, 34, 38, 53,
    76, 78, 87, 90, 92, 94–7, 104,
    112, 119, 122–3, 126, 131,
    140–2, 153, 158–64, 166–8,

182–8, 190, 198, 200–1, 206, 209–10, 260, 266

accessible 164

cloud-based 165, 182

cloud based business 78, 97, 126, 128, 155, 159, 165, 169, 182, 207, 209, 220

cloud computing 82, 119, 155, 171

cloud ecosystem enablement 164

cloud-enabled 131, 150, 158, 160, 170, 174, 179, 205, 266

cloud enablement 160, 162, 218

easy-to-access 207

emerging cloud 199

foundational cloud infrastructure enablement 166

fundamental 264–5

individual Amazon 185

integrate 198

interface-accessible cloud 36

internal 131

necessary cloud-enabled 205

operational 132, 192

organizational 122

private 78, 201

private internal 159

public 123, 200–1, 205, 222

public infrastructure 223

self-service 30, 63

service-enabled 96

service-enablement of 91, 96

technical 127, 179, 181

capacity 13, 30, 32, 47, 66, 73, 75–6, 79, 159, 171, 230, 254

Carr, Nicholas 21, 42, 44, 68

Catholic Church 19

CC-BoR (Cloud Computing Bill of Rights) 152–3

CC-RA *see* Cloud Computing Reference Architecture

CC-RM Cloud Ecosystem Model 180, 212

CCIF (Cloud Computing Interoperability Form) 41, 151

CCMF (Cloud Computing Manifesto) 152–3

choreography 113, 142–3, 196

Cisco 8

cloud
external *see* external cloud
first public *see* public cloud, first
hybrid *see* hybrid cloud
multi-tenant 33, 37
private *see* private cloud
public *see* public cloud
vertical *see* vertical cloud

Cloud Adoption Lifecycle Model *see* model, Cloud Adoption Lifecycle

cloud application platform 29, 34–6, 43, 54, 56, 63, 67, 169, 268

Cloud Business Adoption Patterns 204–5, 207

cloud business solution 128

cloud business tier 157, 162–3, 168–72, 184–7, 189, 210, 213–23

cloud computing, development of 18, 20 *see also* history, cloud

cloud computing community 152–3

Cloud Computing Community Wiki 161, 191

Cloud Computing Interoperability Forum (CCIF) 41, 151

Cloud Computing Logical Architecture 157, 159, 161

Cloud Computing Manifesto (CCMF) 152–3

Cloud Computing Reference Architecture 100, 113, 123, 129–30, 135, 196–7

Cloud Computing Reference Model
(CC-RM) 35, 113–14, 123–7,
130, 135, 138, 144–5, 148–9,
152, 155–7, 162–5, 170, 179–80,
182–5, 187–8, 190–2, 197, 210,
212–13, 225
Cloud Computing Reference
Model, summary 187
Cloud Computing Technical
Reference Architecture 188–9,
191
Cloud Deployment & Provisioning
Plan 113, 196
Cloud Deployment Model 113,
123–4, 126, 128, 135–6, 139,
148, 156–7, 170–1, 173, 176,
178, 187, 190, 196, 215–16,
218–19, 221–2, 224
cloud dial tone 108, 126, 156, 180–2
Cloud Ecosystem Model 126, 156–7,
179–81, 183, 187, 190–2, 214,
216–21, 223–4
Cloud-Enabled New Business Unit
85
cloud enablement see enablement
Cloud Enablement Model see
model, Cloud Enablement
216–17
Cloud Governance & Lifecycle
Planning 113, 196
Cloud Governance and Operations
Model 123, 126, 156–7, 174–5,
177, 179, 187, 190, 214–15,
217–24
cloud modeling see modeling
Cloud Modeling Framework see
framework, cloud modeling
cloud network 126, 156
Cloud OS (Operating System) 164,
166, 169, 192, 222
cloud OS, capabilities 167, 221
Cloud OS, tier 36, 163, 166–7, 180,
182, 192, 222

Cloud Physical Access 180, 183
Cloud Physical Tier 162–3, 171, 183,
210
Cloud Platform/PaaS Sub-tier
167–8
cloud platforms see platform
cloud program 113, 118, 141, 196 see
also implementation
Cloud Provider Analysis see
providers, analysis
cloud push 77, 96
cloud ramp 122
cloud reference architecture see
Cloud Computing Reference
Architecture
cloud reference implementation
113, 134–6, 196, 198
successful 130, 140, 198
Cloud Reference Model see model,
Cloud Reference
cloud service providers (CSPs) see
service providers
cloud services 38, 124, 132, 149, 159,
161–2, 186, 189, 201
cloud solution providers 82–3, 127,
142, 153
cloud sprints 205–6
Cloud Steady State 113, 196, 199
cloud storage 161, 188–9
cloud strategy see strategy, cloud
Cloud Strategy & Planning 113, 196
Cloud Strategy and Roadmap 113,
118, 196
cloud success see success
cloud technology provider (CTPs)
83, 131, 153, 174, 176, 264 see
also vendors
cloud technology stack 35–6, 43,
161, 263
logical 161, 172
cloud tiers see tiers, cloud
cloud virtualization tier see tier,
cloud virtualization

clusters 10, 45, 58, 105, 228
COBIT (Control Objectives for
    Information and related
    Technology) 139, 178
Codd 243–4
collaboration 108, 113, 115, 141–3,
    176, 196, 223
commoditization 39–40, 253–4, 258,
    264
commodity 28, 32, 52, 63, 77, 234,
    241, 246, 253, 258, 264
  components 13–14, 32, 60
  infrastructure 12–13, 16, 32, 60,
    78, 227, 234, 240, 242, 246, 253,
    264
competitive advantage 77–8, 83, 86,
    88, 202
competitors, cloud–based 86–8, 91
complete virtualization 31, 39, 41
complexity 35–6, 38, 49, 53–4, 60,
    62, 94, 209, 238
computers 17, 21, 35, 44, 47, 229,
    246
connectivity, pervasive 247 see also
    access, ubiquitous
consistency, eventual 56, 238
consolidation, server see server
    consolidation
consumers
  cloud 73, 82–3, 108, 126, 129,
    156–7, 159, 161, 163–6, 180–2,
    184, 186–7, 192, 209–24
  internal 209
consumption 53, 92, 140, 149, 159,
    177, 182, 184–6, 214–18, 220,
    247
containerized datacenter 39
control, losing 248
cores, multi see multi-core
cost savings 61, 69–70, 76, 78–9, 217
costs 4, 6, 12–13, 16, 23, 32–4, 36, 45,
    59, 61, 63, 72–4, 76–9, 81, 83–4,
    90, 95, 99, 118, 128, 154, 204–7,

    223, 241, 243, 245–6, 249–50,
    255, 260
  fixed 23, 72–3, 79–80, 86, 99, 215
  lower 34, 229–30
  variable 72–3, 79–80, 99
critical dimension, cloud
    computing 129–30
CRM (customer relationship
    management) 15, 148, 213–14
cross-cloud collaboration 111, 142,
    198
culture 2–3, 8, 19–20, 64, 89, 96–7,
    144, 157, 175–7
customers xiii, 7, 9, 14–15, 18, 38,
    41, 66, 80, 100, 104, 200, 213,
    220, 222, 224, 238, 240, 245,
    252, 259

D
DaaS (Data as a Service) 159–60,
    169, 189
data
  services 37, 106, 219
  services layer 99, 138, 219
  services platform 106, 218, 222
  storing 230, 232, 241
  warehouses 57–8, 228
databases 7, 36, 57–9, 161, 189,
    230–1, 234–5, 239–40, 261
datacenter 16, 21–2, 27, 32, 39–40,
    64–5, 71–4, 79, 85–6, 89, 101,
    133, 170, 183, 201, 216–17, 229,
    235, 237–8
  containerized 39
  low-density 40
  operations 217, 221, 223 see also
    operations
dependencies, false 235
deployment 35, 37, 40, 47, 84–5,
    107, 111, 124–5, 129–30, 132,
    136–9, 142, 149, 166, 176–8,
    187–8, 197, 199, 207, 259
  choice 124, 128, 131–2

deployment (*continued*)
  hybrid 112, 147, 203, 205
  model 27–8, 36–7, 43, 116, 124,
    128, 130–1, 165, 170, 181, 183,
    197, 200, 204, 211
  models
  external public cloud 172
  hybrid cloud 173, 202–3
  private cloud 202
  various cloud 127, 171, 200
  options 128, 132, 148
  pattern 127, 129, 154
  plan 128, 132
  scenarios 126–8, 148, 156, 178,
    204
Deployment Model Scenarios
  200–1, 203
design 38, 47, 229
developers 10, 47, 50, 53–4, 60, 82,
  188, 191–2, 220, 222
development 53, 258
  agile 52, 225
dial tone, cloud 108, 126, 156, 180–2
disaster recovery 228, 243
discovery, cloud business 119–20,
  122, 206
DMTF (Distributed Management
  Task Force) 152
dynamic languages 56–7

E
eBay 8
economics 5, 13, 32–3
ecosystem 9, 126, 149, 151–3, 156,
  159, 177, 180–3, 186–7, 191,
  214, 216, 220, 229, 241
  enablement 157, 180
EDA (event–driven architecture)
  218–19
efficiency 64, 217, 254
efforts, cloud computing 33,
  109
elasticity 30, 41–2, 62–3, 97, 265

enablement 84, 101, 106, 126,
  139–40, 150, 164–6, 182, 190,
  204, 215–18, 220
  capabilities 140, 162, 198, 218
  category 164, 182
  cloud technologies 82, 126, 156,
    163, 181
  continuum 182
enablers, broad 15, 17, 19
energy 71, 254–5, 266
ENIAC 2
enterprise 8–9, 31, 45–6, 59, 61–3,
  66–7, 73, 76, 78–9, 83–4, 97,
  99–101, 103, 109–10, 115–16,
  124–6, 132–3, 140, 144–5, 147,
  154, 156, 172, 175–6, 179,
  190–2, 198–200, 204–6, 228,
  250–2, 259
  applications 53–4, 58, 101, 170,
    234, 246
  existing 58
  applications organization 101
  architecture 103
  business objectives 95
  cloud ethos 66
  deployment 177
  existing 84–5
  larger 79–80, 86–7, 144, 205
  requirements 144, 225
  technology infrastructure 45
enterprise service bus 54, 103
entrepreneurs 89–90, 268
Eucalyptus 83, 265
event-driven architecture (EDA)
  218–19
events, cloud 138, 178
eventual consistency 56, 238 *see also*
  transactional integrity
evolution 6, 66, 85, 89, 152, 231, 237,
  243
evolving, SOA to cloud 91
exabyte 2, 255–6
exascale 255–7

expansion, cloud 113, 115, 140–1, 196, 198

expenses 15, 62, 72–3, 255

exploitation 164

external cloud 141, 173, 221, 224 *see also* public cloud

External Cloud Provider 131

F

Facebook 90, 193, 250, 256–7, 261, 265

failure 10, 14, 63, 68, 104, 116, 177, 246

false dependencies 235

FEAF (Federal Enterprise Architecture Framework) 190

Federal Enterprise Architecture Framework (FEAF) 190

feedback 135, 139, 145

fixed costs *see* costs, fixed

flexibility 20, 22, 29, 48, 50, 52, 62, 69, 86, 92, 95, 99, 229–30, 241, 251

force.com 167–8, 176, 183, 214–15

foundation
cloud 150, 164, 182, 215, 218
cloud computing 126, 190, 247

framework 100, 130
cloud modeling 112, 114
Cloud Modeling 112, 114

frameworks, cloud computing reference model 113

G

GFS (Google File System) 14, 239

Google 13–14, 18–19, 22, 27, 34, 37, 51–2, 90, 108, 124, 172, 187, 200, 233, 236, 240–1, 250, 265

Google File System (GFS) 14, 239

governance 38, 80, 107–8, 113, 125–6, 129–30, 135–9, 145, 156–7, 160–1, 174–5, 177, 179, 187–8, 196, 214–15, 218

application lifecycle 176, 215

cloud-based application lifecycle 176

lifecycle 129, 139, 145

model 127–9

requirements 118, 133, 138

H

Hadoop 14, 241

Hadoop File System (HDFS) 239, 241

HDFS (Hadoop File System) 239, 241

history, cloud 5–6, 31, 60, 88, 264, 266, 268

Holistic Cloud Computing Reference Model 162–3, 165, 167, 169

hybrid cloud 38, 53, 58, 63–5, 83, 86, 122, 126, 129, 131, 140–3, 156–7, 170–4, 198, 200–4, 206, 209, 221–2, 224

I

IaaS (Infrastructure as a Service) 35, 43, 66, 81, 148, 154, 158–9, 190, 264

IDE 167

implementation 15, 113, 115, 120, 122–3, 129–30, 134–6, 140, 144, 187, 196–8, 205, 207, 211, 240
plan 134, 197
planning stage 130, 134, 197
stage 135, 139, 198
successful 125, 135, 144

Implementation, Planning 113, 115, 130, 196, 211

implications, strategic xii, 48, 69–70, 72, 74, 76, 78, 80, 82, 84, 86–90, 92, 94, 96, 98, 100, 102, 104, 106, 108, 110, 264

industry
  cloud 172–3, 191, 203
  cloud computing 119, 187
inevitability xiii, 21, 44, 245–6, 248,
    250, 252, 254, 256, 258, 260
inevitable 245–6, 248, 254, 256, 260
Information Technology
    Infrastructure Library (ITIL)
    139, 178
infrastructure 6–7, 10, 14, 20, 29–37,
    40–1, 43, 50, 52–4, 60, 63–4, 66,
    72–82, 84–90, 95, 101, 103–5,
    112, 121, 150, 158–9, 161–2,
    165, 182–3, 185, 188–90, 219,
    221, 251–2, 254–5, 264–5
  aggregated 244
  avoidance 89
  capabilities 181, 205
  cloud–based 64, 159
  cloud–enabled SOA 100
  costs 6, 76, 78, 85
  enterprise technology 45
  investment 64, 89
  layer 35, 39
  outsourced 222
  physical 166, 182
  public 65
  services 80, 94, 119
  services layer 99
  shared services 92–3, 102
  storage 18, 58, 218, 228, 243
  virtualization 132, 159–61
Infrastructure as a Service see IaaS
initiative 19, 69–71, 92–4, 99, 103,
    105, 107, 120–1, 195, 201–2,
    209
  cloud 111–13, 196, 202–3, 210
  successful 104–5
innovations 1, 10, 21, 23, 28, 33, 35,
    38–9, 53, 70, 81, 88–9, 92, 253,
    257, 259, 266
integrated development
    environment (IDE) 167

integration 59, 108, 111, 113, 115,
    141–2, 149, 151, 157, 168,
    173–4, 180, 183, 189, 196,
    198, 221–4
integration & interoperability 113,
    196
integration, tools 174
interface 17, 108, 151, 161, 173,
    184–5, 200
  application see API
  self–service user 164, 172, 184
intermediaries 126, 156
internal cloud provider 131, 136,
    209, 220, 222
Internet 2–4, 7–11, 13–14, 17, 23,
    27–8, 30, 39, 46, 49–51, 183,
    200, 219, 232–3, 238, 245, 247,
    253, 256–7, 259–60, 265
Internet Bubble 9, 14, 50–1, 233,
    245
interoperability 65, 108, 141–2, 149,
    151–2, 173–4, 198, 257
  challenges 141–2
  issues 142
ITIL (Information Technology
    Infrastructure Library) 139,
    178

J
J2EE 10

K
KaaS (Knowledge as a Service) 160,
    169–70, 189
Kent, Clark 3

L
languages, dynamic see dynamic
    languages
layers 34–6, 63, 135, 157–62, 166,
    210, 248, 252
  logical 158–9, 161, 167
  major 34–5, 263

shared core enterprise services 102
legacy applications 58–9, 86–7
    migrating 176
legacy business models 84, 87
leverage, cloud 77–8, 83–4, 86–7, 90, 95, 100–2, 113, 121, 123–4, 136, 138, 141, 154, 178, 181, 195, 200, 202, 205, 212–14, 219, 222
lifecycle
    complete 175, 197
    end-to-end 133
lock-in 251–2, 257
low-density datacenter 40
lower costs *see* costs, lower

M
mainframe 7, 9, 13, 31–2, 39, 58–9, 228–9, 248
management 100, 106, 126, 129–30, 134, 136–7, 149, 156–7, 166, 174–6, 178, 197, 215, 218, 224, 264–5, 268
    cloud 107, 135, 137–8, 152, 178
management processes 138, 221, 223–4
market 46, 50, 70, 74–5, 77, 80, 83, 87–8, 99, 102, 144, 203–5, 207, 215
maturation 140, 198
    logical phases 140, 198
matures, cloud computing 98, 141, 198
maturity 113, 115, 119–20, 176, 196
    stage 143–4
measured service 33
messaging 105, 167–8, 189
metrics 113, 116–17, 122, 135, 139–40, 196–7
    cloud business 140
mobilization 119, 122
model 27, 30, 35, 71, 76, 81, 86, 100–1, 108, 125–6, 141, 144,

149, 155, 159, 163, 167, 188, 222, 231, 257
application platform 171
cloud 27, 74, 154
Cloud Adoption Lifecycle 111–15, 117, 123, 136, 144, 147, 178, 192, 195–6, 199, 205, 210
cloud computing 73, 136, 138, 187
Cloud Computing Reference (CC-RM) 35, 113–14, 123–7, 130, 135, 138, 144–5, 148–9, 152, 155–7, 162–5, 170, 179–80, 182–5, 187–8, 190–2, 197, 210, 212–13, 225
cloud consumer business 83
Cloud Deployment 113, 123–4, 126, 128, 135–6, 139, 148, 156–7, 170–1, 173, 176, 178, 187, 190, 196, 215–16, 218–19, 221–2, 224
Cloud Ecosystem 126, 156–7, 179–81, 183, 187, 190–2, 214, 216–21, 223–4
cloud-enabled application delivery 169
Cloud Enablement 126, 138, 155, 157, 162–5, 168, 173, 178–9, 183, 185–90, 210, 215–17, 219–20, 222, 224
Cloud Governance and Operations 123, 126, 156–7, 174–5, 177, 179, 187, 190, 214–15, 217–24
Cloud Reference 113, 135, 179, 211, 213
deployment 27–8, 36–7, 43, 116, 124, 128, 130–1, 165, 170, 181, 183, 197, 200, 204, 211
external public cloud 172
hybrid cloud 173, 202–3
private cloud 202

model (*continued*)
Deployment, scenarios 200–1, 203
deployment, various cloud 127, 171, 200
logical 159–61
operational xi, xiii, 20, 33, 227
operations 123, 125–6, 156–7, 174–5, 177, 179, 187, 190, 203, 212, 214–15, 217–24
organizational 107, 120
support cloud computing resource acquisition 80
trust-based 96–7, 108
modeling xii, 113, 115, 123–5, 129–30, 134–5, 145, 147–50, 152, 154–6, 158, 160, 162, 164, 166, 168, 170, 172, 174–6, 178, 180, 182, 184, 186, 188, 190–2, 196–8, 211, 213, 224–5
approach 124, 127
necessary 123, 147, 197
process 126, 128, 155
monitoring 107, 125, 129–30, 134–5, 137–9, 149, 157, 166, 175–6, 178, 197
Moore's Law 6
Mosaic 8
multi-core 12, 242, 244

N
NAS (Network Attached Storage) 31, 228–30, 232
National Institute of Standards and Technology *see* NIST
Netscape 8
network 6–7, 9–10, 16–17, 27–8, 31–2, 35, 46–7, 61, 66, 71, 75, 77, 82, 90, 95, 132, 137, 160–1, 163–5, 170, 181–2, 184, 219, 228, 236–7, 242, 244, 247, 253
distance 237, 242
infrastructure 71, 75

resources 76, 131, 165, 201
virtualization 159–60, 164, 182
new business models 71, 75, 80, 82–3, 85, 87–9, 144, 203, 219
news delivery 3–4
newspapers 2–4
NIST (National Institute of Standards and Technology) 27, 41, 150–1, 158, 163, 174, 190
nominal cloud adoption approach 207–8

O
OASIS (Organization for the Advancement of Structured Information Standards) 150, 155
objections 248–9, 251–2
objectives 90, 98, 116, 121, 140, 150, 197
obstacles, adoption 107
offboarding 137, 175, 179
offerings cloud computing 249
onboarding 108, 128–9, 133–4, 137, 149, 166, 169, 175, 179, 217
Open Cloud Computing Interface (OCCI) 154, 185
Open Cloud Consortium 151
open source 67, 90, 264
Open Virtualization Format (OVF) 152, 154
Operating System *see* OS
operational requirements 111, 118, 124–5, 127–9, 132–3, 141, 144
operations 125, 129, 138–9, 176, 178
business 97, 125, 128, 130, 132–3, 180, 218
Operations Model 123, 125–6, 156–7, 174–5, 177, 179, 187, 190, 203, 212, 214–15, 217–24
orchestration 95, 108, 112, 141–2, 166, 173

Organization for the Advancement of Structured Information Standards (OASIS) 150, 155
OS (Operating System) 1, 16–18, 32, 36, 61–2, 79, 81–3, 157, 162–6, 168, 171–2, 182, 184–6, 189, 192, 201, 210, 214–18, 220–3
outages 14, 137, 139, 178
OVF (Open Virtualization Format) 152, 154

P
PaaS (Platform as a Service) 29, 35–6, 42–3, 54, 63–4, 66–7, 73, 77, 79, 81, 102–3, 132, 153, 158–60, 167–8, 189–90, 201, 207, 209, 215, 247, 250, 261, 264
Papadopolous, Greg 21
paradigm, cloud computing 86, 94–5, 170
pattern
  cloud enablement 127, 213
  cloud transition 93–5
patterns 77, 79, 124–8, 130–2, 139, 142, 145, 148, 165, 178, 183, 213–14, 221, 224
  appropriate 124–5, 127
  cloud computing 106, 109–10, 112
  multiple 124, 201
  new 140, 198
  various 78, 142, 145, 149, 151, 166, 170, 185
pervasive connectivity 247 *see also* ubiquitous access
petabytes 255–6
physical infrastructure 17, 62–3, 90, 229–30, 242, 255
pilot 116–17, 135, 200
Pilot *see* POC

pilot projects 115–16, 118, 201, 205, 212
planning xiii, 39, 47, 111–13, 121–2, 124, 129, 133, 136–8, 144, 147–8, 161, 175, 178, 187, 196, 205–8, 224
  framework 139, 178
  tools 144–5
platform 29, 33, 35–6, 41–3, 53–4, 56, 65–7, 73, 75, 77, 81–3, 93, 100, 102–3, 106, 126, 128, 132, 143, 153, 155, 158–61, 163, 165–8, 179, 182–3, 188–90, 192–3, 215, 247, 250–4
  application 57, 65, 103, 106, 163, 167–9, 185
  cloud 80, 82, 85, 95, 100, 166, 176
  cloud application 29, 34–6, 43, 54, 56, 63, 67, 169, 268
  cloud-enabled application development 215
  cloud middleware 99, 167–8
  cloud provider 142, 200
  cloud services 132
  hosted 206, 215
  layers 251, 255
  pattern 106
  provider 166
  pure-play cloud enablement 81, 250–1
  as a service *see* PaaS (Platform as a Service)
  service providers 82–3
  tier 157, 162–5, 167–9, 171–2, 182, 184–7, 189, 210, 214–23
  virtualization 159–60
Platform as a Service *see* PaaS (Platform as a Service)
platforms
  internal 101
  new 163, 246
  third party 100

POC (Proof of Concept) 92, 113,
    115–18, 122, 134, 155, 195–6,
    200–1, 205–6, 212, 225
  implementation 115
  project 113, 118, 196
principles, cloud computing 22, 265
privacy 22, 37, 108, 126, 149, 157,
    170, 172, 175, 177–8, 197, 202,
    208
private cloud 22, 37, 42, 58–9, 63, 65,
    78, 83, 86, 100, 108, 123–6, 129,
    133, 137–8, 140–1, 143, 148,
    156–7, 170–3, 178, 197–8,
    200–4, 206, 208–9, 216–22, 224,
    248–9, 265
procurement 80–1
projects, skunk works 205–6
Proof of Concept see POCs
provider, internal cloud see internal
  cloud provider
providers 46, 76, 78, 82, 126, 128–9,
    131–3, 136–7, 149, 152, 156–7,
    161, 164, 180–2, 186, 206, 209,
    213–17, 219–24, 250, 252
  analysis 113, 130–1, 196
  enterprise-oriented private 249
  internal 209
  platform 216
  public 63, 65, 134
  third–party 74–5, 84, 169, 174,
    209, 222, 224
provisioning 39, 66, 91, 100, 102,
    106, 128, 133, 159, 167, 180,
    264
public cloud xiii, 21–2, 33, 37–8, 42,
    60, 64–5, 83, 86, 121, 123–4,
    126, 129, 131, 133–4, 139, 141,
    148, 156–7, 170–3, 178, 197,
    200–2, 204, 208–9, 212, 214–15,
    220–5, 249–50
  deployment model 214, 219
  deployment pattern 172
  deployments 134, 200, 222

  first 30, 121
  leveraging 206
  use cases 203

Q
quality of service (QoS) 46–7,
    107–8, 123, 134, 136, 149, 164,
    176, 181–2, 248

R
rationality 253, 255
RDF (Resource Description
    Framework) 151
readiness 117, 119–20
Redshift Computing 21
reference architecture, master 100
relational databases 1, 10, 18, 227–8,
    230–2, 235, 238–9, 243–4 see also
    databases
reliability xiii, 22, 32, 34, 36, 40, 43,
    48, 54, 56, 60, 62–3, 68, 106,
    108, 181, 227, 246
requirements 27, 46–7, 52–3, 56, 74,
    77, 96, 107, 111, 125–7, 130,
    133, 142–3, 148, 153, 156, 172,
    174, 183, 187–8, 204, 206–7,
    209–12, 255
  business 75, 118, 133, 148–9, 160,
    165, 175, 183, 199, 204, 206–7,
    211–12
  cloud enablement 210–11
  organization's 131, 185
Resource Description Framework
    (RDF) 151
resources 27–9, 35–6, 61, 72, 74–8,
    93, 97, 123, 130–4, 150, 152,
    154, 159, 164, 166, 169–71,
    173–4, 181–4, 187–8, 190, 221,
    223, 238
  cloud-enabled 74, 79, 81–3, 108,
    126–7, 132, 158, 164, 183–4,
    187
  cloud enablement 184

provision 78, 133
public 63, 131, 220, 222
ReST 50, 67
  interfaces 41, 50–1
  web services 50, 56
reusable services 96, 99
Rightscale 265
risk 15, 41, 82, 117–18, 142,
    154, 173, 195, 203–4, 206–9,
    260
  mitigation 81, 207, 209
ROA 73–4, 79
ROA calculation 74
roadmap 109, 113, 115, 118–20, 122,
    134, 140, 196, 206, 212
  standards 153
Ruby on Rails 252

S
SaaS 35–6, 44, 51, 73, 77, 79, 81, 102,
    132, 153, 158–61, 169–70,
    189–90, 201, 207, 209, 214, 248,
    252, 265
sales 15, 72–3, 213
  cloud-enabled 84–5
  volume 73
salesforce.com 15, 82, 148, 167, 169,
    183, 213–14, 223, 250
SANs (storage area network) 31,
    228–30, 232
scalability xiii, 29, 42, 48, 62–3, 238,
    240, 243
  application 106, 216
scale 4–5, 11, 14–15, 20, 22–3, 28–9,
    31–2, 34, 51–2, 57–8, 60, 62, 65,
    216, 219, 227, 232, 240–1,
    245–7, 249, 253, 255–7, 265
  web 34, 234
scarcity 5
scenarios 72, 75–6, 78, 84, 101, 137,
    142–3, 172, 209–10, 212–13,
    216–19, 224
  business 116, 196, 201

hybrid 128, 220, 222
synopsis 213, 215–21, 223
search 14
security 22, 37–8, 46, 64, 75, 91, 95,
    105, 107–8, 113, 118, 123, 126,
    136–8, 149, 151–3, 157, 160,
    162, 166, 170, 172, 174–8, 196–
    7, 202, 227, 246, 249, 252
  challenges 108, 130, 138, 197, 200
  resources 163–6, 182
SEI (Software Engineering
    Institute) 267
self-organize 10
self-service 30, 66
semantic web 259, 261
server 4, 7, 17, 21, 26–7, 31–2, 35, 40,
    58, 61–3, 95, 121, 189, 218, 229–
    30, 232, 235, 237, 239, 241–2,
    248, 253–4, 258
  sprawl 61–2
  utilization 79
server consolidation 29, 61, 78, 183,
    217
as a service 158, 162, 167, 187
service
  as a 158, 162, 167, 187
  ad–supported free 52, 257
  application 102
  application container 168
  application hosting 160
  cloud-based 19, 38–9, 41
  cloud enablement 82
  cloud queuing 188
  common 53, 103
  contract 46–7, 136, 164, 172, 182,
    260
  core enterprise 92–3, 99, 105
  enablement 95, 97, 161
  external provider 74, 78, 97, 101,
    131–2, 148, 172, 187, 221–2
  financial 38, 260
  implementation 46, 95
  individual 14, 47, 50, 67, 185

service (*continued*)
 managed 65, 264
 measured 33
 new 48, 51, 75
 platform 102
 presentation 102, 106
 provider 38, 47, 120, 126, 152,
   162, 179, 181–2, 215, 266
 reusable 96, 99
 standard cloud provider 219
 web-based 41, 51
service contract 132, 181
service level agreement *see* SLAs
service-oriented architecture *see*
   SOA
service provider, third–party cloud
   108, 124, 128, 131–3, 136–7,
   147, 173, 202
service providers 76, 78, 81–3, 85,
   100, 105, 124–5, 127, 130–3,
   136–7, 142, 147–8, 153, 155,
   170, 172–3, 187, 197, 208–11,
   215, 220
services 14–16, 18–19, 27–31, 35–8,
   43–4, 46–8, 51–2, 57, 66–7,
   72–3, 77, 81, 86–8, 91–7, 100,
   102–4, 106, 136, 148–9, 153,
   158–60, 164–9, 179, 181–3, 185,
   189–90, 201, 215–16, 218–19,
   247–8, 264–5
 web *see* web services
Services-Driven Enterprise 267
Simple Queue Service (SQS) 172,
   185
simplicity 239–41
skunk works 205–6
SLAs (service level agreement)
   (*see also* QoS) 46–8, 108,
   119–20, 132, 134, 136–7, 140,
   149, 172, 176, 181–2, 200
SOA xii, 10, 17, 43, 45–6, 48, 67,
   69–70, 91–110, 119–20, 123,
   137–8, 142, 145, 147, 155, 161,

167, 176–7, 181, 200, 219, 258,
   267
 adoption 92, 94, 104
 enablement by cloud 162
 evolve to cloud 91
 failure 94, 103–4
 infrastructure 99–101, 105–6
 initiatives 69, 92–5, 99, 102–5, 108
 patterns 105, 107, 109
 service provider capabilities 104
 service virtualization 107, 160
 success 93, 103–4, 107, 109
SOAP 49, 67
social media 19
social network 19, 70, 256, 265
software 4, 11–13, 17, 30, 35–7, 40,
   45, 52, 56–7, 71, 73, 75, 77, 81,
   90, 152–3, 158–60, 163, 169,
   171, 189–90, 193, 201, 214, 235,
   247, 258–9, 265, 268
 cloud–based 34, 48
Software as a Service *see* SaaS
software development 53, 258
Software Engineering Institute
   (SEI) 267
solution 81–2, 125, 151–3, 159, 165,
   200, 203, 239
 cloud–enabled 179, 185
 cloud–enabled business 185
solutions 81–2, 113–14, 124, 128,
   130, 142, 152, 166, 176, 179–80,
   197, 203
source, open 67, 90, 264
stack 21, 35–6, 66, 71, 150, 152, 191,
   241, 258, 265
 logical 161–2, 191
standards xii, 21, 25–6, 28, 30, 32,
   34, 36–8, 40–4, 49, 67, 108–9,
   136, 142–3, 149–55, 163, 174,
   176, 193, 198, 264
 cloud 142, 149–51, 153
 cloud security 153
 de facto 41–2, 67, 150

proprietary cloud 135
web services overview poster 67
web services security 200
standards roadmap *see* roadmap,
   standards
startup xii, 53, 60, 65, 71–3, 75, 80,
   89, 94, 144, 219–20, 245, 257,
   259, 263–4
state 28, 56, 121, 143, 152, 203, 228
storage 4–5, 7, 15–16, 27, 31–2,
   35–6, 40, 54, 57, 75–6, 95, 106,
   121, 131–2, 159–64, 173, 182,
   184, 189, 201, 218–19, 228–30,
   235–6, 238, 242, 244, 255
   approaches 238–9
   area network *see* SANs
   cloud 161, 188–9
   cloud patterns 106, 151
   enterprise facilities 57–8
   infrastructure 18, 58, 218, 228,
      243
   infrastructure (specialized) 7, 242
   pools 35, 229, 242–3
   resources 165
   technologies 234, 237–8
strategic implications xii, 48, 69–70,
   72, 74, 76, 78, 80, 82, 84, 86–90,
   92, 94, 96, 98, 100, 102, 104,
   106, 108, 110, 264
strategies 71, 97, 101, 109–10, 116,
   120, 188, 197, 202, 225
   defined cloud 77, 117, 119, 123,
      144, 196–7
   failed SOA 92, 94
   formal cloud 117, 120, 134, 200,
      205, 211–12
strategy
   cloud 39, 74, 77, 100–1, 115–23,
      125, 128–31, 134–6, 138, 140,
      177, 184, 192, 196–200, 202,
      206–7, 213
   formal cloud development 117,
      196

sub-tier, Cloud Platform/PaaS
   167–8
success 33, 92–3, 103, 105–7,
   109–10, 112, 114, 116, 119–20,
   122, 137–8, 147, 177–9, 183,
   212, 257
Sun 8
supply chain, cloud-enabled
   84
support xiii, 52, 57, 70, 74–5,
   77–8, 85, 90, 97, 99, 101–2, 108,
   113, 115, 118, 120, 123, 130,
   138–9, 143, 148–9, 153,
   156–7, 169–75, 177–8, 196–7,
   205–6, 211–13, 218–19, 224–5,
   234
   applications 103
   models 125, 176, 217
   requirements 107, 125, 139, 178,
      197

T
technologies 3, 8, 28, 35–6, 41–3, 50,
   62, 69–70, 82–3, 92, 96, 99,
   111–12, 115–16, 119, 124,
   126–8, 130, 132, 135, 141–3,
   145, 150–2, 158–9, 167–9,
   181–3, 190, 210–11, 239, 243–4,
   267
   applying 204
   emerging 112
   selection of appropriate 130,
      197
technology
   cloud-based 61
   cloud-enabled 124, 126, 131, 155,
      204
   emerging 142, 144, 151, 154, 195,
      198, 206, 267
   trends 70–1, 91, 110–11, 144, 181,
      236
terabyte 251, 255–6
third parties 96–7, 131–2

tier 126, 158–62, 164–6, 168–9, 171,
    173, 180, 182, 184–6, 188–91,
    210, 214–18, 220–4
  cloud business 157, 162–3,
    168–72, 184–7, 189, 210,
    213–23
  cloud client 161
  cloud enablement 139, 164, 169,
    173, 178, 182, 190, 220
  cloud enablement model 162,
    165, 219
  Cloud OS 36, 163, 166–7, 180,
    182, 192, 222
  Cloud Physical 162–3, 171, 183,
    210
  Cloud Platform 36, 163
  cloud virtualization 157, 163,
    165–9, 171–2, 184–6, 189–90,
    210, 219
  operating system 157, 216–17
  physical 163
  platform 157, 162–5, 167–9,
    171–2, 182, 184–7, 189, 210,
    214–23
  virtualization 162, 166–7, 214–18,
    220–3
tiers, cloud 164–5, 168–9, 183–4
time-to-market 77, 83, 121, 207, 209
  faster 69, 78, 102, 104
transactional integrity 60, 228 *see
    also* eventual consistency
transactions 235, 240, 246
transition 3–4, 13, 15, 19, 48, 54,
    56–7, 59, 61, 63–5, 69, 79, 91–4,
    98, 103–5, 107, 112, 122–4,
    135–6, 142, 149, 192–3, 210–11,
    248, 250, 255, 265
trends xii, 16, 54, 56, 67, 70, 111–12,
    258–9, 264
  technology 70–1, 91, 110–11, 144,
    181, 236
trust 15, 108, 136, 177, 181
Twitter xiii, 19, 250, 265, 268

U
ubiquitous access 30 *see also*
    pervasive connectivity
UCI (Unified Cloud Interface) 151
unstructured 57, 231–2
USA Today 3
use case
  business 126, 200, 204, 212, 224
  development 211, 224
  patterns mapped 213, 215, 217,
    219, 221, 223
  public cloud 203
use cases 126–7, 211–13, 216,
    225
  common 213

V
value 63, 82, 84, 93, 100, 102,
    109–10, 138, 145, 150, 152, 172,
    204, 224–5, 232
variable costs *see* costs, variable
vendor, community 139, 178
vendors 68, 111, 177, 211, 257–8,
    263–5
vertical cloud 37–8, 65, 126, 156,
    170–1, 174
virtualization xii, 16–17, 26, 31,
    61–3, 142, 150, 159–60, 165,
    170, 182–3, 201, 253
  cloud 165, 216–17, 220, 222
  cloud technologies 163
  complete 31, 39, 41
  leveraging cloud 99
  platform 159–60
  successful infrastructure pattern
    105
  system 152, 154
  tier *see* tier, virtualization
vision, persistent 5, 15
Voice over Internet Protocol (VoIP)
    85
VoIP (Voice over Internet Protocol)
    85

W
Wall Street Journal 4
web 1.0 8
web 2.0 4, 50–2, 67, 70, 176, 189
web scale 34, 234
web services 17, 45, 48–50, 52–4, 57,
    59, 67, 95, 103, 108, 161–2, 177,
    193, 200, 267
  management (WSM) 177
Web Services Standards Overview
    poster 67
WS–* 49 *see also* web services

WSM (web services management)
    177
www.execsguidetocloud.com xiii,
    266

X
Xerox Altos 9
Xerox PARC 9

Y
Yahoo 8
Youtube 19, 250, 265